Dialogues
of Paul Tillich

Paul Tillich, 1886–1965

Dialogues
of Paul Tillich

by
Mary Ann Stenger
Ronald H. Stone

Mercer University Press 2002

ISBN 0-86554-784-X
ISBN 0-86554-833-1

MUP/H591
MUP/P235

Dialogues of Paul Tillich
Copyright ©2002
Mercer University Press
All rights reserved
Printed in the United States of America

Library of Congress Cataloging-in-Publication Data

Stenger, Mary Ann, 1947–
Dialogues of Paul Tillich /
by Mary Ann Stenger, Ronald H. Stone.
p. cm.
Includes bibliographical references and indexes.
ISBN 0-86554-784-X (alk. paper) — ISBN 0-86554-833-1 (pbk. : alk. paper)
1. Tillich, Paul, 1886–1965. I. Stone, Ronald H. II. Title.
BX4827.T53 S82 2002
230'.092—dc21

2002009162

Contents

Preface

Several essays in this volume have been published previously. We are grateful to the editors of these journals and books for permission to reprint these essays, with some revisions.

Chapter 1, section A, was published originally as "The Understanding of Christ as Final Revelation," in *Christianity and the Wider Ecumenism*, edited by Peter Phan (New York: Paragon House, 1990) 191-205. Discussion of Barth and Tillich from that essay is included in section B, with extensive unpublished material.

Chapter 3 was published originally as "Paulas, Reinie, und die Judenfrage," in the *North American Paul Tillich Society Newsletter* 20/2 (April 1994): 2-8.

Chapter 4 originally appeared as "The Significance of Tillich's Epistemology for Cross-cultural Religious Truth," in *Religion et Culture*, edited by Michel Despland, Jean-Claude Petit, and Jean Richard (Quebec: Les Presses de L'Université Laval, les Editions du Cerf, 1987) 589-603.

Chapter 5 was published as "The Limits and Possibilities of Tillich's Ontology for Cross-cultural and Feminist Theology," in *God and Being/Gott und Sein*, edited by Gert Hummel (Berlin/New York: Walter De Gruyter, 1989) 250-68.

Chapter 6, section A, was first published with the title "A Critical Analysis of the Influence of Paul Tillich on Mary Daly's Feminist Theology," in *Encounter* 43/3 (Summer 1982): 219-38, and then later included in *Theonomy and Autonomy: Studies in Tillich's Engagement with Modern Culture*, edited by John J. Carey (Macon GA: Mercer University Press, 1984) 243-65.

Chapter 6, section B, was published as "Male Over Female or Female Over Male: A Critique of Idolatry," *Soundings* 69/4 (Winter 1987): 464-78.

Chapter 7 was published as "Paul Tillich and the Feminist Critique of Roman Catholic Theology," in *Paul Tillich: A New Catholic Assessment*, edited by Raymond F. Bulman and Frederick J. Parrella (Collegeville MN: Liturgical Press, 1994) 174-88.

Chapter 8 was published originally as "Paul Tillich: On the Boundary between Protestantism and Marxism," in *Laval theologique et philosophique* 45/3 (October 1989): 393-404.

Chapter 10 was published originally as "Paulus and Gustavo: Religious Socialism and Liberation Theology," in *Laval theologique et philosophique* 44/2 (June 1988): 155-67.

Authorship of the thirteen essays in this collection is as follows: chapters 1, 2, 4, 5, 6, 7, and 11 are by Mary Ann Stenger; chapters 3, 8, 9, 10, 12, and 13 are by Ronald H. Stone.

Mary Ann Stenger wishes to thank Christopher M. Jones and Genevieve Petty for their help in the preparation of her part of the manuscript and her husband, Robert L. Stenger, for his constant support and encouragement.

Ronald Stone thanks Sheryl Gilliland and Anita Sattler for their work on the manuscript and the membership of the North American Paul Tillich Society for its comradeship.

August 2002

Mary Ann Stenger
Ronald H. Stone

A Candid Album

The photographs reproduced on these four pages are from the collection of Mutie Tillich Farris. Mutie selected these photos as representative of her father, from student days in Germany to later times in America. Exact dates and sources are unknown, Mutie remarks, but she identifies some subjects and general time periods as indicated. These unique Tillich candids (as readily apparent, only the photograph of Tillich as a student is "professionally" posed) are by the gracious permission of Mutie Tillich Farris.

Paul Tillich, late teens or 20s.
Student days in Germany.

A moody Tillich in Germany, in his 30s or 40s (?).

Hannah, Mutie, and Paulus, in Germany, before 1933.

Hannah and Paulus, in the same general time period as the two candids above.

*With students at Union
Theological Seminary, New York.*

*With Leo Lowenthal & his wife
& holding Mutie's son, ca. 1955.*

With Susan Sontag, 1950s (?).

In Japan, "with the president" (?), Hannah wrote.

Relaxed dialogue with Rollo May.

Introduction

Paul Tillich's life was one of conversation seeking understanding. From his doctoral dissertation to his last lecture, he wrestled with the meanings to be found in conversations among the world's great religions. Students who gathered at his apartment remarked on how he always sought out their ideas and enriched them by drawing their concepts into the world of his mind. Professional colleagues chided his method of learning through conversation, suggesting that he often learned essential ideas by talking with authors rather than reading their books.

Some of his dialogues with religious leaders and with students have been published.[1] In addition to these recorded conversations, Tillich engaged in dialogue with minds from the past and with contemporary religious thinkers through letters, articles, and books. Since his death in 1965, religious thinkers have continued to dialogue with Tillich's works in their own writings and conversations. Regular meetings of three scholarly societies (North American, French, and German) are devoted to analysis of Tillich's thought, both looking at the past and projecting possibilities for present and future theological developments. As scholars of Tillich's thought, we have carried his writings into our own theological conversations and shared in the richness of the dialogues of the scholarly societies. We have chosen for this work some of his dialogues with past thought, reflection on his own conversations, and contributions to present and future theology. We have centered on questions raised by our own primary work in religion, politics, and ethics, focussing on the topics of religious pluralism, feminism, politics, and war.

Tillich named his distinctive method of raising existential questions from culture to be answered by an essentialist reading of classical Christian

---

[1]Paul Tillich's dialogues with faculty and students at the University of California in Santa Barbara are published in *Ultimate Concern: Tillich in Dialogue*, ed. D. Mackenzie Brown (New York: Harper & Row, 1965). Three dialogues with Hisamatsu Shin'ichi are published in Paul Tillich, *The Encounter of Religions and Quasi-Religions*, ed. Terence Thomas (Lewiston NY: Edwin Mellen Press, 1990) 75-170.

theology "the method of correlation." It too was a form of dialogue and a method that invites others, past, present, and future, into the conversation. In an early discussion of how theological norms are developed, Tillich spoke of considering past theological norms in relation to the present culture and historical situation as necessary in creating contemporary theology.[2] His dialogues with biblical material, past theologies, and the contemporary historical situation involve critically analyzing their messages and pulling their truths into his own theology.

During his lectures at Columbia University in 1961, he mentioned four presuppositions for interreligious dialogue. Both sides in the dialogue recognize the value of the other's perspective as necessary for conversation. Both participants must present their perspectives with conviction. Some common ground is required for the meeting to be fruitful, and finally both perspectives have to be open to criticism.[3] Such guides to dialogue insure that dialogue involves risk. Not everyone or every position is available for dialogue as it presupposes willingness to risk one's own presuppositions or even one's identity.

Conversations with the texts of past thinkers involve interpretation of their work brought into our own time and language. Hans Gadamer uses the concept of *conversation* to describe the interpreter's relationship with a text. The interpreter's *horizon* is his or her own understandings along with an openness to the particular text and its author. In the course of the conversation, there is a *fusion* of horizons, where past and present understandings are brought together to form present views.[4] This dialogical structure and fusion of horizons applies to Tillich's conversations with other thinkers as well as to our engagements of his thought in relation to contemporary theological questions.

---

[2]See Paul Tillich, *Das System der Wissenschaften nach Gegenständen und Methoden* (1923), vol. 1 of *Gesammelte Werke* (Stuttgart: Evangelisches Verlagswerk, 1959) 210-45, 269-83; "On the Idea of a Theology of Culture," in *What Is Religion?* ed. James Luther Adams, trans. William B. Green (New York: Harper & Row, 1969) 55-181.

[3]Paul Tillich, *Christianity and the Encounter of World Religions* (Minneapolis: Fortress Press, 1974) 39.

[4]Hans Gadamer, *Truth and Method* (New York: Seabury Press, 1975) 258-78, 305-41.

Tillich's significant dialogues range from his vocation as a theologian in dialogue with world religions in Berlin, Chicago, and Japan to his engagement of Lutheranism and socialism in revolutionary Berlin in 1918. Like the constructed conversations of Socrates we know as Plato's dialogues, Tillich's 'dialogues' exhibit a great deal of variety in form and content. Even the pursuit of one term like virtue leads through a genuine dialogue representing different perspectives in the *Gorgias* through a utopia in the *Republic* to totalitarian enforcement in the *Laws*. Although not structured as formal dialogues, our dialogues of Tillich bring his thought into conversation with other significant thinkers to explicate its relevance.

Continually in the study of religion, Tillich's formulations appear—as a basis for approaching the history of religions or understanding the dynamics of religion,[5] as a conversational partner in developing a theology rooted in love,[6] or influencing some feminist theology. Legal struggles over church-state issues and Supreme Court decisions on conscientious objection to war reflect his definitions of religion. On one occasion in South India, a Hindu philosopher interpreted religious symbolism in terms of Tillich's distinctions between symbol and sign. He responded to his Western friend beside the pool in the Menakshi temple when his use of Tillich was pointed out: "Of course we are all Tillichians in this Hindu-Christian dialogue." In Kenya a young theologian attempted to relate African socialism to his Christian-theological roots in conversation. Recognizing a possible post-Christian and a probable postsocialist age, he still seeks a synthesis for himself and his work through the thought of Paul Tillich. The Tillich band of conversation around the world is both wide and deep, and these essays are a reflection of and contribution to it.

Essays in part I focus on Tillich's theology confronting the issues of religious pluralism in dialogue with other Christian thinkers. The first chapter looks at the understanding of Christ and final revelation as a crucial issue for approaching non-Christian religious traditions. Section A of chapter 1 places Tillich in conversation with Karl Rahner and John Hick, with section B providing more depth to Tillich in dialogue with Barth on this issue.

---

[5]See Robert D. Baird, *Category Formation and the History of Religions* (The Hague: Mouton, 1971) and Peter Slater, *The Dynamics of Religion* (New York: Harper & Row, 1978) xii-xiv.

[6]See Sallie McFague, *Models of God* (Philadelphia: Fortress Press, 1987) chaps. 4–6.

Chapter 2 continues the conversation with Barth but broadens it to include two Buddhist thinkers, Masao Abe and Keiji Nishitani, focussing on the primacy of being versus nothingness in their understandings of ultimacy. Relationships with Jews, support for Zionism, and a socialist religious approach form the basis of a dialogue between Reinhold Niebuhr and Tillich in chapter 2. The final chapter in part I focuses on epistemological contributions that Tillich can make to current philosophical discussions of religious pluralism. Key issues are the problem of relativism, judging among religious truth claims, and the challenge of diverse truth claims to the understanding of ultimacy. Placing Tillich in these dialogues moves the discussion beyond his publications on encountering world religions or his specific dialogues with Hisamatsu Shin'ichi to issues of religious pluralism that are debated today.

Part II brings Tillich's ontology into conversation with both pluralist and feminist theological discussions, demonstrating several shared issues. Tillich, for the most part, did not address directly feminist concerns. He did show an awareness of patriarchy and talked about the female symbolism in his term, the ground of being.[7] But in the 1970s and later, several female theologians who had studied Tillich and later became engaged by feminism, brought elements of Tillich's theological method and content into dialogue with feminist issues. Chapter 6 focuses on Tillich in dialogue with Mary Daly's feminist theology, showing his extensive influence on her approach in *Beyond God the Father* and then her individual theological developments, intentionally separated from Tillich. Chapter 7 places Tillich in dialogue with Roman Catholic feminism, showing both his influence on some thinkers and limits and possibilities for future feminist thought rooted in his theology.

Conversations focused on religious-political and social issues center part III. The dialogue between Protestantism and Marxism engaged Tillich politically and intellectually, as we see in chapter 8. Tillich's religious socialism blends elements of Max Weber, Lutheranism, and Marxism, in part as a counter to Nazism but also as support for a critical-prophetic approach

---

[7]For an analysis of his awareness of patriarchy, see Guy Hammond, *Conscience and Its Recovery: From the Frankfurt School to Feminism* (Charlottesville VA: University Press of Virginia, 1993). Tillich's discussion of female symbolism in the 'ground of being' is found in his *Systematic Theology*, 3 vols. (Chicago: University of Chicago Press, 1951–1963) 3:293-94.

to politics. His religious socialism was developed with dialogue partners, particularly members of the Kairos Circle, the Frankfurt School, and the Fellowship of Socialist Christians, reviewed in chapter 9. Although liberation theologian Gustavo Gutiérrez was not influenced by Tillich, their alternative models of religious socialism in chapter 10 are suggestive in dialogue for developing a politically viable social theology.

Current involvement of religion in politics on the American scene is animated by a fundamentalist religious approach rather than religious socialism. Major differences between fundamentalists and Tillich make them uneasy dialogue partners, but as shown in chapter 11, there are some points of common ground in their approaches to the event of Christ and the Cross. Building on a set of Protestant principles for connecting faith and political action, Tillich develops a critical theological approach to the aims of war (chapter 12). The use of the atomic bomb and the buildup of nuclear weapons provided specific issues for both Reinhold Niebuhr and Tillich to apply their specific forms of Christian realism, as the dialogue in chapter 13 shows. Having participated in and responded to a wide variety of political situations, Tillich's work becomes a helpful dialogue partner for many issues of our current religious, political situation.

Dialogues occupied Tillich's life from his original teaching in Berlin to his last lecture in Chicago. But they never were concluded, as the essays here show. In *Theology of Culture*, he wrote in concluding his reflections on Martin Buber:

> The interrelation and conversation, the "I-Thou" encounter of Judaism and Christianity, has not yet and never should come to an end.[8]

As interpreters of Tillich, we continue the conversations and encounters, and we invite you into this process of conversation with and about these Tillichian ideas.

---

[8]Paul Tillich, *Theology of Culture* (New York: Oxford University Press, 1964) 199.

Part I

Interreligious Dialogue

Chapter 1

Christ as Final Revelation and Other Religions

With technologies and communication networks connecting us to peoples around the world, we can think in terms of a global community. With increased mobility of peoples, our own neighborhoods have become a microcosm of that community, with cultural and religious diversity. In such a context, any form of Christian imperialism seems offensive and archaic. But the theological issues involved in avoiding Christian imperialism are complex and reach to the very center of Christian doctrine.

One such central issue is the understanding of Christ as final revelation and its significance for dealing with religious pluralism. This issue raises at least the following interdependent questions for discussion. (1) Can the understanding of Christ as final revelation include revelation and truth in non-Christian religions? (2) Does emphasis on the universality of Christ over the particularity of Jesus allow for more openness to non-Christian religions? (3) To what extent is the doctrine of Christ as final revelation diluted by a move to theocentrism in cross-cultural theological discussions (Christocentrism versus theocentrism)?

Traditionally, the Christian belief in Jesus as the Christ and as final revelation has been a motivating factor in proselytizing non-Christians, the primary form of Christian interaction with non-Christian religions. Focus on the finality of Christian revelation can lead to a self-righteousness which sees other religions as preliminary to the final revelation in Christ or sees Christianity as the exclusive bearer of final revelation. Such a position reduces non-Christian religions to a lame-duck position: you were important for a while but ultimately your positions are or will be surpassed and eliminated.[1] "Final" can mean "last," which suggests revelation is over and that

---

[1]This type of supersessionism has been of particular concern in Jewish-Christian dialogue. See R. Kendall Soulen, *The God of Israel and Christian Theology* (Minneapolis: Fortress Press, 1996).

there will be no other revelation. Such a view cuts off further revelatory moments within Christianity as well as outside and leaves Christianity looking backward for its understandings, with forward efforts related to a life or process beyond the ordinary world.

Traditionally, in Christianity final revelation has been tied up with the centrality of God's revelation in Jesus as the Christ. Many who grew up with this "Christian" outlook are uncomfortable today with such an imperialist approach that often went hand in hand with economic and political imperialism.[2] From a popular, liberal standpoint, some resolve this discomfort by rejecting all efforts at conversion and saying, "To each, his or her own." But if we look at this stance more deeply, we are dissatisfied with an unthought-out pure relativism. To give up the claim of final revelation or the centrality of the Christ would be to drastically change the focus and direction of Christian theology from its self-understood position of absoluteness to a relativized position of one truth among the many.

Is there a way to mediate the difference between the imperialism of an absolutist approach and the indifference of a relativist approach? How can we be open to non-Christian religious persons and still maintain a critical religious stance? How can an ecumenical Christian deal with the claim of final revelation in Jesus Christ? With these questions defining the issues for our discussion, in section A we will explore Tillich's ideas in relation to those of Karl Rahner and John Hick. Section B then will offer a more in-depth dialogue between Karl Barth and Tillich on these questions.

A. Rahner, Tillich, and Hick

Final Revelation in Jesus as the Christ

Karl Rahner: Christian Inclusivism with Anonymous Christians. Karl Rahner wants to retain the centrality and absoluteness of final revelation in Christ, but he is more concerned about including rather than condemning non-Christians. The basis of this more inclusive stance is his belief in the universality of Christ's redemption. He develops the idea of "anonymous Christian" to do justice to the Christian view that salvation cannot come

---

[2]See Rosemary Radford Ruether, *To Change the World: Christology and Cultural Criticism* (London: SCM Press, 1981).

apart from the theistic God and Christ and to include the possibility of super-natural salvation and faith for non-Christians.[3]

In "Christianity and the Non-Christian Religions," Karl Rahner accepts Christianity's self-understanding as the absolute religion, intended for all people, which cannot accept any other religion as equal to itself.[4] The basis of this stance is rooted in God's own action for humans in Christ,[5] but Rahner states strongly that non-Christian religions do contain supernatural elements of grace because of God's gift in Christ.[6] Some non-Christians can be called "anonymous Christians" because their experience of grace is rooted in Christ.

Such a position may satisfy the Christian's concern to love one's neighbor and avoid an imperialist condemnation of non-Christians. But Rahner's inclusiveness is rooted in God's gift in Christ rather than any quality in non-Christian religions themselves. To a non-Christian, this may appear as a somewhat more subtle and therefore more offensive claim of Christian superiority. Any positive religious value in their traditions is seen as coming from Christ, not from the religious and spiritual actions set forth by their own scriptures and leaders. On a practical level, Rahner's Christian inclusivism fails to take the non-Christian seriously on his or her own terms.

Paul Tillich: Paradox in Final Revelation as Criterion. Paul Tillich's discussions of final revelation and universal revelation provide another example of Christian inclusivism, but the concept of paradox used in his analysis can be developed more universally. When Tillich focuses on the concrete content of the Christ or the Cross, he retains the traditional sense of Christian superiority. But his formal abstractions of meaning from those events need not be tied to the specific Christian content.

In his *Systematic Theology*[7] Tillich defines revelation as "the manifesta-

---

[3]Karl Rahner, "The One Christ and the Universality of Salvation," *Theological Investigations* 16 (London: Darton, Longman, & Todd; New York: Seabury, 1979) 218.

[4]Karl Rahner, "Christianity and the Non-Christian Religions," *Theological Investigations* 5 (London: Darton, Longman & Todd; New York: Seabury, 1966) 118.

[5]Ibid.

[6]Ibid., 121.

[7]Paul Tillich, *Systematic Theology*, 3 vols. (Chicago: University of Chicago Press, 1951-1963). References will be in the form of ST volume number:page

tion of what concerns us ultimately" (ST 1:110). Such manifestation is always a concrete event for someone in a particular situation of concern (ST 1:111). Tillich does not accept a general revelation but does affirm the universal possibility of revelation. Because every person and thing participates in the ground, meaning, and power of being-itself, anything can bear revelation (ST 1:118).

This view of revelation has significant implications for developing an inclusive ecumenical understanding. Krishna, Buddha, and the Qur'an, like all beings, participate in the ground of being and can express and reveal it. The universal possibility of revelation is not tied to a Christian context, even though Tillich develops it from Christianity.

Final revelation is a specific form of revelation, in Tillich's view, not just the last genuine revelation. It is "the decisive, fulfilling, unsurpassable revelation, that which is the criterion of all the others" (ST 1:133). That criterion, based in Jesus as the Christ or the New Being, is that "a revelation is final if it has the power of negating itself without losing itself" (ST 1:133). Jesus' sacrifice to himself as the Christ is particularly seen in the Cross; in the negation of Jesus on the Cross is his affirmation as the Christ.[8]

Jesus as the Christ is the final revelation, but because of the grounding of all in the power of being-itself and the transforming power of the New Being (ST 2:167), other events outside Christianity can be revelatory of that power. Also, Tillich accepts the possibility of divine self-manifestation in other ways before and/or after our history (ST 2:101). In "The Significance of the History of Religions for the Systematic Theologian," Tillich suggests other possibilities of transforming revelation. What happened in the Cross in a symbolic way "also happens fragmentarily in other places, in other moments, has happened and will happen even though they are not historically or empirically connected with the cross."[9]

The paradoxical content of the criterion of final revelation relates to the paradoxical structure of all revelation that occurs in any unity of the ultimate with the finite.[10] A finite symbol of the ultimate is both conditioned and yet

---

number, e.g., ST 1:234.

[8]Paul Tillich, *The Dynamics of Faith* (New York: Harper & Row, 1957) 97-98.

[9]Paul Tillich, "The Significance of the History of Religions for the Systematic Theologian," *The Future of Religions*, ed. Jerald C. Brauer (New York: Harper & Row, 1966) 89.

[10]See Paul Tillich, "The Conquest of the Concept of Religion in the Philosophy

points to and bears the unconditioned. But even more, this paradox of final revelation involves the negation of ultimacy which is yet an affirmation of ultimacy.[11] The negation of ultimacy for Jesus on the Cross is yet the affirmation of ultimacy for Jesus as the Christ.

As with Tillich's affirmation of the universal possibility of revelation, so also his paradoxical criterion of final revelation can provide a basis for judging final revelation outside the Christian tradition. Many non-Christian symbols and ideas involve a paradoxical unity of the conditioned and the unconditioned, the finite and the ultimate. And some may even involve the paradoxical content of negation/affirmation specified in Tillich's criterion of final revelation.[12] Thus, the move to abstract formal meaning from specific content allows more openness to non-Christian traditions and may prevent the absolutization of the concrete content itself.

John Hick: Absoluteness of Christ for Christians. John Hick has called for a switch from a Ptolemaic understanding of religion to a Copernican viewpoint. Often this discussion has focussed on the center of all religions as the Real, with salvation in any religion as the transformation of the person from self-centeredness to Reality-centeredness.[13] Christianity, then, is just "one of a number of worlds of faith which circle around and reflect that Reality."[14] Religious truth and moral goodness can be found in all the major religious traditions.[15]

Hick's emphasis on one divine center does not mean he has abandoned the significance of Christ for Christians. But he has moved away from the

---

of Religion," *What Is Religion?*, ed. James Luther Adams (New York: Harper & Row, 1969) 123.

[11]See Robert P. Scharlemann, *Reflection and Doubt in the Thought of Paul Tillich* (New Haven CT: Yale University Press, 1969) 179-82.

[12]For further development of this idea, see my discussion in Mary Ann Stenger, "The Significance of Paradox for Theological Verification: Difficulties and Possibilities," *International Journal for Philosophy of Religion* 14 (1983): 171-82.

[13]John Hick, "On Grading Religions," *Religious Studies* 17 (1981): 467; John Hick, "Religious Pluralism," *The World's Religious Traditions*, ed. Frank Whaling (Edinburgh: T.&T. Clark, 1984) 158. See also Hick's discussions in *An Interpretation of Religion* (New Haven CT: Yale University Press, 1989) and in *A Christian Theology of Religions* (Louisville KY: Westminster/John Knox Press, 1995).

[14]John Hick, "Religious Pluralism and Absolute Claims," *Religious Pluralism*, ed. Leroy S. Rouner (Notre Dame IN: University of Notre Dame Press, 1984) 200.

[15]See Hick, "On Grading Religions."

traditional view of universal finality in Christ. He applauds those modern Christologies which judge the Christ event historically, seeing the historical Jesus as an exemplification of a specific religious quality and as one who leads others to respond to that truth.[16] Such Christologies cannot argue historically for absolute truth in Jesus even though they do assert the absoluteness of Christ for Christians.

Hick prefers metaphorical to literal understandings of the incarnation. Viewed metaphorically, the incarnation can be understood as one human way of expressing the Christian contact with God's presence, love, and power through Jesus. That view allows the possibility of other ways of salvation outside of Christ while still affirming salvation in Christ.[17] With such interpretations, Hick accepts the psychological absoluteness of Christ for Christians but asks that this not be turned into a claim of objective absoluteness and superiority that rejects all claims from non-Christian religious traditions.[18] His position affirms religious pluralism rather than just including non-Christians into his Christian framework.

Preliminary Comparisons. In all three approaches, we see an affirmation of revelation in Christ and an effort to accept some truth in all religions. Like Rahner, Tillich is a Christian inclusivist, affirming the finality of revelation in Christ and a sense of superiority in Christianity while also including truth from other religions. Hick takes further the acceptance of truth in all religions by not tying that truth to revelation in any one religion.

All of these positions do affirm a center in God, the ultimate/unconditioned, or the Real. For each, that center is the absolute which grounds all truth and all reality. All would also agree on an integral relationship between Jesus Christ and that divine center. But for Rahner, Christ is in the center with God; there is no revelation of God apart from Christ. Parts of Tillich's position suggest he agrees with Rahner: all reality is grounded in the ultimate, being-itself, and all saving transformation of people is grounded in the New Being manifested in Jesus as the Christ. But to the extent that Tillich's discussion abstracts from the concrete New Being in Jesus Christ and offers more universal, formal meaning for the Cross and the Christ, his ideas can be applied more universally—both inside and outside Christianity. Hick, like

---

[16]Hick, "Religious Pluralism and Absolute Claims," 193-213.

[17]John Hick, *God Has Many Names* (Philadelphia: Westminster Press, 1980) 75.

[18]Ibid., 57.

the others, retains absoluteness in Jesus Christ; but unlike them, the absoluteness affirmed is not objective but psychological for Christians. Similarly, he would see other religious truth claims as psychologically absolute for members of that tradition but not objectively or universally absolute.

Final revelation in Jesus as the Christ, then, may be understood as *inclusive* of non-Christians when it emphasizes the universal significance of the Christ and the Cross for all people. But such inclusion does not take the non-Christian seriously in his or her own terms but simply brings the non-Christian into the "Christian fold." An understanding of revelation that is open to revelation outside the Christian context (such as Tillich's position) is a necessary beginning of genuine openness to non-Christians. But we may also need to move beyond that to a deeper relativization of the understanding of Christ, such as Hick proposes in his affirmation of pluralism. Such relativization of the doctrine of Christ will involve analyzing the relationship between the historical Jesus and the universal Christ as well as reconsidering the role of that doctrine within Christian theology.

Universality of the Christ versus Particularity of Jesus: Rahner and Tillich

Even if Rahner and Tillich affirm the finality of God's revelation in Christ, they can still develop a theology which is open to non-Christian religious traditions by focusing on universal meaning in Christ. How possible it is to focus on the universality of Christ depends on how the relationship between the Christ and the historical Jesus is understood.

· Rahner affirms the centrality of Jesus Christ but allows inclusiveness based on the universality of Christ and the wide-spread efficacy of grace-filled salvation through Christ. The anonymous Christian is the person who lives in the grace of Christ through faith, hope and love but who does not explicitly recognize its source in Jesus Christ and who is not explicitly oriented to salvation through Christ.[19] Thus, Rahner is not using the term to refer to every person (universal salvation) but to persons whose beliefs and actions reflect the grace of Christ. It is Rahner's strong acceptance of the universality of Christ's redeeming action that grounds his position on

---

[19]Karl Rahner, "Observations on the Problems of the 'Anonymous Christian,' " *Theological Investigations* 14 (London: Darton, Longman & Todd; New York: Seabury, 1976) 283.

anonymous Christians.[20] His Spirit/Logos christology, i.e. his emphasis on the universal Christ, more than the particular historical Jesus provides the basis for his inclusion and openness.

Tillich attempts to maintain a dynamic tension between the particularity of the historical Jesus (including the Cross) and the universal meaning of the Christ or the New Being. But like Rahner he emphasizes the Christ more than the historical Jesus throughout his theology. When defining the essence of the Christ event or the meaning of the Cross or setting forth criteria of religious truth, Tillich focuses on the universal meaning derived from the concrete event more than the historical Jesus himself. In fact, he sees final revelation in Jesus as the Christ precisely because the particularities of the finite Jesus are sacrificed to the universal Christ. "The decisive trait in his picture is the continuous self-surrender of Jesus who is Jesus to Jesus who is the Christ" (ST 1:134).

When Tillich discusses the historical Jesus in relation to the New Being, he is quite clear that historical research about the historical Jesus does not guarantee us the reality of the New Being, nor that Jesus of Nazareth is that person, nor that the biblical details are correct (ST 2:114-15). Faith and participation in the transforming power of the New Being can guarantee that the biblical picture of Jesus is an adequate expression of that transforming power, but they cannot guarantee that Jesus is the name of the person who is the New Being (ST 2:107, 115). While it is important to Tillich that some historical reality bear the transforming power of the New Being, he does not focus on the certainty of the historical Jesus as such.

Tillich specifically discusses the interrelationship of particularity and universality in Jesus as the Christ and the significance of that for judging religious truth. Jesus is a particular historical life, but he makes no claims for himself based on his particularity. "What is particular in him is that he crucified the particular in himself for the sake of the universal."[21] Tillich applies this negation of particularities to all religions.

> Religion cannot come to an end, and a particular religion will be lasting to the degree in which it negates itself as a religion. . . . In the depth of every living religion there is a point at which the

---

[20]Rahner, "The One Christ and the Universality of Salvation," 218.

[21]Paul Tillich, *Christianity and the Encounter of the World Religions* (New York: Columbia University Press, 1963) 81.

religion itself loses its importance, and that to which it points breaks through its particularity, elevating it to spiritual freedom and with it to a vision of the spiritual presence in other expressions of the ultimate meaning of man's existence.[22]

Once again, Tillich's criterion of religion builds on the paradoxical significance he derives from Jesus as the Christ. He pushes to the depth of the religion, to the underlying spiritual presence and a spiritual freedom which is found by breaking through the finite particularities of religion (parallel to the Christ revealed by breaking through the finite particularities of the historical Jesus). This criterion applies to all religions, including Christianity, out of whose center the criterion is developed. It is important to recognize that Tillich is not advocating a universal religion outside of traditional religions; rather, he is calling people to experience the depth within each living tradition. In that depth, he believes that they will be spiritually free from the finite particularities of their own tradition and therefore open to that possibility in other religious traditions.

In a similar way, Tillich's critique of idolatry develops from the symbol of the Cross but then is applied to all religious symbols. The self-negation of Jesus to himself as the Christ leads to a criterion of a true religious symbol as one in which the finite aspects are transparent to the ultimate, without the finite elements themselves being taken as absolute. When people instead absolutize the finite medium itself, it ceases to be a medium of revelation and becomes an idol. Although developed from the Cross, this critique of idolatry can be applied outside Christianity.

At one point, Tillich uses this criterion to claim the superiority of Protestant Christianity.[23] But it would seem that he has overstated the claim since elsewhere he applies the critique within the Protestant tradition as well as to all of Christianity and other traditions. Still, there is little doubt that for Tillich, the Cross and Jesus' sacrifice of himself to himself as the Christ on the Cross did insure the unsurpassability of Christian revelation. Yet, his statement of a Yes and No judgment, that the most adequate symbol

---

[22]Ibid., 97.

[23]Tillich, *Dynamics of Faith*, 98. See Tom Driver's discussion of Tillich's position in "The Case for Pluralism," *The Myth of Christian Uniqueness*, ed. John Hick and Paul Knitter (Maryknoll NY: Orbis Books, 1987) 215.

expresses the ultimate (yes) but also its own lack of ultimacy (no),[24] is not stated in Christian terms and could be applied cross-culturally, even to his own view of the Cross and Christ.

Once again, we see that emphasis on the universality of the Christ and the universal meaning developed from the event of the Christ leads to more openness towards religious truth and spiritual meaning in non-Christian religious traditions. For Tillich, one cannot really separate that meaning and truth from the Cross, from the picture of Jesus as the Christ. But we suggest that these meanings might be developed for application across all religious traditions, without simply imposing a Christian standard or Christian meaning.

Christocentrism versus Theocentrism: Hick

Recognizing that the particularity of Christian claims can be a blocking point in dealing with non-Christian religions, John Hick has proposed an understanding which shifts the emphasis to the Real from the Christ. His call for a Copernican revolution in the Christian attitude toward other religions involves "a shift from the dogma that Christianity is at the center to the thought that it is *God* who is at the center and that all the religions of mankind, including our own, serve and revolve around him."[25] Hick proposes one transcendent, divine noumenon, which transcends all human conceptions of it and a plurality of divine phenomena (God as a personal god, the impersonal Absolute, etc.).[26] This imagery clearly calls into question any Christian claim of superiority over other religious traditions.

But Hick's shift to theocentrism here does not ignore the Christian center in Christ. As we have seen earlier, he allows for a psychological absoluteness but rejects the traditional claim of "objective absoluteness and superiority of our own faith in comparison with all others."[27] He also uses a metaphorical interpretation of Jesus Christ to relativize but retain the incarnation in Christ in relationship to the Real.

Hick is particularly interested in what he calls "degree Christologies" which talk about "the activity of God's Spirit or of God's grace" in varying

---

[24]Tillich, *Dynamics of Faith*, 97.
[25]Hick, *God Has Many Names*, 36.
[26]Ibid., 53.
[27]Ibid., 57-58.

degrees in human lives.[28] Although the authors of such Christological theories often affirm the superiority of revelation in Jesus Christ, Hick points out that such superiority can no longer be claimed a priori. Therefore, Christian claims of revelation are put on the same level with other claims. It is possible to see "God's activity in Jesus as being of the same kind as God's activity in other great human mediators of the divine."[29] By emphasizing God's activity, theocentrism can replace Christocentrism without giving up the central significance of Christ in Christianity. Only the Real itself is beyond the metaphors, myths, and cultures which attempt to express that Reality. Hick takes history seriously in emphasizing the diverse human cultural situations in which the different religious images and traditions operate. "It is the variations of the human cultural situation that concretize the notion of deity as specific images of God."[30]

Hick's theocentrism is more accurately Reality-centeredness since he does recognize that "God" is not an accurate name for the ultimate in all religious traditions. Hick does believe that across religious traditions there are many people who "experience life in relation to a limitlessly greater transcendent Reality—whether the direction of transcendence be beyond our present existence or within its hidden depths."[31] With the center in that Reality, religious pluralism can be affirmed in such a way that diverse concepts, images, practices, and forms of religious awareness can be seen as based on and directed toward the Real. These diverse ways are authentic to the extent that they are effective in transforming people from self- to Reality-centeredness.[32]

Hick's approach, then, maintains its openness to non-Christian religions by relativizing all human forms of religion, a move that we shall see in section B is shared by Barth's critique of religion and Tillich's critique of idolatry. He affirms pluralism rather than inclusivism by understanding Jesus Christ metaphorically rather than literally and by shifting absoluteness to the Real which is beyond the human forms of specific religious conceptions or practices. It is important to note that Hick's pluralism does not come from

---

[28]Hick, "Religious Pluralism," 154-55. Also see his discussion in "Religious Pluralism and Absolute Claims."

[29]Ibid., 155.

[30]Hick, God Has Many Names, 105.

[31]John Hick, "Religious Pluralism," 156-57.

[32]Ibid., 163-64.

simply emphasizing universal meaning in Christ (as do Rahner and Tillich) but rather from understanding all religious traditions as centered in the one transcendent Real.

From our discussions of Rahner, Tillich, and Hick, we can clearly see the tension between final revelation in Christ and a desire to be open to truth in non-Christian religions. For those who retain the centrality of final revelation in Christ and a close tie to the historical Jesus Christ, openness will most likely be expressed as some form of Christian inclusivism, including non-Christians under Christian rubrics. Even most of Tillich's writings, although more open than Rahner because of his formal abstractions of universal meaning, basically express a Christian inclusivism centered in Jesus as the Christ as final revelation.

Any form of Christian inclusivism, Tillich's or Rahner's, fails to take the non-Christian religions seriously, on their own terms. It dismisses their teachers, scriptures, prophets, deities, and ultimates as secondary and finally irrelevant to Christian truths. With such a position, dialogue is a sharing of ideas but not an openness to new ideas. But real engagement with another person involves openness to adjusting one's ideas.

In fact, both Tillich and Hick have engaged in dialogue with non-Christians, and one can see ongoing shifts in their thought as a result of those conversations. Both make similar moves in their thinking, toward one underlying Reality or depth beneath the particular phenomena of the religions. This position has the advantage of allowing individual religions to have their truths but makes all religious truths relative to the one underlying or centering Real or depth. This approach does not destroy the acceptance of final revelation in Christ but relativizes it in relation to other revelations in non-Christian traditions. Christians can still retain the absoluteness of Christ for themselves, but they do not assert it in relation to the non-Christian.

One can develop criteria out of one's own tradition and state them in ways that are not tied to the particular tradition (for example, Tillich's criterion of "affirmation in negation"). But the real test of such criteria is not just how they fit with final revelation in Christ but how applicable they can be in dialogue with non-Christians. Many traditions might agree with Tillich's critique of idolatry even though they would not accept the concrete content from which the critique arises.

B. Barth and Tillich

Unlike the theologians discussed in section A, Karl Barth sometimes has been linked with a conservative evangelical approach that proclaims Christianity as the one true religion over against all others.[33] Thus, it might seem that there would be little basis for dialogue between Barth's position and Tillich's. Yet they share some key ideas in their analysis of religion, final revelation, and the Christ; in the end, however, their differences establish contrasting approaches to non-Christian religions.

We will first compare Barth's and Tillich's critiques of religion itself, relating that to their approaches to non-Christian religions. Second, we will discuss the role of Christ in those critiques and compare their understandings of Christ as final revelation. The final section will evaluate their approaches in the context of our prior discussion of Rahner and Hick, with respect to the degree of openness to truth in non-Christian religions.

Critiques of Religion Itself

Developing out of the theological climate of post-World War I Germany, both Barth and Tillich were critical of religion itself as a human activity with idolatrous elements. Those critiques continued throughout their careers but were modified in relation to other theological concerns in their later writings. Since their critiques are applicable to discussion of Christ as final revelation in relation to non-Christian religions, we shall analyze those arguments as our starting point for their "dialogue."

Karl Barth: Human Religion versus Divine Revelation. In his commentary on Romans, Barth's critique of religion is rooted in his affirmation of God as Other and Holy judging humans in their unbelief. Religion is judged with a Yes and a No although the No is clearly stronger. To the extent that religion is directed toward faith, it can be judged with a Yes; of course, that direction is really the divine possibility of religion, related to

---

[33]See Paul Knitter, *No Other Name? A Critical Survey of Christian Attitudes Toward the World Religions* (Maryknoll NY: Orbis Books, 1985) 80-87. Also see Daniel B. Clendenin, *Many Gods, Many Lords; Christianity Encounters World Religions* (Grand Rapids MI: Baker Books, 1995) where Barth is cited as "a prime example of Christian exclusivism" (61).

God's revelation and transformation of the old world.[34] But to the extent that as a human possibility, it claims to be more than human and to possess ultimate reality, it stands under sin and death and is subject to the No of God's wrath. As the latter, religion must be abandoned because its claims made on its own behalf are worthless.[35] As arrogant human effort, religion is contrasted to God's grace and shows the distance between God's righteousness and human self-righteousness. Instead of responding to God's grace, through religion humans try to do things for themselves; in their pride and despair, they lose sight of God's eternal righteousness.[36]

Behind this understanding of God's righteousness versus human self-righteousness is Barth's understanding of Jesus as the Christ, as the revelation of God's righteousness. In the Christ, God's power, sovereignty, and faithfulness are shown.[37] In Jesus' death on the Cross, the otherness of God and yet also God's indissoluble union with humanity is presented.[38] Both the Yes and No of God's judgment are seen in Jesus as the Christ, in his Cross and Resurrection.

In Barth's *Church Dogmatics*,[39] the contrast of human and divine righteousness is stated as the contrast between revelation and religion. Revelation shows the distance between religion which starts with humans and revelation which originates in God.[40] Religion "contradicts" revelation, and God's revelation "denies that any religion is true."[41] Thus, Christianity as well as non-Christian religions stand under the judgment of religion as unbelief, including idolatry and self-righteousness.[42]

But revelation also can pick out a religion as true religion, not on its own basis but on the basis of divine judgment and revelation.[43] Thus, one

---

[34]Karl Barth, *The Epistle to the Romans*, trans. from the 6th ed. by Edwyn C. Hoskyn) (London: Oxford University Press, 1933) 130, 135-36, 183-84, 231.

[35]Ibid., 184-85.

[36]Karl Barth, "The Righteousness of God," *The Word of God and the Word of Man* (New York: Harper & Row, 1956/1928) 20, 23.

[37]Ibid., 94-97.

[38]Ibid., 162.

[39]Karl Barth, *Church Dogmatics*, 4 vols., ed. G. W. Bromiley and T. F. Torrance (Edinburgh: T.&T. Clark, 1958).

[40]Ibid. 1/2:293.

[41]Ibid. 1/2:325.

[42]Ibid. 1/2:326-27.

[43]Ibid. 1/2:325-26.

cannot say that Christianity is the true religion in and of itself although Barth does say that Christianity is the bearer of true religion by the grace of God through His revelation in Christ.[44] It is not that Christians have earned that status through their own merit or actions; it is simply God's free choice and righteous judgment.

Barth draws several conclusions from this understanding of Christianity as the bearer of true religion. First, since it is not through the merits of Christian action that Christianity has that status, one cannot gain higher status for non-Christian religions which have similar historical forms in doctrine, ethics, or ritual.[45] Another religion's emphasis on grace, love, and devotion does not mean it contains partial Christian truth. For Barth, because other religions do not have their focus in Jesus Christ as God's revelation, they continue to stand under the judgment of all religion as unbelief.[46]

Second, that Christianity has been chosen as the bearer of true religion does not mean that Christ's actions were for Christians only. Rather, Jesus Christ did die and rise for all people, but non-Christians do not recognize that or accept that gift. "It is not as though Jesus Christ did not die and rise again for them, or as though they were not reconciled, justified, and sanctified to God and before Him and for Him. It is simply that they have turned away from this benefit so fully and unreservedly proffered to them, so that it is of no avail."[47] Barth argues that it is not that God has condemned non-Christians but rather that they have condemned themselves to their unspiritual life.

Third, people should not say that another religion could have been chosen, that things could be otherwise, but they should accept God's decision and judgment which offers all people acquittal through Jesus Christ.[48] God acts freely and justly, and humans cannot second-guess those actions but must respond by accepting God's free gift of grace. Human judgment and tolerance of non-Christian religions is simply human decision and action and remains on the level of sin, self-righteousness, and idolatry in contrast to God's righteous judgment for humans in Christ.

---

[44]Ibid. 1/2:331, 345-46, 350.
[45]Ibid. 1/2:432-43.
[46]Ibid. 1/2:343.
[47]Ibid. 4/3/1:354.
[48]Ibid. 1/2:354.

Paul Tillich: Critique of Idolatry. Tillich's concept of religion as ultimate concern can be compared with Barth's discussion of human and divine possibilities in religion. The element of concern points to the subjective and existential aspect of religion as a human response to ultimacy (ST 1:11-12). The adjective *ultimate* points to the object of that concern as beyond ordinary human concerns and as that which determines our being and not-being (ST 1:13-14). Thus, both Barth and Tillich recognize the human and the divine or ultimate in religion—for Barth, the basis of a Yes and No judgment of religion.

For Tillich, the Yes and No judgment stems from the relationship between religion and idolatry. Revelation is the manifestation of the ultimate or divine through something finite. If that finite object, person, or experience maintains its status as a *medium* of revelation, then its finite status will continue to be recognized along with its transparency to the infinite. But if people forget or ignore the finite, limited status of the object as medium, they turn the object into the ultimate revelation itself and respond idolatrously.

It is important to note that while Tillich is criticizing the idolatrous response for elevating the finite to ultimacy, he is also recognizing the element of divine revelation that underlies that response. Because all things participate in the power of being and the power of being in them, anything can become a bearer of the mystery of being (ST 1:118). Second, since all people are oriented beyond their immediate situation toward ultimacy,[49] concern about the ultimate is behind even idolatrous responses. Third, the response of people to what they see as ultimate involves the risk of personal commitment that may turn out to be existentially disappointing, frustrating, and destructive if the object of commitment is not really ultimate. But the structure and personal risk of commitment is the same in idolatrous and nonidolatrous responses. Finally, the revelation of the holy can be experienced as creative or as destructive, as divine or as demonic.[50] Thus, the revelation and demand of the ultimate stands behind both idolatrous and demonic possibilities as well as nonidolatrous and divine possibilities of religion.

Tillich states his critique of idolatry in various versions of the Protestant Principle which protests against absolute claims for relative, finite realities.

---

[49]Tillich, *Dynamics of Faith*, 9.
[50]Ibid., 14-16.

True bearers of revelation and true symbols of faith should both express the ultimate and deny their own ultimacy (see discussion of this above in section A). This criterion of faith "contains a Yes—it does not reject any truth of faith in whatever form it may appear in the history of faith—and it contains a No—it does not accept any truth of faith as ultimate except the one that no man possesses it."[51] For Tillich, this criterion of self-negation is realized in the Cross of Christ; Jesus sacrifices himself (negates himself) in bearing the revelation of the Christ. The acceptance of Jesus as the Christ must include Jesus the crucified.[52] In one sense, it is the event of the Cross that has given Tillich the criterion of self-negation, and yet the paradoxical criterion of self-negation can be developed outside of a specifically Christian focus.

Just as Barth's critique of religion focuses on the human attempt to do what only God can do, Tillich's critique of idolatry focuses on the human elevation of something finite to ultimacy. Both critiques protect the ultimate as ultimate or God as God and recognize the human tendency to usurp that status. In Tillich's terms, both would be operating from the standpoint of the Protestant principle "that the sacred sphere is not nearer to the Ultimate than the secular sphere. It denies that either of them has a greater claim to grace than the other; both are infinitely distant from and infinitely near to the Divine."[53]

But Tillich's critique of idolatry recognizes the element of divine revelation underlying all religion, including idolatrous types. In contrast, Barth focuses on the human efforts as unbelief and ignoring of God's revelation rather than seeing revelation underlying the idolatrous response. This difference stems in part from Tillich's view that any reality can be the medium of revelation while Barth sees God's revelation in Jesus as the Christ through Scriptures.

Tillich's critique of religion expands on his critique of idolatry. He continues to recognize the universal revelation which can be found in all religions but also the dangers of absolutizing a particular concrete form of religion. In *Christianity and the Encounter of the World Religions*, Tillich focuses on this relationship between universality and particularity. To the extent that a religion can break through its own particularity, it can be a

---

[51]Ibid., 98.
[52]Ibid.
[53]Tillich, *Christianity and the Encounter of the World Religions*, 47.

bearer of the religious answer.[54] This does not mean that a person should replace one's particular religious tradition with some kind of universal concept; rather one breaks through the particularity by penetrating the depth of one's own religious tradition and recognizing and experiencing what underlies the particularity: ultimate meaning rooted in the power of being-itself which participates in all being.

In his last essay, "The Significance of the History of Religions for the Systematic Theologian," Tillich states that "the universal religious basis is the experience of the Holy within the finite."[55] This universal revelation or experience of the Holy is the basis of sacramental and mystical elements in all religions and grounds the ethical or prophetic critique which judges concrete phenomena in terms of destructive, demonic results of injustice. Tillich calls the unity of these three elements in one religion the "Religion of the Concrete Spirit" and sees such a religion, as the inner *telos* of the history of religions.[56] But one cannot identify any particular religion as the Religion of the Concrete Spirit; rather "we can see the whole history of religions in this sense as a fight for the Religion of the Concrete Spirit, a fight of God against religion within religion."[57] This discussion is a fuller and more specific application of Tillich's critique of idolatry. Barth would agree with the "fight of God against religion within religion" but would disagree with Tillich's stronger Yes to an underlying presence or power of God in all religions.

Tillich continues to use the Cross of the Christ as the basis for criteria of judgment and as the example of religious truth. In relation to particularity and universality, he argues that the particularity of the Christ is crucified for the sake of the universal.[58] Jesus as the Christ is religious, yet free from religion, and particular, yet free from particularity.[59] Similarly, the event of the Cross of Christ is a manifestation of the religion of the concrete spirit.[60]

---

[54]Ibid., 97.

[55]Tillich, "The Significance of the History of Religions for the Systematic Theologian," 86.

[56]Ibid., 87-88.

[57]Ibid., 88.

[58]Tillich, *Christianity and the Encounter of the World Religions*, 81.

[59]Ibid., 82.

[60]Tillich, "The Significance of the History of Religions for the Systematic Theologian," 88-89.

But Tillich also allows for other actualizations of religious truth that are not specifically Christian or tied to the Cross. As we shall explore further, Tillich's openness to revelation and religious truth anywhere creates a tension in his thought between the recognition of revelation and truth in non-Christian religions and the assertion of Jesus as the Christ as final revelation. This tension is coupled with Tillich's growing respect for and contact with non-Christian religious possibilities. Barth's form of Christocentrism avoids such a tension, but it does raise questions about the universality and finality of God's revelation in Christ.

Final Revelation and the Christ

The Role of Christ in Barth's Critique. In both his early and later discussions of religion, Barth stresses the freedom and righteousness of God in contrast to human self-righteousness and idolatry. God's faithfulness, righteous judgment and free decision in Christ show human decisions and actions to be sinful, distorted, and self-oriented. Barth's emphasis on the negative human condition serves to highlight the glory and righteousness of God. The human activities of religion serve to highlight *human* glory rather than God's and thus are called unbelief.

God's revelation through Christ does not change this judgment of human efforts for their own merit, but it does offer acquittal and acceptance of humans in spite of that ongoing judgment of sin and unbelief. Thus, it is the role of Christ that enables Barth to see Christianity as the bearer of true religion. Barth is clear that without Christ, Christianity would be nothing.[61] In divine freedom and righteousness, God marked out Christianity to be the bearer of true religion although its human efforts are still held under the judgment of sinfulness and idolatry, just as non-Christian religions are.

This universal critique of religion is coupled with the universal significance of Jesus as the Christ. Jesus as the Christ did die and rise for non-Christians as for all people, but that gift of reconciliation is not effective if not recognized and accepted. The objective reality and finality of God's redeeming revelation is present in Christ, and that redemption is the basis for creation and provides the center for the history of the world. God's grace in Christ is universal as a part of His eternal covenant with humanity.

For Barth, then, it is only God through Christ who can reconcile non-Christians and Christians. Without the name of Christ, their human efforts

---

[61]Barth, *Church Dogmatics* 1/2:347.

count for nothing toward religious truth or salvation. Religious truth and salvation stem from *divine* action, not human actions, but what God does affects all humans, not just Christians. To speak of revelation or religious truth apart from Christ would also mean to speak of it apart from God, for Barth. Revelation of God in Christ is final and will not—indeed cannot—be surpassed.

Since the gift of Christ and salvation is not based on human merit and is given by God for all humanity, then one can ask why God would choose to mark out some people and not others for that gift. Barth sees such a question as an expression of human idolatry and self-righteousness—putting our knowledge, logic, and understanding against the righteous judgment that God has already made. Instead, Barth wants the response to be free acceptance of that gift for oneself and recognition that those who do not accept the gift condemn themselves. But since it is divine action which initiates and sustains faith in Jesus Christ, the question is merely ignored by Barth, not answered.

God's gift in Christ shows a universal and unmerited love for all humanity, but it does not imply a tolerance of views and actions which are not centered in Christ. Barth tries to avoid a self-righteousness for Christianity by applying his critique of religion to Christianity as well as non-Christian religions. But since the practical effect of his position is to deny truth to non-Christian religions and therefore to see non-Christians as condemned, it is difficult not to see Barth's exclusivity as implying a self-righteousness for Christianity - even if its source is God in Christ, not human efforts. Of course, Barth has argued that God's decision for Christianity in His revelation in Christ should not be the source of any such self-righteousness since it only expresses divine righteousness, not human righteousness.[62]

---

[62]Following Barth, Robert Jenson has argued that Christians should affirm pluralism by cultivating their Christian identity (Robert W. Jenson, "Religious Pluralism, Christology, and Barth," *Dialog* [Winter 1981]: 32). Jenson sees Barth asserting the universality of the revelation in Christ's resurrection: the reconciliation between God and humans has occurred in that event (33). But Jenson pulls out more from Barth's affirmation of the universal significance of Christ's resurrection. He argues that in Barth's emphasis on God's eternal covenant with humanity, which includes creation as well as reconciliation, "all persons are *summoned into being by the Resurrection-proclamation,* and thus by their mere being are qualified as witnesses" to Christ (33). In other words, all religions are in the same situation in

The Role of Christ in Tillich's Critique. For Tillich, as we have seen in section A, there is a dynamic tension between the particularity of Jesus as the Christ and the Cross and the universal significance of the Christ or the New Being. His criteria of evaluating religions and religious symbols are developed out of his understanding of the Christ and the Cross but are stated in forms which are not tied to the Christ and the Cross and therefore can be more universally applicable. The criteria of self-negation to avoid idolatry, the paradox of Yes-No for religious truth, and the interrelationship of universality and particularity need not be tied to Christianity even though the basis of their formulation was the event of the Christ. Tillich does not deny the circularity in this argument: the criteria are developed out of the Christian events, and then the Christian events are judged to be true in light of those criteria.[63] But we will suggest later that the criteria could be separated from that specifically Christian foundation.

Tillich and Barth agree on the centrality of the Christ and the reality of God's revelation and action in the Christ. And both agree on free divine activity as the basis of any revelation at all. It is not human action that determines salvation or brings about union with one's essential self, others, and God; it is God's action—free gift of grace in Christ—which reconciles and reunites beings to their root in God. Both also see the need to protect the absoluteness of God against human efforts at self-salvation and the idolatry of human or finite concerns. In preserving God's absoluteness, Barth notes the freedom of God to choose Christianity to be the bearer and to righteously judge other religions against the revelation in Christ. But we can ask whether such a viewpoint adequately protects the freedom of God or in fact binds God to "our" "Christian" viewpoint. Barth's view of the exclusivity of God's revelation in Christ does retain the sovereignty and righteousness of God's action as well as the universal significance of the Christ, but it also denies God the possibility of other equally righteous action in non-Christian bearers.

For Tillich, centrality does not mean the exclusivity of God's revelation in Jesus as the Christ as it does for Barth. For Tillich, there is the possibility

---

relation to Christ, but Jenson recognizes that this does not solve the political problem of pluralism (35).

[63]"In accord with the circular character of systematic theology, the criterion of final revelation is derived from what Christianity considers to be the final revelation, the appearance of Jesus as the Christ" (ST 1:135).

of revelation in other events, persons or realms, although for historical humanity, the revelation in Jesus as the Christ will not be surpassed. Other bearers of revelation could be partial manifestations or at best equal to the revelation in Jesus as the Christ but not greater than the Christ. In his last essay, Tillich does assert that "there are revealing and saving powers in all religions."[64] But this openness creates a tension in Tillich's theology between the recognition of revelation and truth in non-Christian religions and the assertion of Jesus as the Christ as final revelation.

Final revelation for Tillich does not necessarily mean the last but rather complete fulfillment for historical humanity. Final revelation means "the decisive, fulfilling, unsurpassable revelation, that which is the criterion of all the others" (ST 1:133). But when Tillich pursues the understanding of final revelation, he relates it to the criteria of self-negation and argues strongly that the particularities of Jesus (his finite characteristics, individual piety, first century worldview, etc.) are not absolute but part of his finitude. Thus, there could be non-Christian revelations that approach finality or are final according to the same criteria.

From this analysis of the positions of Barth and Tillich, we can see two different ways of approaching God's revelation in Christ as final. Barth's understanding of the finality of God's revelation in Christ demands exclusivity because he wants to affirm the sovereignty and righteousness of God over against all human religious attempts to know God and be like God. But it can be argued that Tillich's more universal approach to final revelation better preserves the sovereignty and righteousness of God by allowing the possibility of divine revelation outside of Christianity. For Barth, such a position is unbelief, for it denies the universality of God's covenant with humanity in Christ, from redemption through creation. Tillich tries to retain the central significance of God's transforming, healing power in the Christ or the New Being, but his position downplays the particularity of the historical person of Jesus. Jesus becomes a particular bearer of the New Being, not the bearer. That manifestation may not be surpassed, but it could be just one among others.

---

[64]Tillich, "The Significance of the History of Religions for the Systematic Theologian," 81.

Evaluation of Barth and Tillich—
Exclusivity versus Inclusivity versus Pluralism

As we have seen in section A, John Hick has argued for a relativizing of Christian claims to finality in the face of religious pluralism.[65] His Copernican model of religious revelation and truth that sees God at the center, with the different religious traditions based in and reflecting that center, has been criticized for giving up the centrality of Christ in Christianity.[66] He argues that traditional christology does not work for the modern perspective on religious pluralism: "It is hard to hold together our modern awareness that God is savingly at work within all the great world religions with our inherited orthodox christology."[67] Hick states well the crux of the issue when he argues that cutting out the exclusivity and uniqueness of the divine incarnation in Christ decreases its power, and yet not to cut that out violates the understanding of God as the Creator and loving parent of all humankind.[68] It can be argued that Hick has carried the sovereignty and freedom of God that are posited in Christian theology to its logical conclusion, that God need not be tied to only revealing truth in one way and one person. Hick's position is more radically relativized than Tillich's and could be used to critique Tillich's retention of the centrality of final revelation in the Christ. Hick's position is perhaps the polar opposite of Barth's but would agree with Barth's emphasis on God as absolute. Barth shares with Karl Rahner the centrality and absoluteness of final revelation in Christ and the sovereignty of God's action for humans in Christ, but Rahner allows for more manifestations of God's grace in non-Christian religions than does Barth.

---

[65]John Hick, "Whatever Path Men Choose Is Mine," *Christianity and Other Religions*, ed. John Hick and Brian Hebblethwaite (Philadelphia: Fortress Press, 1980) 171-90. Also in *God Has Many Names* (Philadelphia: Westminster Press, 1980) 60-78.

[66]For example, see Kenneth Surin, "Revelation, Salvation, the Uniqueness of Christ, and Other Religions," *Religious Studies* 19 (Summer 1983): 323-43. Also see Jenson, "Religious Pluralism, Christology, and Barth."

[67]John Hick, "Christology in an Age of Religious Pluralism," *Journal of Theology for Southern Africa* 35 (June 1981): 6.

[68]Ibid., 7-8.

For Barth, God's revelation in Jesus Christ is directly connected with the historical Jesus' birth, death and resurrection which brought the reconciliation of humans to God. With Barth, there is little separation of the historical Jesus from the universal Christ. It is not just that Jesus is a particular example of religious perfection or some other ideal quality. Barth is quite clear that "theology must begin with Jesus Christ, and not with general principles" as if Jesus Christ "were a continuation of the knowledge and Word of God, and not its root and origin, not indeed the very Word of God itself."[69] In Barth's discussions of Jesus Christ, he moves back and forth between references to the historical events in Jesus' life and the reconciliation and liberation for humanity that were achieved through those events. He rejects a formal meaning for Christ and focuses instead on Christ's salvific meaning for the Christian in faith.

But, as Rahner would agree, this salvific meaning was meant for all people; all are called into the light of Jesus Christ.[70] Barth speaks of Jesus Christ as the one light of the world but also of reflecting lights both inside and outside the church.[71] True words that reflect the light of Christ can occur in Christian communities but also outside Christian communities— perhaps in other religious or secular settings. The basis for such a view is in Barth's acceptance of the preexistence of Jesus Christ. God's covenant from the beginning included God's redemptive choice to be unified with humans through Jesus Christ. God wills redemption first, then creation. The universal significance of Jesus Christ then relates to all persons through creation and may be reflected in some particular words which point to God's word in Christ.[72]

The positive side of Barth's position is that it does have a universal, inclusive dimension. Theoretically and theologically, all persons of the world are included as capable of expressing at least a possible reflection of Christ's truth. But Barth is also clear that for someone to reflect the light of Christ, that person must have had some contact with Christ,[73] a position that sets him apart from Rahner's view of anonymous Christians. Thus, Barth's

---

[69]Barth, *Church Dogmatics* 2/2:5.

[70]Ibid. 4/3B:875; 4/3-1:354.

[71]Ibid. 4/3-1:¶69.

[72]For fuller discussion of Barth on this issue, see Jenson, "Religious Pluralism, Christology, and Barth," 31-38.

[73]Barth, *Church Dogmatics* 4/3-1:124, 344-45.

suggested inclusiveness is not an inclusion of non-Christian religions in their own right but only if there is some reflection of Christ's truth. Nor does this inclusiveness imply a tolerance of non-Christian ideas and practices that are not centered in Christ. Practically, Barth's position excludes non-Christians except for some reflections of *Christ's truth* or as witnesses to the *light of Christ*.

Barth's understanding of the universality of Christ is centered in the historical Jesus. He does not see the reconciliation between humans and God occurring through any other person than Jesus Christ. Thus, the universal Christ does not include Gautama Buddha, Amida Buddha, Krishna or Brahman, and so forth. For Barth and for Rahner, Christ is in the center with God; there is no revelation of God apart from Christ. Barth commentator Robert Jenson has suggested that Barth would see the view that all religions lead to the same place not as mediating the difference between Christianity and other religions but rather adopting an alternative religion to Christianity.[74]

Also important in Barth's position is his concern for the absoluteness of God over against finite, human efforts. The idolatry and absolutization of human religion have supported injustice, oppression, and destruction of individuals. But it is not clear that Barth's critique of religion and preservation of God's righteousness demands the kind of practical exclusivism which Barth suggests. If God is really absolute and free and we did not earn the revelation in Christ, then there is the possibility of God's righteous, free activity outside of Christianity. Of course, it is here that Barth's Christocentrism overtakes his theocentrism; the choice for humanity in Christ was made prior to and through creation, and thus there cannot be another revelation. The practical exclusivism that stems from Barth's position does not fit the situation of religious pluralism today and has made Barth's position an easy target for criticism. But we should not lose his concern to protect the absoluteness of God and the significance of Christ.

From Tillich, present discussion of cross-cultural religious truth should consider his view of anything finite as a medium of revelation, his universal application of criteria developed in relation to the Cross, and elements of his critique of idolatry. For some, Tillich's approach is still too closely tied to the Christ—expanding the applicability of the Christ but basically drawing other traditions into the fold through the Cross of the Christ. For non-Christians,

---

[74]Jenson, "Religious Pluralism, Christology, and Barth," 32.

such an approach is no more palatable than Hindu arguments that Christian religious forms are relegated to the phenomenal level in relation to the Absolute Brahman would be to Christians. Yet for those within the Christian tradition, Tillich does offer an open approach which yet retains the importance of Christ, an attempt at balancing universality with particularity in the event of Christ.

Tillich's approach has a strong theocentric approach in his concern for the ultimate, but this is coupled clearly with a strong emphasis on Christ that does not diminish as he becomes more open to non-Christian revelation and religious truth. Rather, his increasing openness is accompanied by a more universal application of his understanding of the Christ and God's revelation. Hick and Tillich both emphasize God as the center, but for Tillich, as also for Barth and Rahner, Christ is also the center and not relativized as in Hick's position.

Although Tillich's critique of idolatry and Barth's critique of religion are tied into their understandings of the Cross and Christ, the basic root of those critiques is the unconditionality of God or the ultimate in contrast to the conditioned, finite world. Tillich's understanding of symbols and his use of paradox express that concern for God's unconditionality and can be used to develop a criterion against idolatry (see section A).

The Unconditional is beyond the subject-object split of ordinary knowledge, but in religious expression we bring the ultimate into that relation. Thus, the expression both expresses and does not express the Unconditional.[75] This paradoxical form, then, is the basic structure of religious expression; in idolatry, the basic structure of religious expression or the paradoxical form is violated when the finite object or expression is taken as ultimate in itself.

The criterion of paradox may have application to the Cross of the Christ but it does not need to be tied to that symbol. The application of this criterion can protect the ultimate from being identified with the finite itself and thereby also work against the destructive results of idolatry. When finite aspects of a religious expression are absolutized (race, maleness, nation, etc.) or when one expression is absolutized as the only true expression (one literal interpretation of the Bible, one acceptable understanding of Christ, Christ

---

[75]Tillich, "The Conquest of the Concept of Religion in the Philosophy of Religion," 123. Similarly, Tillich says: "Every religious symbol negates itself in its literal meaning, but it affirms itself in its self-transcending meaning" (ST 2:9).

as the only revelation, etc.), then something finite has been absolutized. Often this has led to negative results for people who are somehow outside the finite area that has been absolutized. Blacks, women, and non-Christians could testify to the destructive consequences of such idolatry in Christianity, and similar results could be documented in other religious traditions as well.

This criterion of paradox in religious expression shares the concern for the absoluteness of God or the ultimate found in Barth's critique of religion and Tillich's critique of idolatry. In its application within Christianity and outside of Christianity and its tie to the universal structure of religious symbol, it goes beyond their specific critiques and yet it maintains that ultimacy and absoluteness of God or the ultimate. This criterion of truth is theocentrically based rather than christocentrically, but it will work well with a Christocentric theology that is not exclusivist. This theocentric base can be brought forward from both Barth's and Tillich's critiques of religion and idolatry and retained in the criterion of paradox applied cross-culturally as well as within Christianity.

Our future, then, is not for Christians to abandon their centering in Christ as final revelation but to relate that center finally to ultimacy that is beyond finite expressions and forms. There are some who call for an even more radical relativism, seeing each tradition operating within its historical-cultural context, without claiming one underlying absolute. But that direction toward ultimacy and truth in all religions is a structural commonality even if people do not agree on the nature of that ultimacy. Consequently, people of faith can work out of their own traditions and cultures but must continue in conversation and dialogue that is based on their common search for truth and transcendence. As they do so, core doctrines like final revelation in Christ are not abandoned but interpreted anew for our present pluralistic situation, as in the development of the criterion of paradox.

Chapter 2

Buddhism, Barth, and Ultimacy

Scholars of religious experience have been intrigued by the question of whether the different languages of religious traditions express real differences in the religious experiences or are mere linguistic variations. Even if we recognize that there is a gap between the experience and the expression of the experience, we are still left with major differences in expression that raise the issue of the nature of the basic experience of ultimacy. Is that basic experience different when it is expressed in terms of "reality" or "being" from the basic experience that is expressed in terms of "nothingness"? Are the differences in terminology simply that or do they express truly different understandings and experiences?

Although the traditional Christian starting point of religious expression is usually *being* or *reality* and a common Buddhist beginning point is *nothingness*, we cannot assume there is no common ground in the ultimacy that underlies those expressions. In this essay, I explore the relationship of affirmation (grounded in being) and negation (grounded in nothingness) in the root understandings of ultimacy for two Christian thinkers (Paul Tillich and Karl Barth) and two Buddhist thinkers (Masao Abe and Keiji Nishitani). I focus on affirmation and negation because these opposites suggest contradiction rather than equivalency and therefore present a challenge to any discussion of God-equivalents and to interreligious dialogue.

Tillich and Barth

For Paul Tillich, the relationship of affirmation and negation in ultimacy is based on the interaction of being and nonbeing. In his *Systematic Theology*, he suggests that being is prior to and more primary than nonbeing. "Being precedes nonbeing in ontological validity, as the word 'nonbeing' itself indicates."[1] And in *The Courage to Be*, he states that nonbeing is "the negation of every concept,"[2] with the negative living from the positive it negates.[3] Again, expressing the priority of being over nonbeing, he states that "being has nonbeing 'within' itself."[4]

This relationship of being and nonbeing is tied to Tillich's understanding of ultimacy as "being-itself." Tillich uses the term "being-itself" to conceptualize God without treating God as *a* being like or above other beings and to express God as the infinite power and meaning of being which underlies all beings.[5] It is important that Tillich emphasizes being-itself as the power of being since otherwise one might understand being-itself as a static concept. All other beings experience the threat of nonbeing, but being-itself is the power of being which continues to resist nonbeing in everything that is.[6]

So in being-itself, being is prior to nonbeing, yet continually overcoming it. Interestingly enough, this understanding leads Tillich to suggest an almost equal status of being and nonbeng or even a priority for nonbeing. For example, as part of his explanation of being-itself as the power of being in *The Courage to Be*, Tillich states:

> We could not even think "being" without a double negation: being must be thought as the negation of the negation of being. . . . The self-affirmation of being without nonbeing would not even be self-affirmation but an immovable self-identity. Nothing would be manifest, nothing expressed, nothing revealed. But nonbeing drives being out of its seclusion, it forces it to affirm itself dynamically.[7]

If being is the negation of nonbeing, then being gets its character from an ongoing relationship with nonbeing. Similarly, nonbeing "lives" off of the being it negates.

---

[1]Paul Tillich, *Systematic Theology*, 3 vols. (Chicago: University of Chicago Press, 1951–1963) 1:189. Hereafter *Systematic Theology* will be cited as ST followed by volume and page numbers.

[2]Paul Tillich, *The Courage to Be* (New Haven CT: Yale University Press, 1952) 34.

[3]Ibid., 176.

[4]Ibid., 34.

[5]ST 1:235.

[6]ST 1:236.

[7]*The Courage to Be*, 179.

For Tillich, this ontology is rooted in the experience of absolute faith. God as being-itself is experienced as the power that enables a person to resist nonbeing in the forms of fate, doubt, and guilt. The experience of nonbeing is an ordinary part of life; the awareness of one's possibly not being, of one's finitude is natural anxiety.[8] But also the experience of courage, of the power of being which enables a person to affirm himself/herself is an ordinary part of life. Faith, for Tillich, is the "state of being grasped by the power of being which transcends everything that is and in which everything that is participates."[9] Faith is not an opinion but a state of being, an underlying basis of life. Faith is experiencing one's basic connections with being-itself.

In Tillich's view, then, the experience of ultimacy is a dynamic experience of courage, of being able to affirm being by resisting and overcoming nonbeing. Continually, we are aware of our limits—physically, psychologically, intellectually, morally, spiritually. But as part of our living, we also affirm and live through the power of the positive—physical life, psychological health, religious and ethical meanings and values. But this power of the positive is not a human power; rather it is rooted in the divine, ultimate power—the power of being-itself resisting and negating nonbeing. "The divine self-affirmation is the power that makes the self-affirmation of the finite being, the courage to be, possible."[10]

Nonbeing is not just a necessary evil of finite life, but it is important in drawing out the dynamic power of God as being-itself. "Nonbeing makes God a living God. Without the No he has to overcome in himself and in his creature, the divine Yes to himself would be lifeless."[11] Still Tillich retains his understanding of being as more powerful, more basic than nonbeing. "The infinite embraces itself and the finite, the Yes includes itself and the No which it takes into itself."[12] The Yes is greater than the No, and that relationship is the root of all faith, the basis of the experience of ultimacy.

Karl Barth's discussion of God is not expressed in ontological terms, but he does talk about the relationship between affirmation and negation in God. For Barth, God's Yes and No does not seem to be internal to the

---

[8]Ibid., 35.
[9]Ibid., 173.
[10]Ibid., 180-81.
[11]Ibid., 180.
[12]Ibid.

divine life but related externally to human lives and actions. Barth rejects the more mystical understanding of God as participating in all beings and all beings participating in God as being-itself, as Tillich holds. Although Tillich does show the relationship between being-itself and the biblical God,[13] Barth prefers the biblical language as most accurate in portraying God. God as Other and Holy relates to humans not only with the Yes of grace but also the No of wrath. In their experience of ultimacy, humans can encounter either the Yes or the No or both. But the Yes of grace and revelation is more powerful and enduring than the No of judgment and wrath.

For Barth, both God's Yes and God's No are revealed in Jesus as the Christ. In the Cross and the Resurrection, God is seen as indissolubly tied with humanity and yet more powerful and more sovereign than human limits.[14] God has freely chosen to be related to human beings in this way but does not in any way depend on humans, or even on the No to them, for God's Yes. Barth's emphasis on the negative human condition of sin and selfishness helps bring out the glory and righteousness of God. God's gift in Christ shows a universal and unmerited love for all humanity, but that Yes in Christ is in spite of the No rather than living because of the No.

This relationship of affirmation and negation in God can be more nuanced when one considers that Barth emphasizes redemption as more primary than creation. This suggests that the Yes of God, the grace of God, is always experienced as a Yes over the No. From the beginning God wills the Yes over the No, with the Yes more fundamental. God is in need of nothing and yet is the source of being of everything else.[15] God is the one being for whom this is true; all other beings are in need of something. Also, there is no evil in the divine nature itself. "It is a mark of the divine nature as distinct from that of the creature that in it a conflict with Himself is not merely ruled out, but is inherently impossible."[16]

Barth does speak of evil as "nothingness." Nothingness is not just a negative principle but is that which opposes or negates grace, that which

---

[13]See Paul Tillich, *Biblical Religion and the Search for Ultimate Reality* (Chicago: University of Chicago Press, 1955).

[14]Karl Barth, *The Epistle to the Romans*, trans. and ed. Edwyn C. Hoskyn (London: Oxford University Press, 1933) 94-97, 162.

[15]Karl Barth, *Church Dogmatics*, 4 vols., ed. G. W. Bromiley and T. F. Torrance (Edinburgh: T.&T. Clark, 1958) 2/1:458.

[16]*Church Dogmatics* 2/1:503.

offends God.[17] "Nothingness is that which God does not will. It lives only by the fact that it is that which God does not will."[18] Nothingness has no power of its own against God; God's ongoing effort is fighting nothingness.[19] Humans fall prey to nothingness and cannot resist it on their own. "In face of real nothingness the creature is already defeated and lost."[20]

For Barth, the victory over nothingness is accomplished through Jesus Christ, through God making the cause of the creature God's own cause.[21] Humans then are to choose God and thereby show their opposition to nothingness. Even that ability to choose God and oppose nothingness is possible through God's free gift. But Barth also recognizes that we do not observe the overcoming of nothingness in our selves or our world.[22] The claim of victory over it is based on the resurrection of Jesus and the promise of His coming in glory, not on ordinary human experience.[23] Because of God's action in Jesus Christ, one affirms in faith that nothingness does not last.

Barth and Tillich, then, share a basic stance of the divine Yes as more primary than the No. Both understand God's Yes or grace as the divine gift to humanity, enabling them to cope with nonbeing or nothingness. Thus, they also recognize the No, the negative, as a basic part of human experience. The dialectical movement of the Yes over against the No is part of the dynamic quality of life for Tillich and of grace over sin for Barth.

But Barth's theology sees God's No as the No to nothingness or the No to evil and sin. God's No is not part of God's essence for Barth, just as nonbeing is not part of being-itself for Tillich. Yet for both, the ongoing action of God is a resistance of nonbeing or nothingness. Although Barth does not use this phrasing, one could say for Barth that God's action is a negation of the negation of nothingness which resists God's will. The affirmation of God's will is secured through the overcoming of nothingness. For both Barth and Tillich, the positive essence of God (the being of God)

---

[17]Ibid. 3/3:353ff.
[18]Ibid. 3/3:352.
[19]Ibid. 3/3:357.
[20]Ibid. 3/3:357.
[21]Ibid. 3/3:358.
[22]Ibid. 3/3:363.
[23]Ibid. 3/3:358.

is prior to and superior to and more powerful than the negative activity of nonbeing or nothingness.

Masao Abe and Keiji Nishitani

Masao Abe has raised questions about the claim of the ontological priority of being over nonbeing. He recognizes it as a basic understanding of being and nonbeing in the West, but he points out that "in reality there is no ontological ground on which being has priority over nonbeing."[24] Abe suggests that it is a Western *assumption* that being embraces itself and nonbeing (using Tillich's terminology). In contrast, he sees the Eastern traditions of Taoism and Buddhism asserting nothingness or emptiness as ultimate and seeing the positive and negative principles as equal in force.

Abe recognizes that for the Christian tradition the relation of being and nonbeing has ethical implications as well as ontological meaning. Being is associated with the good and nonbeing with a privation of good and, even more strongly for some, the negative principle (e.g. sin) undermines God's goodness.[25] Even death is seen as the result of sin; privation of being is related to privation of the good, as we have seen above in Barth's theology. Abe understands that people do prefer life to death and goodness over sin and evil. But he points out the difference between wanting that to be the case (or saying that being and the good should be superior to nonbeing and evil) and the actual human situation which he sees as mutual interaction of the positive and negative.[26] Consequently, Abe characterizes this traditional Western view as idealistic in contrast to his Buddhist view as realistic.[27]

Following his Buddhist roots, Abe accepts nothingness or emptiness as ultimate and speaks of negation as a crucial element of the experience of ultimacy. However, ultimacy is not experienced just as nothingness or emptiness but also as suchness or fullness. In Abe's understanding, the basic Buddhist principles of impermanence (*anitya*) and no permanent self (*anātman*) point to the principle of dependent origination, that everything

---

[24]Masao Abe, *Zen and Western Thought* (Honolulu: University of Hawaii Press, 1985) 121.

[25]Ibid., 123.

[26]Ibid.

[27]Ibid., 131.

is dependent in its arising rather than independent.[28] Concretely, this means realizing the limits of one's things, relationships, and knowledge. We usually treat these things and persons as if they were permanent, and that treatment leads us to suffer with each awareness of their impermanence.

One's goal is to experience or realize Śunyatā, often translated emptiness but more accurately understood as a paradoxical experience of emptiness and fullness.[29] "Emptiness as Śunyatā transcends and embraces both emptiness and fullness."[30] Śunyatā is beyond form and formlessness, beyond the duality of being and nonbeing (see Tillich's "being-itself" above), beyond all dualities.[31] It is the negation of negation which is also affirmation.[32] Absolute affirmation only comes through the absolute or double negation (negation of negation). Thus, the paradoxical relation of affirmation and negation is also a dynamic and dialectical relation which is experienced.[33] "In order to attain true Emptiness, Emptiness must empty itself. Emptiness must become non-Emptiness. Thus true Emptiness is wondrous Being, . . . the fullness and suchness of everything."[34] This true Emptiness which is wondrous Being needs to be experienced existentially and subjectively in one's own life as "a self-contradictory oneness of being and nonbeing."[35]

There is here an underlying monistic principle, but the monistic principle includes the mutual and equal interaction of being and nonbeing. Although Abe argues that "the negativity of human life is felt more seriously and deeply in Buddhism than among the followers of Western intellectual traditions," he also states that negativity is considered equal to positivity rather than inferior to it as in the traditional Western view.[36] But most important to Abe is that in Buddhism the contradiction between the positive and negative is to be overcome. It is not a victory of one over the other (as in the traditional Christian view of redemption—see Barth above) but a liberation from the

---

[28]Ibid., 125-26.
[29]Ibid., 127.
[30]Ibid., 126.
[31]Ibid., 128-29.
[32]Ibid., 127.
[33]Ibid.
[34]Ibid., 128.
[35]Ibid., 129.
[36]Ibid., 130.

contradiction and tension between the positive and negative.[37] Nirvana, then, is a liberation from the contradiction of life and death, from the wheel of life and death in which we are caught, and an awakening to a freedom that can be experienced right here and now.[38] In this freedom, "one can be master of, rather than enslaved by, good and evil."[39]

Although he argues strongly for the equal and mutual interaction of positive and negative, Abe concludes that in general negativity is the primary and central principle in the East in contrast to the priority of the positive in the West. "In short, the ultimate which is beyond the opposition between positive and negative is realized in the East in terms of negativity and in the West in terms of positivity."[40] This characterization reflects what is emphasized while recognizing exceptions in both the East and the West.

Keiji Nishitani also focuses on nothingness or emptiness as most basic and absolute. In *Religion and Nothingness*, he argues that we experience nothingness or emptiness when our ordinary mental processes are transcended in the realization that they are ultimately unreal.[41] All ordinary truths and distinctions are relativized by the experience of emptiness. This experience of emptiness opens up the experience of suchness, of the ground of all things including life and death. It is an experience of being with nonbeing, of life with death; it is a realization of the intersection and identity of these opposites.[42] "The point at which emptiness is emptied to become true emptiness is the very point at which each and every thing becomes manifest in possession of its own suchness."[43] For Nishitani, this absolute self-identity of emptiness and being is neither monistic nor dualistic but "the absolute self-identity of the absolutely two."[44] Thus, the intersection and identity of emptiness and suchness is a dynamic and paradoxical relationship.

---

[37]Ibid., 131.

[38]Ibid., 132.

[39]Ibid.

[40]Ibid., 133.

[41]Keiji Nishitani, *Religious and Nothingness* (Berkeley: University of California Press, 1982) 29.

[42]Ibid., 96-97.

[43]Ibid., 106.

[44]Ibid., 107.

Like Abe, Nishitani posits Śunyatā as a real and lived experience rather than an abstract emptiness.[45] Ordinarily, we are tied to the standpoint of being, to things which are ultimately impermanent. When we transcend this standpoint and recognize the impermanence and nihility of it all, we move to a standpoint of nothingness. But this standpoint also needs to be negated, and it is this final negation of nihility which is Śunyatā and experienced as a positive.[46] "Pressed to give it a name, we might call it a 'seeing of not-seeing,' a seeing that sees without seeing."[47] Elsewhere, Nishitani speaks of a "knowing of nonknowing."[48] "The emptiness of Śunyatā is not an emptiness represented as some 'thing' outside of being and other than being. It is not simply an 'empty nothing,' but rather an absolute emptiness, emptied even of these representations of emptiness. And for that reason, it is at bottom one with being, even as being is at bottom one with emptiness."[49] Absolute negation is in reality absolute affirmation.

Comparisons

For all four thinkers, the experience of ultimacy involves both affirmation and negation understood dynamically rather than statically, with both dialectical and paradoxical elements. The interaction of the negative and positive is a dialectical relation for Nishitani and Abe, with a back and forth relation between two mutual aspects—being and nonbeing. In the depth of that dialectical relation is the paradox of being and nonbeing as intersecting points. For Tillich and for Barth, there is an ongoing back and forth relation of being and nonbeing, affirmation and negation, but the underlying basis is not a mutual relation but the priority of being and affirmation. Yet the views of these Western thinkers is not without paradox. For Barth, the paradox is connected with Jesus as the Christ who negates the nothingness of the world. For Tillich, the paradox is rooted in absolute faith, in the experience of meaning in meaninglessness, in the experience of God beyond

---

[45]Ibid., 70-71.
[46]Ibid., 97.
[47]Ibid., 71.
[48]Ibid., 110.
[49]Ibid., 123.

the gods who are doubted, and in the recognition that Jesus both is not and is the Christ (cross and resurrection).[50]

Also, for each thinker, affirmation and negation are experienced relations to ultimacy, not just conceptual abstractions. Although many people may experience affirmation and negation in relation to ultimacy, only a few would express the experience in these ontological terms. But it is important to emphasize that the ontology is rooted in experience itself.

For Abe and for Nishitani and to some extent for Tillich, being and nonbeing have a polar relationship. But for Barth and to some degree for Tillich, the polarity is broken by the claim of the one superior basis in being-itself or God. That puts the ultimate outside of the polarity. Yet even this difference is softened by Abe's statement that Śūnyatā is beyond the duality of being and nonbeing.

For Abe, Nishitani, and Tillich, the emphasis on the participation of ultimacy in everything that is shows the ultimate experienced in the midst of the polarity of being and nonbeing. In Buddhist thinking, one can speak of the interpenetration of ultimacy (absolute nothingness and absolute reality) in all ordinary things. For Tillich, the dynamic activity of being over against nonbeing is ongoing in ordinary things and activities. For Barth, God's resistance to nothingness is for the creature but not in the midst of the creature's being. Nishitani connects the love of neighbor to the standpoint of Buddhism which sees one's self in all things (and therefore one's self as no thing).[51] He goes on to compare his Buddhist stance to the approach of St. Francis of Assisi who saw all things in creation as related to himself as God's creatures.

In spite of these very close descriptions of the root experiences of ultimacy among these thinkers, we are still left with significant differences. Most obvious is the difference that Masao Abe continues to emphasize—the issue of the priority of being or of nothingness (nonbeing). A related difference is that between an emphasis on effort and an emphasis on grace. The superiority of the Yes over the No is the basis for the gift of affirmation or redemption. The priority of being grounds the free gift of grace—generally but most specifically in Jesus as the Christ—overcoming nonbeing and nothingness for all people. The priority of nothingness or nonbeing emphasizes the activity of negation which is carried out by the creature in

---

[50]Paul Tillich, *Dynamics of Faith* (New York: Harper & Row, 1957) 97-98.
[51]Keiji Nishitani, *Religion and Nothingness*, 281.

an effort to reach ultimacy (absolute negation which is absolute affirmation). The experience of ultimacy is described as an awakening or a liberation rather than redemption, and the experience is not dependent on the action of being-itself or God but rather on human discipline and effort.

We have seen enough similarities in the conceptualizations of the experiences of ultimacy to suggest that people may experience similar dialectical movements of affirmation and negation, being and nothingness. But we have also seen enough differences to be wary of concluding that the experiences are the same. The roots out of which one comes (religious tradition and culture) do affect the understanding of the experience to the point that one feels most aware of being and affirmation or most aware of nothingness and negation.

Because of the gap between the experience of ultimacy and the verbal representation of it, much religious expression is symbolic rather than a literal description. But religious symbols are more than arbitrarily chosen words. For a religious symbol to be effective, it must be able to convey something of the ultimacy experienced. Paul Tillich suggests that religious symbols are able to convey ultimacy because they participate in the power of the ultimate.[52] "The religious symbol, the symbol which points to the divine, can be a true symbol only if it participates in the power of the divine to which it points."[53] This power of ultimacy is expressed through the concrete symbol, with the concrete language tied to a particular experience, religious tradition, time and culture. The combination of particularity and symbolic character should make us cautious about any easy, formal agreement between symbols from different traditions but also open to comparing the underlying experiences towards which religious symbols point.

We must remember that the conceptualizations of these four thinkers are symbolic—pointing beyond the words to a deeper experience of ultimacy. But the symbolic character of this religious speech should warn us against absolutizing the descriptions, turning the descriptions themselves into idols. All four thinkers would be opposed to an absolutization of concepts, rejecting such an idolatry. Our human concepts are limited; we can hope for truth within our understandings but should be warned against taking those conceptualizations as absolute truth in themselves. Therefore, we cannot

---

[52]Paul Tillich, "The Religious Symbol," trans. James Luther Adams, *Journal of Liberal Religion* 2 (Summer 1940): 14.
[53]ST 1:239.

take the differences in views to necessarily entail different ultimates. But most importantly, we should take the differences as challenges to one point of view as absolutely true in itself.

Finally, the agreements here are specific to these individual thinkers and cannot be extrapolated to make claims for the whole traditions of Christianity and Buddhism. Yet these agreements and differences supply a basis for further discussion and interreligious dialogue. All four are concerned to express an experience that transcends ordinary human categories, to give some expression to the experience of ultimacy. But they also give specific content to that ultimacy in their choice of concepts to convey it. We cannot ignore the differences between starting from being versus starting from nothingness. But our discussion here shows that there may be more similarities in the root experience than these opposite terms would suggest. For all four thinkers, ultimacy transcends these differences of being and nonbeing and yet is involved in the midst of the dialectical and sometimes paradoxical relation of being and nonbeing. Thus we cannot resolve the question of whether different paths (different experiences and expressions) lead to the same ultimate, but we can suggest that the differences are not total and when explored reveal important similarities. The intersection of affirmation and negation, of being and nothingness, in each of the four thinkers points to the possibility of further interreligious dialogue on this issue.

> Forgetting mind, its complications,
> My hand is free. The All appears.
> I use devices, simultaneously.
> Look—a halo penetrates the void.[54]

---

[54]This Zen poem is attributed to Kakua in *Zen Poems of China and Japan: The Crane's Bill*, trans. Lucien Stryk and Takashi Ikemoto (New York: Grove Press, 1973) 50.

Chapter 3

Niebuhr and Tillich on the Jewish Question

Paul Tillich recorded in his *Travel Diary: 1936* his warm associations with Niebuhr in Geneva. They breakfasted together, lunched together by the lake, and worked on lectures together. Tillich translated Niebuhr's lecture, and they reflected together on European politics at that fateful hour. Tillich remembered asking Niebuhr about academic positions at Ann Arbor and Manchester, England. He recorded that Niebuhr advised him to stay at Union Theological Seminary and "We will found a school of theology there." He noted in his reflection for July 30: "I have a feeling of warmth with him such as I had never experienced before."[1]

They were at their closest intellectually when they were working on questions of religion and society. Tillich's belief-ful realism and Niebuhr's Christian realism bound them together to support religious socialism during the 1930s. Niebuhr's movement away from socialism in the late 1940s and early 1950s led Tillich and Niebuhr to diverge politically. But the impossibility of Tillich carrying religious socialism forward in the Eisenhower years meant their divergences were not widely known. For years they shared the Fellowship of Socialist Christians.[2] They also shared teaching responsibilities in "Philosophy of Religion" at Union Theological Seminary while Niebuhr taught "Christian Ethics" and Tillich "Systematic Theology." Tillich wrote appreciatively of Ursula Niebuhr's welcoming them to Union Theological Seminary the day they arrived in New York as well as his debt to Reinhold for conveying the offer to come to Union after he was dismissed in Frankfurt. But despite friendships and three decades of shared scholarly and political causes no one at Union could have regarded them as sharing a school of theology. On the other hand, by their greatness they did contribute to

---

[1]Paul Tillich, *My Travel Diary: 1936* (New York: Harper & Row, 1970) 145.

[2]See: John C. Bennett "Tillich and the 'Fellowship of Socialist Christians,' " *North American Paul Tillich Society Newsletter* 16/4 (1 October 1990): 3.

strengthening Union and increasing its importance, so they did strengthen a school.

The differences between them became clearer with the publication of volume 1 of Tillich's *Systematic Theology* in 1951. The end of religious socialist commitments occurred roughly at the same time as the differences between them as representatives of biblically based pragmatism and ontologically developed existentialism became clearer.

Roger Shinn, as a student of both Paulus and Reinie, has put this divergence as clearly as anyone:

> When Tillich arrived in this country, knowing no English, Reinie was one person with whom he could converse. As late as my time, I heard them occasionally exchange comments, in German, as they passed each other in the halls. Each had a genuine admiration for the other. See Gilkey's angry review of Fox for an example of Tillich's admiration for Reinie. Many people glibly associated the two as "neoorthodox," a bad categorization for both. I think I once wrote in *C&C* [*Christianity and Crisis*], back in the days when I was one of their regulars, that I long puzzled over this categorization of Tillich until the reason dawned on me: he spoke with a German accent. There's one other possible reason: As Niebuhr once said in a friendly, jovial way, "Whatever heresies Paul Tillich goes wandering among, he always comes home to 'justification by faith.' "

> But to back up, the two became strongly associated in the public mind. A second reason is that each of them defended the other against critics of the prevailing liberal-rational type. So the critics of both tended to merge them. The phrase, "Niebuhr-and-Tillich," became almost one word in some circles, even sometimes at Union. But it was foolish.

> There was one more reason for the popular association. When Tillich arrived in this country, Niebuhr immediately welcomed him and many of his friends (including Eduard Heimann and others from the New School) into the Fellowship of Socialist Christians, and they there found something of an American base. Actually, as Tillich's book on religious socialism shows, there was a considerable difference between the continental group and Niebuhr's American group. But they shared many criticisms of the dominant American culture, and from the mainstream of American politics they looked

alike.One night (somewhere in my 1945–1949 period at Union) I found myself helping Reinie and Ursula clean up their kitchen after a party. We combined intellectual conversation with dishwashing in a very Niebuhrian way. Something led Reinie to comment, "You know, I've just begun to realize how really different Paul and I are." I replied brashly—it was easy to be brash around Reinie—"Your students have known it for a long time." He laughed in his friendly way. We students knew it because we were getting Tillich's "system" in his lectures; Niebuhr, reading Tillich's early publications and entering conversation with him, was slower in getting the impact of "the system."[3]

Tillich's work had been called to Reinhold's attention by his brother. Tillich would at a later date credit H. Richard Niebuhr for saving his life by translating *Die religiöse Lage der Gegenwart* (1926) and thereby winning an invitation for him to come to the U.S.[4] Reinhold's reviews in 1932 and 1936 of Tillich's earliest translations into English[5] were full of praise as was his 1937 essay, "The Contribution of Paul Tillich."[6] These early pieces did not prefigure the later arguments, the last and major essay from the 1930s only raised a question about the need for more attention to the historical Jesus. He celebrated Paulus; after all, he had sponsored his immigration.

For he is not only one of the most brilliant theologians in the Western world, but one whose thought is strikingly relevant to every major problem of culture and civilization. His terms may be abstract, but his thought is not. It deals in terms of rigorous realism with the very stuff of life.[7]

---

[3]Roger Shinn, letter (in author's possession) responding to Ronald Stone's questionnaire (November 1990).

[4]*Die religiöse Lage der Gegenwart* (Berlin: Ullstein, 1926). ET: *The Religious Situation*, trans. H. Richard Niebuhr (New York: Henry Holt and Co., 1932).

[5]Review of *The Religious Situation*, in *World Tomorrow* 15/23 (21 December 1932): 596; review of *Interpretation of History*, in *Radical Religion* 2 (Winter 1936): 41-42.

[6]*Religion in Life* 6/4 (Autumn 1937): 574-81.

[7]Ibid., 581.

Tillich's review of volume 1 of Niebuhr's *Nature and Destiny of Man* returned the compliments and raised questions primarily about historical judgments and some of Niebuhr's comparisons. Tillich concluded, "It is a masterpiece," and applauded its chapters on sin.

Niebuhr's critique of Tillich in the Charles Kegley and Robert Bretall essay collection[8] moved their discussion into the deeper areas of disagreement. Until the end, Niebuhr remained suspicious of Tillich's ontology. He wanted to preserve poetic-dramatic language concerning the human condition and he feared Tillich's language reduced both human responsibility and the difference between their positions. Niebuhr would concede an implicit ontology in interpretations of biblical insight and in the Bible itself, but he wanted to keep the ontology implicit. Tillich wanted to make it explicit and Niebuhr called such explication, speculation. Tillich was certainly correct in asking for more careful definitions. Niebuhr feared too much precision regarding reduced faith/reduced mystery which was important to his sense of the Christian faith. More than that he feared that Tillich's understanding of estrangement made human sin more subject to fate and less to responsibility than he believed the human situation warranted. Niebuhr's critique of Tillich was at its strongest in this prestroke essay. His later responses in a 1956 review of *Biblical Religion and the Search for Ultimate Reality*,[9] certainly in part a response to Niebuhr's "Biblical Thought and Ontological Speculation,"[10] was weaker as was his response to Tillich's criticism in Charles Kegley and Robert Bretall's Niebuhr volume.[11]

Tillich kept up the attack in the Harold Landon volume, *Reinhold Niebuhr: A Prophetic Voice in Our Time*.[12] While confessing his indebted-

---

[8]Reinhold Niebuhr, "Biblical Thought and Ontological Speculation in Tillich's Theology," in *The Theology of Paul Tillich*, ed. Charles W. Kegley and Robert W. Bretall, 216-27 (New York: Macmillan, 1964).

[9]Reinhold Niebuhr, in *Union Seminary Quarterly Review* 11/2 (January 1956): 59-60.

[10]In *The Theology of Paul Tillich*, 216-27.

[11]Reinhold Niebuhr, "Reply to Interpretation and Criticism," in *Reinhold Niebuhr: His Religious, Social, and Political Thought*, ed. Charles W. Kegley and Robert W. Bretall (New York: Macmillan, 1961) 429-51.

[12]Paul Tillich, "Sin and Grace in the Theology of Reinhold Niebuhr," in *Reinhold Niebuhr: A Prophetic Voice in Our Time*, ed. Harold Landon (Greenwich CT: Seabury Press, 1962) 27-41.

ness to Niebuhr and his appreciation for their lifelong conversation he criticized him relentlessly for not turning to ontology. He criticized him first for taking philosophic opinions out of context and out of time and finding them to be in error in comparison to biblical views. He tried to suggest that Niebuhr was accepting of *universal estrangement* as descriptive of the human condition. He urged Niebuhr to use ontology in thinking about freedom and destiny, pride, and self. In Niebuhr's response he merely suggested he preferred not to use Plotinus's concepts and that he now preferred to use the symbols descriptively rather than ontologically.[13]

At that point in the argument, Tillich had certainly won. But the resultant discussion by their common friends and colleagues denied Tillich the victory. John Hutchision, Wilhelm Pauck, and Richard Kroner all defended Niebuhr's right to use his terms without needing to use Tillich's ontology. My own reading of the debate is that Tillich was correct to push Niebuhr for more careful definition of his terms and very mistaken in thinking this meant Niebuhr should use Tillich's terms. In these exchanges they both were careful to say how they appreciated the realism of the other's position.

Tillich and Niebuhr kept most of their disagreements private though an exchange about the religious meaning of Picasso's "Guernica" broke into the open.[14] In correspondence Niebuhr would recognize Tillich as the greater theologian,[15] and Tillich in the Fellowship of Socialist Christians would recognize Niebuhr as the genius in political thought.[16]

The most famous difference between them, of course, was the anecdotal gap between them on the appreciation of nature. Tillich referred to it as Niebuhr accusing him of being a German romanticist as he appreciated a tree in Riverside Park. Other students' versions have Niebuhr referring to him as a "damned nature mystic" or of Tillich quoting Niebuhr's rumored description of him as such when Niebuhr asked him why he stopped either in front of a tree in Riverside Park or the flowers in the Union quadrangle.

---

[13]Reinhold Niebuhr, "The Response of Reinhold Niebuhr," in *Reinhold Niebuhr: A Prophetic Voice in Our Time*, 120.

[14]*Christianity and Crisis* 16/1 (6 February 1956): 2-3; and 16/3 (5 March 1956): 24.

[15]Letter of Reinhold Niebuhr to Will Scarlett (5 November 1968). Washington papers of Reinhold Niebuhr, Library of Congress.

[16]Langdon Gilkey, "A Critical Review Article." Draft of essay (August 1987) 24. In author's possession.

Christian Zionism

The meaning of the term "Zionism" has varied according to the differing positions of those claiming to be Zionists. The term "Christian" also has a variety of meanings. The use of Christian as an adjective modifying Zionism seems peculiar since Zionism is a Jewish movement. Here in reference to Reinhold Niebuhr and Paul Tillich it means that they, as Christian theologians, come to support the establishment of a "Jewish state" in Israel. As a Jew can be a Zionist without migrating to Israel or a Christian may be a Christian-Marxist without subscribing to the metaphysics of Karl Marx, so it is possible for a Christian to be a Zionist in the sense of supporting Jewish migration to Israel and the consolidation of the Jewish people into a state. Following contemporary usage, Zionism implies more than the "national homeland" of the Balfour Declaration and it is not reconcilable with the "unitary, nonsectarian state" of El Fatah.

> Zionism may be summarily defined as the Jewish nationalist movement whose endeavors to solve the "Jewish problem" led to the establishment of the "Jewish state" of Israel.[17]

It is not self-evident that American theologians would be Christians in support of Zionism. None of the major church positions could really be regarded as Zionist though they accept Israel. The tendency of the Christian archaeological community that has worked in Jordan, American missionary interests, liberation theologians, and official church boards to be pro-Palestinian and slightly hostile to Israel is, I think, generally recognized.

Friendships with and Respect for Jews

Both Niebuhr and Tillich found themselves forming close friendships with Jews who were allied in struggling for social justice. Both of them had grown up in parsonages of German parentage, Niebuhr in Missouri and Illinois and Tillich in Eastern Germany and Berlin. Tillich remembered that though anti-Semitism had been discussed in his home, it had been rejected

---

[17]Ben Halpern, "Zionism," *International Encyclopedia of the Social Sciences* (New York: Macmillan, 1968) 593.

by his parents. In their youth, neither, of course, was free from the anti-Judaism sentiments their church contexts encouraged. As an adult, Tillich remarked that as a young boy, particularly during Holy Week, he found the anti-Judaism teaching of the church impressed upon him. Reinhold Niebuhr recorded how as a young boy he observed the stereotyping of Jewish businessmen in his U.S. Midwestern town. The generous, courteous Jewish merchant was thought of by the Gentiles as atypical; the prosperous, rather pushy Jewish capitalist was regarded as typical. As a young boy who knew few Jews, Niebuhr had no basis for ignoring or judging such stereotyping.

Their friendships with Jews that are documented are post-World War I. Niebuhr in his last book documented the importance of his friendship in Detroit with Fred Butzel. Niebuhr liked to quote his mentor, Episcopalian Bishop Charles Williams (a follower of the social gospel), who said: "In the weightier matters of social justice there are only two Christians in Detroit, and they are both Jews."[18] Niebuhr reflected on the sources of the social-righteousness he perceived among Jews. He thought that perhaps it should be attributed to the prophetic tradition. He noted that many of the most religious Jews attributed it to the *Torah*. Butzel, however, who had served with Niebuhr on the Mayor's Race Committee, attributed the passion for social righteousness to their minority status which resulted in suspicion of the establishment and compassion for other minorities. Niebuhr never resolved the issue in his own mind, but noted that Butzel's genius was responsible for the beginning of "my long love affair with the Jewish people."[19] Niebuhr's respect for the Jews had led him in an early article to contrast their concern for social justice with the relative impotence of German-Americans in supporting any progressive causes. The superiority of Jewish social sensitivity to most Protestant social consciousness was to remain a theme throughout Niebuhr's teaching and writing. The urban pastoral of Detroit was essential to developing Niebuhr's own social realism and part of that mixture was his debt to Jewish friends.

Tillich was in Berlin during the 1918 revolution. He spoke at radical political rallies, attempted to move the church to revolutionize its own traditions, and lectured on social problems at the University of Berlin. Soon he found himself evolving as the leader of a small discussion group of

---

[18]*Man's Nature and His Communities* (New York: Charles Scribner's Sons, 1965) 18.

[19]Ibid., 19.

intellectuals for religious socialism. The group—which became known as the *Kairos* circle after Tillich's use of the concept—included Jews, notably Eduard Heimann and Adolf Löwe. They taught the young Christian theologian economics and implanted their influence in his social philosophy. They were to continue as his close friends throughout his life, sharing his exile and his wine, and helping to shape his mind. The context of his friendships with Jews is different than Niebuhr's but also similar in pressing urban social conflicts, alliances with Jewish leaders, and resulting friendships.

In Frankfurt, Tillich was one of the most ardent supporters of the Institute for Social Research which attracted Erich Fromm, Herbert Marcuse, and Max Horkheimmer. These left-Hegelian intellectuals of Jewish origin joined with others and Tillich to form a *Kranzchen* or intimate discussion group. Tillich's social world as well as his intellectual world involved both Jew and Gentile. Hannah Tillich has recounted that in jest Tillich was referred to as "Paulus among the Jews." It was in this group that his socialist writing evolved and that the emerging dangers of anti-Semitism were perceived.

In retrospect the Institute, dominated by assimilated Jews, may be said to have been slow in perceiving the dangers of anti-Semitism prevailing in Germany. After Tillich shared dismissal from the University of Frankfurt with Mannheim, Horkheimmer, and Singheimer of the Institute, and other Jews, he would help to rally them at their home in exile in New York.

Tillich as dean of the philosophy faculty was at the center of the struggle for the University of Frankfurt. When storm troopers attacked Jewish students, he took the students to his office for protection and medical aid. He demanded in print the expulsion of students who joined the storm troopers. He was attacked in the *Frankfurter Zeitung* and passages from his *The Socialist Decision* were quoted to prove him an enemy of the new order. Earlier Max Horkheimmer had warned him that certain sentences in *The Socialist Decision* would cost him his life. He was suspended from his post on 13 April 1933; further consultations with the ministry of education during which Tillich pushed questions concerning governmental attitudes toward Jews and modern culture proved that Tillich's academic career in Germany was over.

Meanwhile, Reinhold Niebuhr had been visiting Germany. He had gotten in an argument with the pastor of his German relatives over the pastor's anti-Semitism and created tension at the family reunion. Niebuhr telephoned Tillich of the offer for him to come to Union Theological Seminary as a visiting faculty member. Eventually, after a near arrest by the Gestapo, Tillich came to New York.

The Jewish friends of Niebuhr and Tillich were not necessarily Zionists, but their friendships laid the ground for a deep empathic reaction to the Holocaust and the founding of Israel. Before Herbert Marcuse moved to California, he was often present at Tillich's apartment as were other Jewish friends from the Berlin and Frankfurt days. In later years Abraham Heschel and Reinhold Niebuhr formed a close friendship, mutually influencing each other's thought. Gradually traffic between Jewish Theological Seminary and Union Theological Seminary across Broadway increased as mutual trust and respect between their institutions deepened. I know from my own experience how differently I have viewed Judaism and the need to save Soviet Jewry, after forming friendships with Jews on an Americans for Democratic Action tour of the Soviet Union. Friendships, particularly friendships formed in the context of the struggle for social justice, may be the most important aspect of Jewish-Christian dialogue.

Social Ethics

The developed political philosophies of Niebuhr and Tillich were both socialist and democratic. They remained socialist inspired even after the socialist option was destroyed in Germany and proved politically barren in the United States. When it emerged, Israel gave every promise of being the most socialist and the most democratic state in the Middle East. This affinity between their goals and the announced goals of the new state made their support natural.

Both political philosophies recognized politics as the struggle for power. Neither was blinded by illusions that states simply pursued a moral cause. They were open to the ambiguity of politics in the Middle East and neither had to reject Israel on moralistic grounds just as they had not rejected the British mandate on moralistic grounds. Niebuhr spoke of pure justice as always being compromised by the pursuit of interest, and a rough justice as being the harmonization of competing interests. For Tillich justice was the state of affairs that would allow the relative power of different centers of power to flourish without crushing each other. Both Christian moralists also recognized that most borders were created in conflict and so they were not subject to the sort of Christian or liberal moralism that proclaims that no borders established through war are to be recognized as Security Council Resolution 242 (1967) implies. Their values of democratic procedures, respect for civil rights, need for social planning, and realism combined to make them potential supporters of Israel.

Another strain of these political thinkers reinforced the above values to incline them to respecting Jewish developments in the land of Israel. Both thinkers relied heavily on the Hebrew prophets in their preaching and teaching. More fundamental, however, was the use of prophetic religion to describe their own social theology. They intended that history be taken seriously but not absolutized. They pleaded for active political involvement of a progressive sort that eschewed all fanaticisms and determinisms. Their sympathies for some of Marx's social thought rested on their detection of genuinely prophetic elements within his own social thought. Their respect for the Hebrew prophets was so great that the term prophet is perhaps the best single tribute to Reinhold Niebuhr. He read the contingent in terms of the eternal and fought and pled for justice. The socialist journal that Niebuhr founded, *Radical Religion*, understood itself to be representing the prophetic spirit under the conditions of the twentieth century. Doom was pronounced on the tottering house of capitalism and justice was demanded in the name of God. Like another prophet before him, Niebuhr was perhaps surprised when Nineveh repented and was spared. He changed with the times, however, and with the old capitalism dying under the pragmatic adjustments of the New Deal he became a defender of the mixed economy or social-welfare capitalism. He remained on the left in encouraging the powers of the state to be used for the disadvantaged.

Tillich's Socialism

The explicit connections between prophetic religion and social criticism are perhaps best seen in Tillich's major work on social theory, *The Socialist Decision* (1933). This volume was written in 1932 to fight the threat of National Socialism. It was banned in 1933 soon after Hitler assumed power. Though it circulated in the underground, most of the printed volumes of it were destroyed when American bombers bombed the warehouse in which they were stored. *The Socialist Decision* is a work of speculative, critical, political philosophy directed against Nazism. In it, Tillich proposes a reformulation of socialism so that it can more effectively combat Nazism.

There are basically two types of political philosophy. They are either grounded in myths of origin or in the prophetic criticism of myths of origin. Political romanticisms (read conservatism and Nazism) are attempts to define political existence as sacred because of its origins in soil, blood, or race. Western capitalism, on the other hand, is an expression of the attacks on the myths of origin. Western capitalism riding the waves of the Enlightenment and bourgeois revolt broke the social order of feudalism grounded in myths of origin. Capitalism was not, however, able to establish harmony. Its rational, controlling mentality could destroy, but not replace the sense of order and purpose of the social order of feudalism. Political romanticism attacked capitalism in the name of the powers of origin—blood, soil, group. Socialism attacked capitalism from within and shared some of the weaknesses it sought to overcome. If socialism as rational social planning were to prevail, it had to reform itself and take on some of the strengths of conservatism and political romanticism. The chaos of contemporary Germany required new answers that conservatism could not give and political romanticism was only a destructive movement with no lasting power to govern. Socialism like capitalism inherited the motif of prophetic criticism which could not surrender to either social resignation or utopia, but it needed to unite its social planning with symbols of expectation to change society. To achieve this, socialism had to affirm its religious dimensions and to demonstrate that it had a place for appreciation of the national homeland as well as internationalism, the family as well as society, traditional organizations as well as rational planning.

Tillich criticized Nazism's pretensions to be scientific. While admitting its philosophy was powerful poetry tending toward ecstatic and revolutionary apocalypticism, he dismissed it as a serious school of thought. It was a demonic movement in its attempt to make sacred: leader, race, party, and space. The only integrity for the church was to oppose Nazism. Nazism was understood as an alternative religious attempt to create a system of meaning and solution by a leap back to myths of origin without critical inquiry.

The spirit of Nazism was essentially opposed to the spirit of Judaism. The spirit of Judaism was located in the worship of the God who transcended blood, soil, and communal loyalties, and demanded justice. The pagan myths of origin were broken in the Hebrew Bible and so the Old Testament was opposed by Nazism. The spirit of Judaism was eternally an adversary to the spirit of political romanticism. Myths of origin could still be found in biblical Jewish faith but only in a criticized mode. Christianity had to join with Judaism in the affirmation of the prophetic critique of romanticism and especially the churches of the reformation. The political romanticism of Nazism was a countermovement against the prophetic in religion and humanism in culture. In Judaism these primitive nations of blood and race found a sharp intellectual critique and a factual denial in Germany.

Tillich's critique included socialism, which neglected its prophetic heritage and so lacked the power of expectation. A rediscovery of eschatology would, he thought, show socialism how it could reform its ideology. There were imminent possibilities within the proletariat that had to be emphasized in a call for the transformation of the human situation. In fact, for Tillich the essence of the socialist principle is the principle of expectation or political eschatology. The essential point for the argument is that Tillich found in the Hebrew prophets a political eschatology that was necessary for the reform of socialism and to save Germany and the world from the barbarism of the Nazi movement. However, 1933 was too late: socialism was exhausted, capitalism was disgraced and fragmented, conservatism was irrelevant, and chaos and war resulted.

In 1933, Niebuhr criticized the churches for their quietism in regard to the "extravagances of Nazi terror." He detailed anti-Semitic atrocities and called for a worldwide Christian protest against the Nazi government. He had only a little respect for the German churches and he thought that sensitivity to the feelings of German Christians ought not to dull the protest. In August 1933, he criticized not only the announced policies of the Nazis but the execution of Jews.

In New York both Tillich and Niebuhr joined with Jewish friends in organizing relief programs for exiles from Germany and joined in criticizing anti-Semitism. After becoming an American citizen, Tillich spoke publicly at political rallies as Niebuhr was doing consistently. Tillich's first public speech against the regime in Germany at Madison Square Garden attacked the regime's anti-Semitism. When Tillich began a series of propaganda broadcasts for the Voice of America, his first one on 31 March 1942 was addressed to *Meine deutschen Freunde* on "The Jewish Question." He addressed himself primarily to German-Protestant church people. He pointed out that the religion of Protestant Christians is of Jewish origin. The Old Testament is part of the Christian Bible and the Reformation was founded in the name and spirit of the Jewish Paul. An attack on Judaism was a surrender of Christianity, and all Christians, he argued, were obligated to defend Jewish people resolutely. The persecution of the Jews was blasphemy and opposition to God. So, throughout his wartime broadcasting dealing with a variety of political and philosophical issues he returned again and again to attack anti-Semitism.

Niebuhr's arguments for a Jewish homeland appeared in *The Nation*[20] in 1942. Recognizing Judaism as a nationality as well as a cultural and religious group, he argued for a homeland after the Holocaust. He regarded it as a solution to be contained within British imperial policy and American foreign policy as part of the postwar settlement. Arguments for Jewish rights were set in the context of the need for settlement of Arab claims. He criticized Zionist claims that there would be no "injustices" to Arabs, but he hoped for an overall settlement that would compensate for losses. These articles and articles by others in his *Christianity and Crisis* set him against the anti-Zionist policies of the *Christian Century* and the immediate past-president and the then-current president of Union Theological Seminary.

The increase in Zionist militancy was reflected in the formation of the Christian Council on Palestine in mid-1942. Paul Tillich and Reinhold Niebuhr were joined by three others as the executive committee. Between 1942 and 1946 when the Council merged into the American Christian Palestine Committee, it recruited 3,000 American clergymen to subscribe to its pro-Zionist principles. In the preface to Waldo Frank's book, *The Jew in Our Day*, Niebuhr argued for political security for the Jews in Palestine "without reference to the final religious problem."[21] Fishman has detailed the political intrigues of these Christian Zionists during the war.[22] Carl Voss, the secretary of the Council, was in the process of writing a book on this story when he died.

When the Anglo-American Committee of Inquiry held hearings in Washington, D.C., on 14 January 1946, Niebuhr testified for the Christian Council on Palestine. He argued for a Jewish state and more openness to Jewish immigration in Palestine. The final report of the Committee essentially agreed as did President Truman, but the British government referred the issue to the United Nations in 1947.

The similarities in the writing of Tillich and Niebuhr on Judaism are striking. They rejected aggressive mission to convert Jews to Christianity. They continued the dialogue with Jewish friends, and they expressed a willingness to help Jews who were alienated from Judaism to find meaning

---

[20]"Jews after the War," *The Nation* (21 February 1942): 214-16, 253-55.

[21]Hertzel Fishman, *American Protestantism and a Jewish State*, (Detroit: Wayne State University Press, 1973) 75.

[22]Ibid.

in Christianity. They both affirmed the need of preserving Judaism against tendencies in Christianity to relapse into paganism.

During the war they both called for the defeat of Germany and urged Western nations to secure the safety of the Jews. Both urged distinctions between the guilt of the regime and the guilt of the German people. Both sought to encourage forces in Germany which could act against Hitler and both urged restraint in the practice of war and for policies which would encourage resistance to mount within Germany. They came to recognize the need for a homeland for the Jewish people, although they were not absolutist about the need for it to be in Israel. As with other Zionists, they debated other options, but the establishment of Israel in 1948 they accepted as fact. Israel was the response to the Holocaust. For them the two are historically tied together. Niebuhr would comment on each of Israel's wars, revealing both his love for Israel and his stance against Arab politics. With the aid of secular and religious Jews, he founded Americans for Democratic Action which continued political support for Israel among American liberals.

Anti-Semitism and Zionism

In Berlin in 1953, Tillich analyzed German guilt for World War II activities against the Jews. Though he knew Germans did not want to think about their guilt, he regarded it as of the first importance for Germans to come to grips with guilt. The primary guilt lay upon those directly responsible for the atrocities and, of course, only some Germans were so responsible. A secondary type of guilt derived from failure to act responsibly, and he affirmed that he was guilty of not acting more boldly as the German political situation deteriorated in 1932–1933. Most Germans he thought participated in some of the other three types of guilt: the guilt of suppressing knowledge, the forgetting of one's responsibility for the past, and the guilt of regarding the past as over with no consequences for the present. He regarded the guilt that was troubling Germany as operating at psychological depths in much of the population. He urged the recognition of the guilt and positive steps be taken to deal with it.

In dealing with Christian anti-Semitism he also used his analysis of five types of guilt. In regard to the question of the guilt of Jews for the death of Jesus, he found none of the types of guilt applicable. The accusation that Jews were guilty for the death of Jesus was absurd. His program to free the churches from anti-Semitism involved the review of church publications to purge them of dangerous stereotypes, the emphasis on the Old Testament in the church, the abandonment of the active missionary movement to Jews, the sharing of worship services, the alliance for the struggle for social justice, theological dialogue, and the acceptance of the continuity and authenticity of Jewish faith. The primary witness of the power of Christ to Judaism would be in the demonstration of the quality of life in Christianity which would eradicate the demon of anti-Semitism in the life of the church.

Tillich had known Judaism as the faith of a dispersed people without a land for most of his life. His acceptance of a pro-Zionist position was after the fact of the establishment of Israel. He joined the American Christian Palestine Committee which promoted sympathy for Israel in the U.S. In explaining his pro-Zionist position he reported how his own position had changed. His earlier teaching that Israel was a people of time without attachment to space was mistaken, he said. Europe was not a secure haven for the Jews; they had to have their own place where they could protect themselves. Assimilation of the Jews in European culture had been a disaster, they had to find their own way. The average Jew was not a prophetic figure who, in dispersion, should suffer for the world; the average Jew was just a person who needed protection.

Tillich accepted Israel as a state, not as fulfillment of a biblical promise. The state of Israel had to be judged as other nations were judged. Israel was a necessary refuge for the survivors of the Holocaust and other expressions of anti-Judaism. His recommendations and hopes for Israel were parallel to his advice to Germans: accept finite borders and develop a sense of national-vocational consciousness within these borders. There is no absolute security; all borders will have some insecurity. Security rests in accepted borders and international understanding across the borders. Solutions will be found through negotiation and compromise that recognize the rights and power of all parties to the dispute.

For Niebuhr, Israel was primarily a refuge for the victims of the Holocaust. He regarded it as a responsibility of the United States to protect Israel for reasons of moral responsibility and for reasons of national interest. He wrote before the Israel-Egypt 1956 war:

> Our nation has a special interest in the preservation of the state of Israel. That interest is not only dictated by national interest in a state devoted to Western democracy and surrounded by Islamic nations in various stages of feudal decay, but is also dictated by humane considerations. For the state of Israel is, whatever its limita-

tions, a heartening adventure in nationhood. It has gathered the Jews of all nations, the remnants of the victims of Hitlerism and other forms of nationalistic persecution, and given them a home of their own. Whatever our political or religious positions may be, it is not possible to withhold admiration, sympathy, and respect for such an achievement.[23]

In writing on the strange mixture of secular and religious forces in the modern world Niebuhr regarded the emergence of Israel "as a kind of penance of the world for the awful atrocities committed against the Jews."[24] Furthermore, while he noted that injury was done to the Arabs, he still wrote, "Many Christians are pro-Zionist in the sense that they believe a homeless people require a homeland."[25] Justice still required further work on the rights of the Palestinians.

Niebuhr's writing on Judaism in *Pious and Secular America* (1958) and his last essay, "Mission and Opportunity: Religion in "Pluralistic Culture" in Louis Finkelstein's volume, *Social Responsibility in an Age of Revolution* (1971), are among the most profound contributions to Christian-Jewish understanding. In the context of the two religious contributions to ethics in the Western world he recognizes that certain issues between the faiths are nonnegotiable and he suggests ways in which both faiths can correct their traditions to promote understanding without proselytizing.

Conclusion

Tillich's death in 1965 and Niebuhr's in 1971 prevent us from knowing how their thought would have evolved vis-à-vis contemporary Israel. A few points are clear, however, their Zionism did not mean that all Jews should live in Zion. Israel was Diaspora Israel as well as Eretz Israel. The creation of modern Israel was the re-creation of a historical nation which was to be evaluated as other nations are evaluated. Israel has a religious history and it is relevant to the present state of Israel, but it is not determinative. For both Tillich and Niebuhr, history is radically free and God judges all nations for their unrighteousness. To want to defend the Jewish choice to return to

---

[23]*Christianity and Crisis* 16/9 (28 May 1956): 65.
[24]*Pious and Secular America* (New York: Charles Scribner's Sons, 1958) 109.
[25]Ibid.

Israel after the Holocaust does not imply absolutism, either biblical or secular. That return can be defended only on the basis that Jews were not welcome or secure elsewhere and that the international community of nations recognized the right of Israel to exist.

The genius of Israel does not depend upon the land but on its relationship to a transcendent God who always requires justice. In neither Tillich nor Niebuhr's thought can borders be regarded as sacrosanct. Borders get changed. They both recognized that our concern for security produces arrogance and blindness, but both recognized the need for security. Defense budgets can tyrannize a people, but people who will not provide for defense in a warring would bear illusions that Jews cannot afford.

Neither theologian dealt adequately with the plight of Palestinians living within Israel, nor did either address themselves at length to the question of Palestinian refugees. Christian ethics, while relating its judgments to historical conditions, must not lose sight of the will of God that all people are to be granted conditions for the flowering of their humanity. Christian reflection favoring the security of Israel must also recognize Palestinian rights and insist that Israel deal more justly with Palestinians inside Israel and on the West Bank.

Neither Tillich nor Niebuhr, both of whom died in their seventy-ninth year, lived to see the beginning of the stabilization of the Middle East with the Camp David Accords. Both would have welcomed movement towards gradual settlement of Palestinian rights. Both would have accepted the reality that not all political refugees would return and the corresponding recognition for the need for reparations and aid for displaced Palestinians.

Regarding this important religious political issue of our time I have been unable to detect how their epistemological, ontological, or aesthetic differences affected their realistic commitment to establishing a Jewish state. Maybe on this issue they did establish a school of thought with consequences.[26]

---

[26]The part of this chapter beginning with "Christian Zionism" and following to the conclusion was published in another form as "The Zionism of Paul Tillich and Reinhold Niebuhr," *Tantur Yearbook 1980–1981* (Jerusalem: Tantur, 1981) 219-33. A comparison of the two will show that this chapter stresses the early Zionism of Niebuhr more than did the previous paper. That correction is due to the helpful critique of Ursula Niebuhr and her calling to my attention certain sources from 1942. This paper was presented at the North American Paul Tillich Society meeting

Chapter 4

Epistemology and Cross-Cultural Religious Truth

Our situation of religious pluralism within cultures and across cultures raises anew the issues of relativism and subjectivism in religious truth. In both his early and later writings, Paul Tillich dealt with the problems of relativism and subjectivism by offering a qualified relativism in relation to the Unconditioned or ultimate. In this chapter, we will discuss to what extent Tillich's theory of normative knowledge, his critique of idolatry, and his understanding of the ultimate can be helpful in dealing with present-day issues of cross-cultural religious truth.

The plurality of religions makes us more aware of the role of personal and cultural perspectives in our understanding of religious truth. In a monopolistic situation of one established religion, it may be easier to assume and assert universal religious truth for all persons. But in the midst of religious pluralism, we recognize our religious differences as culturally and individually rooted and therefore not likely to pass away. Such awareness raises the question of how we can talk about religious truth at all in light of such diversity. Most thinkers dealing with the impact of religious pluralism agree that we cannot ignore individual and cultural perspectives if we are concerned with the persons who hold beliefs and not just the abstract beliefs themselves.[1] But if religious persons and cultures in all their diversity are to

---

in Washington, D.C., on 19 November 1993.

[1]In *Towards a World Theology* (Philadelphia: Westminster Press, 1981), Wilfred Cantwell Smith states: "No statement involving persons is valid, I propose, unless theoretically its validity can be verified both by the persons involved and by critical observers not involved" (60). Also see Smith, *Questions of Religious Truth* (London: Victor Gallancz, 1967) 71, 81, 94-95.

Similarly, John Hick speaks of religious traditions constituting religious *cultures*, "each with its own unique history and ethos" and each creating "human beings in

be taken seriously, then how can we advance beyond religious subjectivism or epistemological relativism? How can our understanding of religious knowledge and truth take account of individual and cultural perspectives and still avoid pure subjectivism and pure relativism?

A second epistemological issue that is crucial to cross-cultural religious truth is the difficulty in judging among conflicting religious truth claims. This difficulty relates to conflicts that arise from change and development *within* as well as *across* religious traditions and cultures. Changing historical situations raise critiques of formerly accepted truths. For example, in our modern period the awareness of racism and sexism or Third World injustices stimulates new theologies and religious truth claims that threaten long-standing religious dogma. Consequently, we need an understanding of religious knowledge and truth that can take account of change and offer a way of dealing with conflicts.

A closely related question involves developing criteria of religious truth that can be cross-cultural. What sort of process of knowledge and judgment is necessary for developing cross-cultural criteria in the situation of religious pluralism? Is it even possible to have a criterion of religious truth that is not tied to a particular personal, cultural, and religious perspective? Some thinkers have offered rational and moral evaluation while others have been concerned with the positive or negative effect of religious traditions on human lives as possible criteria.[2] But the influence of individual and cultural perspectives can affect the understanding of morality, rationality, and humanizing effects as well as the application of these criteria. These questions of cross-cultural criteria are not easy to answer, but they are

---

its own image." John Hick, "Religious Pluralism," in *The World's Religious Traditions: Current Perspectives in Religious Studies*, ed. Frank Whaling (Edinburgh: T.&T. Clark, 1984) 149.

[2]Peter Berger, *The Heretical Imperative* (London: Collins, 1980), suggests rational evaluation in relation to personal decision; John Hick suggests rational and moral evaluation of religious phenomena ("On Grading Religions"); Gordon Kaufman, *The Theological Imagination* (Philadelphia: Westminster Press, 1981), offers contribution to humanization as a cross-cultural criterion; Wilfred Cantwell Smith, *Towards a World Theology*, suggests helping to build a world community; Ninian Smart, *Worldviews* (New York: Scribner's, 1983), offers a test based on the degree of helping those who are threatened by poverty and humiliation.

important to consider since criteria are important in avoiding the disintegration of religious knowledge into pure relativism.

A third issue addresses the relationship between ultimacy and the apparent diversity of religious truth. The claim of ultimacy is important in avoiding a pure relativism and in making theological statements. But we need to ask how ultimacy relates to the plurality of religions and what that diversity implies about the nature and characteristics of ultimacy. Some thinkers such as Wilfred Cantwell Smith and John Hick have suggested one transcendent or divine Reality underlying the diversity of religious traditions. But even they have become increasingly more abstract and less definite in their descriptions of that one ultimate as they have attempted to take account of some Eastern understandings of Emptiness or Nothingness.[3] Clearly, one's understanding of the nature of ultimacy will greatly affect one's judgments of religious truth, and thus an epistemology adequate to religious pluralism must take account of that relationship.

These three issues, then, form the context for discussing Tillich's epistemology. Although our awareness of the impact of religious pluralism has increased since Tillich's time, we find many points in his epistemology that address similar problems of subjectivism and relativism. Both Tillich's early and later discussions offer a theory of normative knowledge for a dynamic religious situation that can be applied to the cross-cultural issues raised here.

---

[3]In *Towards a World Theology*, Wilfred Cantwell Smith often expresses a personalist understanding of God, but he also suggests the more generic term of "transcendence" as more congenial to a variety of traditions (184). Hick moved from the word "God" to "the Real" in an effort to include both personal and nonpersonal understandings (see "The Theology of Religious Pluralism," *Theology* 86 [September 1983]: 337).

Tillich's Theory of Normative Knowledge

In the *System of Sciences*[4] and "Kairos und Logos"[5] Tillich offers a theory of normative knowledge which takes account of the knower as a creative, decision-making person in a particular historical situation. Underlying this theory is Tillich's view of reality as dynamic, that is, changing qualitatively as well as quantitatively.[6] Normative knowledge, including religious truth, changes in relationship to the individual knower and the historical situation.

Producing normative knowledge involves developing norms of meaning which are created through a process of deciding on basic principles and making them concrete for a particular historical situation. The norm of a system of meaning helps to direct the system toward unconditioned meaning or what is universally valid.[7] The knowing subject is faced with the needs and questions of that situation as well as with varying past normative systems and present competing normative systems. In a creative response to that situation and to the demand toward unconditioned meaning and truth, the subject considers past norms and then forms or accepts a principle to use for the present situation. This decision is the beginning of the formation of the norm for the system of meaning that is emerging.

---

[4]Paul Tillich, *Das System der Wissenschaften nach Gegenständen und Methoden* (1923), vol. 1 of *Gesammelte Werke* (GW) (Stuttgart: Evangelisches Verlagswerk, 1959) 109-293. This has been translated into English: *The System of Sciences according to Objects*, trans. Paul Wiebe (Lewisburg PA: Bucknell University Press, 1981). Throughout this essay, references will be to the German text.

[5]Paul Tillich, "Kairos und Logos," *Gesammelte Werke* (GW) (Stuttgart: Evangelisches Verlagswerk, 1961) 4:43-76.

[6]Tillich, *Das System der Wissenschaften*, 123, 134, and "Kairos und Logos," 46-47, 65-66, 76. This view of reality as dynamic underlies his ontology as well as epistemology. Not only our *perception* of reality changes, but reality itself (*Systematic Theology*, 3 vols. [Chicago: University of Chicago Press, 1951–1963] 1:78). (*Systematic Theology* is hereafter cited as ST with volume and pages numbers.)

[7]Tillich, *Das System der Wissenschaften*, 217. Also see Tillich, "The Philosophy of Religion," *What Is Religion?*, ed. James Luther Adams (New York: Harper & Row, 1969) 57-58, where Tillich discusses the demand to fulfill the unconditioned meaning.

This normative decision involves a basic underlying decision with respect to the Unconditioned that includes one's fundamental interpretation of reality expressed through ordinary decisions of knowledge.[8] The knowing subject is both addressed by and directed toward the Unconditioned.[9] As a knowing subject, a person is aware of the possibility of truth and the demand to present it through one's knowledge and systems of meaning. If the person does not follow up on possibilities for truth, then that decision is basically against the Unconditioned. If the subject follows the demand toward truth, the response is for the Unconditioned.

Such a process of normative knowledge can be seen in the recent efforts to deal with religious pluralism. We can legitimately speak about the present situation of religious pluralism demanding a response from religious thinkers. To persevere in traditional dogmatic claims which ignore the possibility of truth in diverse religions and cultures is to turn away from the demands of the moment, to ignore the demand of unconditioned meaning which as unconditioned is not tied to one culture and tradition.

Formal response to religious pluralism generally follows the pattern of decision, judgment, and the positing of a new norm and system of meaning that Tillich has suggested in his epistemology. Religious thinkers such as John Hick or Wilfred Cantwell Smith try to be open to truth in non-Christian traditions but also see the importance of judgments of religious knowledge and truth. They consider past attempts to deal with non-Christian tradition, such as dogmatic exclusivism, judge those attempts in relation to the present situation, and work to develop new normative approaches that are open to a variety of expressions of ultimate truth. But this openness to truth in diverse persons and traditions raises concern about religious subjectivism and epistemological relativism.

Although Tillich's theory of knowledge emphasizes the participation of the subject in knowledge, he is not advocating subjectivism because he also emphasizes the importance of the historical situation and the demand toward the Unconditioned. Also, the decisions of knowledge reflect consideration of past systems, principles, and material in relation to the

---

[8]Tillich, "Kairos und Logos," 50, 52, 56. James Luther Adams says that Tillich makes such religious decision (toward the Unconditioned) the "presupposition of all decision" (*Paul Tillich's Philosophy of Culture, Science, and Religion* [New York: Schocken Books, 1965] 207).

[9]Tillich, "Kairos und Logos," 55.

present situation; thus, these decisions are very involved in the arena of public discussion beyond the individual subject. The truth of the newly posited normative knowledge will also be judged by other thinkers in relation to the historical situation and the demand toward the Unconditioned, just as now the efforts of John Hick and Wilfred Cantwell Smith are evaluated by other scholars dealing with religious pluralism.

Moreover, the dynamic element in Tillich's epistemology allows for ongoing judgment of normative systems and new creative efforts to meet new situations. There is always relation to the past but also a respect for the future, that what is posited now may need changing as people and history change. This same dynamic process suggests that conflicting norms would be dealt with through the development of a new norm which attempts to pull the elements of truth from each of the conflicting norms in relation to the present situation. For example, as we have seen in chapter one, present Christian thinkers dealing with religious pluralism have had to evaluate the position of "no salvation apart from Christ" as well as positions which are open to truth in all religious traditions. The truth and value in both positions has to be taken seriously and judged in relation to the present and the demand for ultimate truth.[10]

Tillich's process of the formation of norms is also expressed in his discussion of the process of experiential verification in his *Systematic Theology*.[11] In experiential verification one is usually dealing with aspects of life that cannot be calculated, easily controlled, or repeated—characteristics that apply to most human experiences. Experiential verification occurs within the life process itself and therefore is affected by many historical-cultural and personal factors.

Tillich speaks of three steps which we repeat over and over again in the life process, with differing contents and situations. The first step is a

---

[10]The use of Tillich's approach for dealing with conflicting norms is somewhat similar to Gadamer's discussion of the fusion of horizons of meaning (*Truth and Method* [New York: Seabury Press, 1975]). For Gadamer, the ongoing hermeneutical process involves awareness of foremeanings and prejudices in relationship to specific material and encounter and play with meanings, resulting in the fusion of horizons. This can be applied to conflicting norms which can interact with our foremeanings and hopefully result in a better understanding of differences or even a transcending of those differences through a fusion of different horizons of meaning.

[11]ST 1:100-105.

preliminary affirmation or judgment on the basis of experience. As a result of more experience or changing historical situation, there is a negation or qualification of the first affirmation. The third step is a final affirmation that reaches a deeper level of truth or reality than the preliminary affirmation.[12] But in the life process, the final affirmation may become a preliminary affirmation, as the dialectical process of affirming truth continues. At each third step or final stage, the truth affirmed holds for that stage of the life process, but it may be negated at another stage.

In forming a norm, one is asserting what is and ought to be the norm for a particular situation. In dealing with past norms and with present conflicts, the process of preliminary affirmation, negation, and final affirmation will be repeated many times. The norm is tested by its effectiveness within the situation for which it was written and for future situations. The more that a past norm is contained in a new norm, the more truth it is judged to have for the past and the present.

This process can be seen in the ongoing discussion of truth in diverse religious traditions. For example, as shown in chapter one, Karl Rahner's proposal of "anonymous Christianity" was an attempt to maintain the truth of salvation in Christ with an appreciation for truth and value in non-Christian religious traditions.[13] Today, thinkers such as John Hick reject the implicit paternalism of Rahner's position as invalid for the present situation of interreligious dialogue.

We also can apply the process to two conflicting religious claims—the understanding of the ultimate as impersonal versus the understanding of the ultimate as personal. Since we do not have an absolute standpoint from which to judge the truth of such claims, we can only consider the claims from our own personal and historical situation. But as we gain more understanding of the claims, we can come to appreciate truth and value in each position and work to develop an understanding of ultimacy that can function for both rather than excluding one. In such development, there will be ongoing affirmation, qualification, and new affirmation. Both John Hick with his term "the Real" and Wilfred Cantwell Smith with his term "transcendence" have attempted such development beyond the usual concept of God although both still have some Western overtones in their

---

[12]ST 1:101.

[13]Karl Rahner, "Christianity and the Non-Christian Religions," *Theological Investigations* 5 (London: Darton, Longman & Todd, 1966) 115-34.

characterizations of ultimacy.[14] The process each follows is a process of verification in relation to expanded understandings and changing religious situations.

Since this ongoing verification is relative to the particular historical-cultural situation, we still can ask whether there can be any verification or a criterion of truth that transcends such relativity to the situation. Tillich makes some effort at answering this in his analysis of the truth of symbols.

The Critique of Idolatry

In "The Religious Symbol," Tillich presents four characteristics of religious symbols that can be treated as criteria.[15] On the subjective side, Tillich points to the importance of response and acceptance. A religious symbol should make the Unconditioned perceptible to people so that there is communication and response.[16] Also, the symbol should be accepted by people as an appropriate and adequate symbol. On the objective side, a religious symbol should point beyond itself to the Unconditioned and be able to really express the Unconditioned. But we need to consider whether there is a criterion which can determine whether the ultimate or Unconditioned is really expressed.

In "Symbol and Knowledge," Tillich says that the criterion for every religious symbol is "the unconditioned character of the unconditioned over against any symbol in which a conditioned, finite, exhaustible reality is made the expression of our ultimate concern."[17] Tillich expresses this criterion more fully in his critique of idolatry which rejects any absolutization of the finite symbol itself. In *Dynamics of Faith*, he states the criterion against idolatry paradoxically: "The criterion of the truth of faith, therefore, is that it implies an element of self-negation. That symbol is most adequate which expresses not only the ultimate but also its own lack of ultimacy."[18] Or,

---

[14]Hick, "The Theology of Religious Pluralism," 338. Smith, *Towards a World Theology*, 183-94.

[15]Paul Tillich, "The Religious Symbol," trans. James Luther Adams, *Journal of Liberal Religion* 2 (Summer 1940): 13-14.

[16]Paul Tillich, *Dynamics of Faith* (New York: Harper & Row, 1957) 96.

[17]Paul Tillich, "Symbol and Knowledge," *Journal of Liberal Religion* 2/4 (1941): 204.

[18]Paul Tillich, *Dynamics of Faith*, 97.

Tillich speaks of a yes and no judgment which recognizes that religious symbols can express the Unconditioned (yes) but that the expression itself is limited and can never fully express the Unconditioned or ultimate (no).

If a religious expression or finite object is taken as absolute in itself, then Tillich would call it idolatrous or demonic.[19] Idolatrous and demonic expressions are destructive to persons because they lead to a loss of the self to the object of idolatrous faith.[20] The self commits to the object of faith as ultimate and therefore life is disrupted when the object is seen as less than ultimate. This can be seen in the effects of questioning dogmatic exclusivism in relation to non-Christian religions. Ordinary thinking and understanding is disrupted and altered as one questions the exclusivity of Christian claims. Some may reject the claim while others may adapt it; still others try to keep the loyalty and also accept other views. Thinkers may ask whether the claim is absolute or perhaps itself idolatrous as a claim for one finite religious form and understanding.

For Tillich, as we have seen in chapter one, part B, the symbol which satisfies the paradoxical criterion against idolatry is the Cross of the Christ.[21] Because it contains both the yes and the no (the yes of the glorified, risen Lord and the no of the self-sacrifice on the cross), the event of the crucified Jesus as the Christ is the criterion of the truths of all faiths for Tillich.[22] This centrality of the Cross raises several issues for our topic of cross-cultural religious truth. Is Tillich merely asserting the central Christian symbol of the Cross as the criterion of all religious truth? If so, that would not be helpful in dealing with non-Christian religious truth. Does the Cross itself then become an idolatrous symbol as the criterion of religious truth?

In *Reflection and Doubt in the Thought of Paul Tillich*,[23] Robert Scharlemann analyzes the significance of the Cross in terms of affirmation and negation to show its nonrelative truth. He argues that to say that Jesus is not the Christ affirms that he is because in dying on the Cross, in negating himself as the Christ, Jesus is the Christ.[24] To deny Jesus as the

---

[19]ST 1:134.

[20]Tillich, *Dynamics of Faith*, 12.

[21]Ibid., 97.

[22]Ibid., 97-98.

[23]Robert P. Scharlemann, *Reflection and Doubt in the Thought of Paul Tillich* (New Haven CT: Yale University Press, 1969).

[24]Ibid., 177-81.

Christ is to point to his self-negation which is simultaneously his being the Christ. By including both its affirmation and denial within itself, Scharlemann argues that the event of Jesus as the Christ anticipates all possible perspectives toward it and thereby overcomes the relativism of individual perspectives and situations. But even such an understanding of the Cross and Jesus as the Christ would be seen as too closely tied to the Christian perspective to deal fully with non-Christian religious truth.

Tillich's use of paradox in his critique of idolatry may be more helpful than his specific discussion of the Cross in developing a cross-cultural criterion of religious truth. The Cross expresses the paradox but so do several other ideas which Tillich uses, both in his earlier and later works. The paradoxical criterion of the yes and no judgment is not necessarily tied to the event of Jesus as the Christ although that event fulfills the criterion. Rather, the criterion against idolatry is tied to the nature of the ultimate or Unconditioned.

The paradoxical *form* can provide one part of a criterion for cross-cultural religious truth—that the paradoxical form be maintained and not be lost in an idolatry of the finite. This criterion of form or critique of idolatry may be the easiest to apply both within one's religious tradition as well as to other religious traditions. Because all religious expression of the ultimate is through the finite, the paradoxical form should be maintained to protect the ultimate from identification with the finite itself.[25]

Tillich's paradoxical *content* provides a further criterion, that the paradoxical relationship of finite and ultimate is part of the content. This content relates to the negation of ultimacy affirming that ultimacy; in other words, the affirmation is assumed and not destroyed by negation, and negation is not destroyed by affirmation, such as the relationship of absolute meaning and meaninglessness. Scharlemann's discussion of the certainty residing in the No implying the Yes and being taken into the Yes so that either a Yes or No stance affirms the Yes is an example of the significance of paradoxical content as distinct from form. Even this criterion of content need not be tied to a specific understanding of the ultimate nor to specific

---

[25]For fuller discussion of the application of the use of paradox and the critique of idolatry, see my discussions in "The Significance of Paradox for Theological Verification: Difficulties and Possibilities," *International Journal for Philosophy of Religion* 14 (1983): 171-82, and, below, chap. 6, section B.

religious or cultural forms of expression, but it is more closely tied to the Cross of Christ than the critique of idolatry based on paradoxical form.

Tillich's critique of idolatry is not just based in a speculative, conceptual understanding of ultimacy but rather on his intuition or experience of the revelation of the ultimate as unconditioned, the limit which nothing conditioned can reach.[26] This experience is expressed as the revelation of the ambiguity of all knowledge in relation to the unconditioned, as a guardian standpoint of the Unconditioned. Because of the centrality of Tillich's understanding of the Unconditioned to his critique of idolatry, we now turn to that topic in Tillich's thought.

The Understanding of the Ultimate

There is an important relationship between the judgment of religious truth, including the judgment of idolatry, and one's understanding of ultimacy. In Tillich's early writings, he most often uses the term "Unconditioned" while in later writings, he uses other terms, such as ground of being, power of being, being-itself, and ultimate, to express ultimacy, but the concern for the paradoxical relation of the ultimate to finite things expressed in his critique of idolatry continues throughout his career.

"The Unconditioned" names the ultimate which is presupposed by and conditions and supports all meaning, being and value.[27] The "Unconditioned" is neither another order of reality nor a part of finite conditioned reality but rather is that which qualifies finite reality as its ground or depth. The Unconditioned in its purity cannot be proved or concretely seen since that would make it a conditioned reality, but it can be dealt with by showing that it is *the* meaning which founds all realizations of meaning.[28] Paradoxically, the Unconditioned cannot be objectified and still be unconditioned, and yet it can only be grasped in the forms and symbols of conditioned things.[29] Tillich also expresses this by describing the unconditional as a quality rather

---

[26]Tillich, "Kairos und Logos," 74.

[27]See Adams, *Paul Tillich's Philosophy of Culture, Science, and Religion*, 37.

[28]Tillich, *Das System der Wissenschaften*, 253.

[29]Ibid., 254. Also see Tillich, "The Conquest of the Concept of Religion in the Philosophy of Religion," *What Is Religion?*, 122-23, 138.

than a being.[30] The unconditioned quality is encountered in reality as that which drives humans to do what is right and good and to search for and try to reach the truth.

James Luther Adams distinguishes three meanings of "the Unconditioned" in Tillich's early writings: (1) a negative limiting concept, distinguishing the Unconditioned from the conditioned and qualifying all finite reality; (2) a positive meaning pointing to the paradoxical participation or manifestation of the Unconditioned in the finite, conditioned order; and (3) a concept of value where the Unconditioned is manifest as a demand in various norms of truth and morality.[31] In all of these the Unconditioned is not static but a dynamic *qualifying* of the conditioned.

The ultimate or Unconditioned is presupposed as the ground of all truth and knowledge—as unconditioned meaning and unconditioned truth and also as the demand for knowledge to be directed toward unconditioned meaning and truth. But the limit concept of experiencing and knowing and yet not fully experiencing and knowing, maintaining the distinction between unconditioned and conditioned, is also there. As source and ground, there is a relationship of ontological participation between the unconditioned and conditioned, finite beings that applies to human knowledge and truth as well as other dimensions of experience. But there is also the important qualitative distinction between the conditioned and the unconditioned that forms the basis of the limit dimension of the ultimate.

The positive meanings of the unconditioned, especially in relationship to ontological participation of the infinite in the finite, raises the question of the relationship between the unconditioned and God. Tillich is not totally clear on this point and seems to fluctuate between saying that the unconditioned is God and saying that the two should not be identified.[32] His

---

[30]Paul Tillich, "Kairos," *The Protestant Era* (Chicago: University of Chicago Press, 1948) 32n.1.

[31]Adams, *Paul Tillich's Philosophy of Culture, Science, and Religion*, 44-45, 48-49.

[32]For example, in "Two Types of Philosophy of Religion," *Theology of Culture* (London: Oxford University Press, 1959) 24, Tillich says: "God is unconditioned, that makes him God; but the 'unconditional' is not God." Yet the opposite view is expressed in "Church and Culture," *Interpretation of History* (New York: Charles Scribner's Sons, 1936) 222: "We can therefore speak of the unconditioned simultaneously as basis of meaning and abyss of meaning [*Sinngrund und -*

doctrine of symbols supplies a key to bringing together the unconditioned and God. In "The Religious Symbol," he suggests that the word "God" has a double meaning:

> It connotes the unconditioned transcendent, the ultimate, and also an object somehow endowed with qualities and actions. The first is not figurative or symbolic, but is rather in the strictest sense what it is said to be. The second, however, is really symbolic, figurative. It is the second that is the object envisaged by the religious consciousness.[33]

When Tillich says that God cannot be identified with the Unconditioned, he is understanding God as the object of religious consciousness who is endowed with qualities and actions. But when he identifies God and the Unconditioned, he is pointing to the unconditioned meaning of God as the nonsymbolic meaning. In volume 1 of the *Systematic Theology*, he argues for the one nonsymbolic statement about God, that "God is being-itself or the absolute."[34] But even this resolution is complicated by Tillich's later statement that "everything we say about God is symbolic"[35] and the identification of being-itself (or the unconditional) and God as the point where the symbolic and nonsymbolic come together.[36]

---

abgrund]. We call this object of the silent belief in the ultimate meaningfulness, this basis and abyss of all meaning which surpasses all that is conceivable, *God*."

In "The Problem of Theological Method," *The Journal of Religion* 27 (January 1947): 16-26, Tillich again suggests that it is wrong to call the transcendent ultimate or the Unconditioned "God": "There is, however, one point (which is only a point, without length or breadth) in which medium and content are identical, because in this point subject and object are identical: it is the awareness of the ultimate itself, the *esse ipsum*, which transcends the difference between subject and object and lies, as the presupposition of all doubts, beyond doubt; it is the *veritas ipsa*, as Augustine has called it. It is wrong to call this point 'God' (as the ontological argument does), but it is necessary to call it 'that in us which makes it impossible for us to escape God.' It is the presence of the element of 'ultimacy' in the structure of our existence, the basis of religious experience" (23).

[33]Paul Tillich, "The Religious Symbol," 27.

[34]ST 1:239.

[35]ST 2:9.

[36]ST 2:10. For a fuller discussion of the underlying basis for Tillich's distinction

This discussion is important for the situation of religious pluralism since the distinction between a personal and impersonal ultimate is often identified as a major difference between Western and Eastern religions. Tillich's discussion of the relationship of symbolic and nonsymbolic suggests a possible way of bringing those diverse views together. Following Tillich, personality would be seen as a symbolic understanding of the ultimate, connected with the positive content side, and the impersonal ultimate or being-itself would be the positive content on the impersonal side. Tillich's statement of a point of identity of the two provides a point of resolution between the personal and the impersonal. But even this point may suggest too much positive content for some understandings of ultimacy. We must also deal with the understanding of ultimacy which emphasizes emptiness and nothingness. As we have seen in chapter two, Tillich's own discussion of the ultimate as the power of being in relation to nonbeing provides some similarities in content to particular Eastern understandings of the relationship of Reality and nothingness.[37]

In attempting to discuss ultimacy cross-culturally, I suggest that the limit/demand side of Tillich's concept of the ultimate could function as a formal demand and limit on finite religious truth apart from Tillich's positive content for the ultimate. This more formal ultimacy would then not be tied to a particular understanding of the ultimate and would therefore be more applicable to diverse views of ultimacy from various religious traditions. If the formal aspect is emphasized rather than the substantive, then emptiness or nothingness as ultimacy can be included without adopting specific understandings of the relationship of emptiness to being and thus can have more universal applicability in cross-cultural discussions and studies.

If we focus on the formal limit and demand of ultimacy, we can also retain Tillich's critique of idolatry and the role of paradox in that critique. This allows the possibility of using the critique of idolatry as a criterion of religious truth cross-culturally. In emphasizing the formal/demand understanding of ultimacy and not the positive content and in focusing on the critique of idolatry without the emphasis on paradoxical content of the

---

between the symbolic and the nonsymbolic, see Robert Scharlemann, "The Scope of Systematics: An Analysis of Tillich's Two Systems," *The Journal of Religion* 48 (April 1968): 136-49.

[37]See Langdon Gilkey's discussion of this point in *Gilkey on Tillich* (New York: Crossroad, 1990) 99-113, esp. 112.

Cross, I am moving away somewhat from Tillich's own understandings. I am asking for a philosophical use of these aspects of Tillich's thought, with a bracketing of the religious dimension that accompanies them in his thought. For cross-cultural philosophy of religion, we need some formal concepts which can be applicable to the diverse religious understandings and expressions. However, in interreligious dialogue as *religious* discussion, the positive content side of ultimacy and the paradoxical content of the Cross will be more significant.

Concluding Comments

We have seen that Tillich's description of the process for developing a creative norm can be helpful in developing an epistemology for cross-cultural philosophy of religion. First, his approach takes seriously the freedom and creativity of the individual person and the impact of the cultural situation. Second, Tillich takes seriously the relationship of the thinker to the past, as well as the present situation and direction toward the future. Third, the dialectical character of the process of forming normative knowledge and of judging experiential truth suggests a way for dealing with conflicting truth claims and for continually developing and refining our religious understandings in relation to diverse religious viewpoints and traditions.

Tillich's epistemological position accepts a historical relativism in relation to changing situations and a theological relativism of the finite in relation to the ultimate. His critique of idolatry and the use of paradox within that critique suggest a criterion for religious truth that is not tied to a particular culture or tradition. Finally, Tillich's limit/demand understanding of the unconditioned can be used in a formal understanding of ultimacy that need not be connected with a particular substantive understanding of ultimacy.

These cross-cultural applications of Tillich's ideas are primarily directed toward philosophy of religion rather than directly to interreligious dialogue. When one moves from the more formal level of philosophical analysis to the personal, religious level of interreligious dialogue, the specific content of the Cross and of ultimacy becomes much more important. The philosophical concerns are preliminary to the more content-oriented dialogue.

Tillich's own opportunities brought him in contact with some Eastern religious traditions and suggested to him the need for revision and further reflection on the relationship of the diverse religious traditions to one another. In that same spirit and with a sense of the ongoing development of normative knowledge, we can pull the truth from Tillich's own epistemology in attempting to develop an approach for religious pluralism today. We continue to accept his openness to the demands of the situation and to the unconditioned, and in light of his own critique and use of paradox suggest the development of a perspective that is not as tied to the Cross and Christianity.

Part II

Theology and Feminism

Chapter 5

Religious Pluralism, Ontology, and Feminism

In part I we explored both Tillich's direct responses to the plurality of world religions as well as ways that his ideas might be expanded to deal more adequately with contemporary interreligious dialogue. In part II we focus on Tillich's influence on feminist theology and elements of his thought that can be helpful to further developments in feminist theology. This chapter provides a transition between the two parts by showing connections between the feminist and pluralist critiques of theology in dialogue with Tillich's ontology. The primary issue here is to what extent Tillich's ontological understanding of ultimacy in relation to his theory of symbols can provide a bridge between the differing directions these two types of contemporary theology have taken.

Major Issues in the Feminist and Cross-cultural Critiques

Language. Both feminism and cross-cultural philosophy of religion have criticized traditional Christian God-language. The feminist critique has focused not only on the patriarchal language about God but also the negative psychological effects of that focus. God as "Father" or "King" is seen as asserting power over others, dominating *his* children and subjects. Exclusively male language for God ceases to be effective symbolism for God and becomes idolatry. As Tillich has noted,[1] idolatry can lead to injustice, where nonfavored beings are seen as inferior and subject to the dominant power, such as females have been to males.[2]

---

[1]For example, in his *Systematic Theology*, 3 vols. (Chicago: University of Chicago Press, 1951–1963) 1:216. (Hereafter, *Systematic Theology* is cited as ST, with volume and page numbers.)

[2]This point is developed more fully in chap. 6, sect. B.

The cross-cultural critique has focused on the exclusivity and narrowness of Christian God-language. Philosophers of religion working cross-culturally have recognized the strongly Western implications of the term "God" and have searched for more neutral terms that both Eastern and Western thinkers could use. For example, both Wilfred Cantwell Smith and John Hick used the term "God" in their early writings on religious pluralism, but more recent essays show a switch to less theistic descriptions, such as "the transcendent" (Smith) or "the Real" (Hick). With these more abstract terms, they hope to include both personal and nonpersonal understandings of the ultimate.

Both the feminist and cross-cultural critiques, then, share a recognition that traditional God-language brings much social and historical baggage with it, baggage which has been associated with patriarchal domination and imperialist missionary efforts. The power of language in defining and structuring thinking and reality cannot be ignored. To the extent that traditional God-language has devalued females, nonwhites, and non-Christians, it needs thorough reworking.

To some extent, Tillich's ontology and theology offered such a reconceptualization well before these critiques became prominent. Tillich's method recognizes historical, cultural relativism and calls for response to the needs of the present situation. His doctrine of symbols works well with the feminist call for new metaphors for God. Also, ontological concepts such as being-itself or ground of being are more neutral than traditional God-language.

But we are not in a position to simply posit Tillich's ontological theology as the already present answer to the feminist and cross-cultural critiques. Rather, we need to investigate more carefully the extent to which Tillich's concepts and symbols resolve these issues. We need to look not only at the form of his language but also the content.

Content—Feminist Challenge. Some feminist theologians have been wary of using abstract images to solve the patriarchy implicit in traditional theology. Rosemary Radford Ruether calls for inclusive images for God that draw from both males and females, but she warns that "abstractions often conceal androcentric assumptions and prevent the shattering of the male monopoly on God-language, as in 'God is not male. He is Spirit.' "[3] While some feminists have responded to this by focusing on female metaphors as

---

[3]Rosemary Radford Ruether, *Sexism and God-Talk; Toward a Feminist Theology* (Boston: Beacon Press, 1983) 67.

a corrective to the dominant patriarchal symbols, Ruether calls for the use of *both* female and male metaphors which can liberate us from stereotypical understandings of male/female roles.

Similarly, in *Models of God*, Sallie McFague states that "one of the serious deficiencies in contemporary theology is that though theologians have attempted to interpret the faith in new concepts appropriate to our time, the basic metaphors and models have remained relatively constant: they are triumphalist, monarchical, patriarchal."[4] McFague then works to develop metaphors that include and affirm all persons and all creation as interdependent. New language that simply restates or covers over old structures does not answer the feminist or pluralist critiques; rather, new metaphors and symbols that avoid the pitfalls of idolatry, patriarchy, and imperialism are necessary.

The emphasis on metaphors in feminist theology is not just a function of doing modern theology, but it also represents a conscious shift away from the popular conceptual identification of the symbol with the reality itself. For too many people, the symbol of God as father is taken literally to refer to God as a dominant male being, or the maleness of Jesus as the Christ is emphasized. McFague argues that the use of metaphors shows the constructive, relative, nondefinitive character of theology.[5] Metaphors suggest and point to possible qualities and aspects of God and Christ rather than describing the way God or Christ is.

It is also recognized that people's concepts and symbols of God influence their conceptions of self, other selves, and world. Consequently, feminists search for metaphors that express mutuality and complementarity rather than hierarchy, liberation and self-realization rather than domination, and inclusivity and interdependence rather than exclusivity. Balance in relationships not only among peoples but also with the plants and animals of our world has been called for as necessary not only for our fulfillment but even for our very survival.[6] The feminist challenge to traditional theology,

---

[4]Sallie McFague, *Models of God; Theology for an Ecological, Nuclear Age* (Philadelphia: Fortress Press, 1987) xi; also see 13.

[5]Ibid., 35ff.

[6]For examples, see McFague, *Models of God*, 6-17, 59-87; Ruether, *Sexism and God-Talk*, 85-92; and Rosemary Radford Ruether, *New Woman New Earth; Sexist Ideologies and Human Liberation* (New York: Seabury/Crossroad, 1975) 186-211.

then, involves not only theological language but also a revision of traditional content.

Content—Pluralist Challenge. The pluralist critique includes a rejection of the claim of Christian superiority and calls for a revisioning of theological doctrines. Some thinkers see a parity among religious traditions and recognize spiritual, transforming power and truth in all. Such a view challenges the traditional understandings of God, Christ, and salvation.

As with the feminist critique, some pluralist thinkers reject abstractions as the solution. For example, Langdon Gilkey argues that there is neither a unifying universal abstracted from a particular tradition nor a neutral philosophical standpoint above and beyond the different traditions.[7] Rather, he proposes a standpoint of relative absoluteness—committing oneself to a particular standpoint in a particular tradition but simultaneously and continuously recognizing the relativity of that standpoint.[8]

But other thinkers have proposed an abstract concept for the ultimate as a neutral category through which dialogue can occur. John Hick uses "the Real" or "Reality"; Wilfred Cantwell Smith uses "the transcendent." All agree that this ultimate is not totally expressed or experienced in specific religious symbols or actions. But each of these concepts works better philosophically than it may theologically. Each is an attempt to name that toward which religious actions and meanings are directed. And each attempts to encompass the diversity of understandings, including both being and nothingness, and yet not be tied to one specific viewpoint. But it is also recognized that all religious meanings and actions are necessarily concrete, historical, and cultural—directed toward ultimacy but not themselves ultimate.

When we focus on the theological content of religious traditions, we recognize important differences that do not disappear easily after a few dialogues on the meaning of terms. Religious pluralism challenges theology

---

[7]Langdon Gilkey, "Plurality and Its Theological Implications," in *The Myth of Christian Uniqueness: Toward a Pluralistic Theology of Religions*, ed. John Hick and Paul F. Knitter (Maryknoll NY: Orbis, 1987) 41.

[8]Ibid., 46-47. Similarly, Gordon Kaufman has argued that there is no universally human position through which we can understand all religious traditions or dialogue about differences. All positions are particular positions, connected to a particular historical, social setting and particular religious beliefs and practices. See Gordon Kaufman, "Religious Diversity, Historical Consciousness, and Christian Theology," *The Myth of Christian Uniqueness*, 5.

to look at God not only personally but impersonally, not only as being or reality but also as nonbeing and nothingness, not only as incarnate in one human but with many incarnations, not only as totally other but as immanent in all reality. Trinitarian understandings of God complicate these views even further.[9]

Such diverse conceptions of the ultimate also impact the Christian view of Christ as the final revelation, as the one incarnation of God, as the perfect human, as we explored in chapter 1, above. Hick and Smith have deliberately chosen theocentric approaches for interacting with non-Christian traditions. The traditional Christian view of Christ is a stumbling block in creating a tolerant, pluralist philosophy or theology. Others have tried to solve this issue through a reconceptualization of the Christ which usually focuses on the formal, structural, and more abstract aspects of the Christ-event rather than on the person Jesus who is the Christ. This allows the possibility of other incarnations or manifestations of similar meaning and effect. There are important differences between the Christ and the Buddha and between Krishna and the Christ, but discovering similarities of meaning, effect, and function leads to more tolerance, more parity, and important revisions in theological truth claims.

Both pluralism and feminism, then, are challenging Christian thought to develop language and content that breaks out of the traditional stance of Christian superiority and male dominance. Although those were not the primary concerns of Tillich's theological and philosophical system, his awareness of historical relativity and dynamics, his concern to advance beyond traditional language, and his creative effort to interrelate concept and symbol influenced him to develop language and content which may be helpful in meeting these challenges of pluralism and feminism.

Application of Tillich's Ontology

The primary focus of this discussion will not be what Tillich said concerning non-Christian religions or feminine symbolism (although that may be brought in on occasion) but rather the extent to which ontological ideas of Tillich may be useful in developing feminist, cross-cultural theology today. To what extent can Tillich's theological method and his understanding of

---

[9]Kaufman, "Religious Diversity, Historical Consciousness, and Christian Theology," 10.

God as being-itself, ground of being, and power of being contribute to these present-day efforts in theology?

Method of Correlation and Theory of Symbols. Tillich's method of correlation allows for response to new questions in the present situation. Today these questions include how to respond to the relativization and critiques of traditional Christian theology by feminism and pluralism. Past theologies not only need development but major revision. As we have explored in chapter 4, Tillich's understanding that theological norms develop out of the interaction of principles and the concrete situation insures dynamic development within theology.[10]

Tillich's theory of symbols assumes his dynamic method and includes the possibility of symbols dying as well as new symbols arising. Such an approach can avoid the popular absolutization of particular symbols and allow for creative response to present situations. Although some feminists prefer to use the term "metaphor" to describe their theological constructs, Tillich's use of "symbol" is similar, even if less "playful" in construction. Tillich's distinction between a symbol and that to which the symbol points, as well as his critique of idolatry, help to answer the feminist hesitation about "symbol" because of the history of identifying reality and symbol.

However, Tillich argues for more of a connection between symbol and that to which it points than the feminist theory of metaphor accepts. For him, the symbol participates in the reality and can only be a true symbol if it does so participate.[11] It is that participation which provides their power. Without such a basis, metaphors are simply imaginative constructs, easily changed or rejected. When we are dealing with theological metaphors, an element of subjective response and commitment is important for the metaphors to be effective. Symbol, understood as Tillich does, can meet the feminist critique of nonidentification and dynamic change. I find it workable within feminist theology, but others may see it as too tied to traditional concepts because of his emphasis on participation in the power of the divine and the connection of his ontology and theology to traditional symbols.

In his efforts to deal with religious pluralism, Langdon Gilkey explores several aspects of Tillich's theory of symbols. Because he recognizes both

---

[10]For further analysis of the dynamic character of Tillich's normative theology, see my discussion in "Paul Tillich's Theory of Theological Norms and the Problems of Relativism and Subjectivism," *Journal of Religion* 62/4 (October 1982): 359-75.

[11]ST 1:239.

commitment and participation in a particular tradition as well as openness to non-Christian truth, Gilkey proposes a relative absoluteness, as describing both our praxis with "the absolute as relatively present in the relative" and the necessary structure for theology.[12] He compares this to Tillich's discussion of the true symbol as both relativizing and sacrificing itself while pointing beyond itself to absoluteness and ultimacy. But Gilkey recognizes the root of that criterion in the Christ as final revelation for Tillich.

Gilkey also speaks of the danger of demonic possibilities in our pluralistic society and calls for the critique of symbols to avoid such possibilities.[13] Although not directly referring to Tillich, his description of the criterion of symbols is certainly close to Tillich's own: "A symbol or a criterion points beyond itself and criticizes itself if it would not be demonic; but it also points *to* itself and *through* itself if it would not be empty, and if we would not be left centerless."[14] This leads Gilkey to critique even the absoluteness of the Christ as final revelation that Tillich accepted. Gilkey accepts Christian symbols as relative and yet transcending themselves, as final and yet not the only symbols.[15] This is a move Tillich does not make, but it is a possible result of applying Tillich's critique of idolatry to his own theology.

Being-itself, Ground of Being, and Power of Being—Immanence and Transcendence. In terms of structure, cross-cultural philosophy of religion stresses transcendence more than immanence although it does not deny the possibility of immanence of the divine across traditions and cultures. For example, both Hick's structure of divine noumenon and human phenomena and Smith's focus on the "transcendent" which is expressed in various cultural and religious forms stress transcendence more than immanence of the ultimate. But in relation to content, the issue is much more complicated for religious pluralism. Whether immanence or transcendence is stressed in

---

[12]Gilkey, "Plurality and Its Theological Implications," 47. For more discussion of Gilkey's doctrine of relative absoluteness, see my discussion in "Relative Absoluteness: An Approach to Religious Pluralism," in *The Theology of Langdon Gilkey: Systematic and Critical Studies*, ed. Kyle Pasewark and Jeff Pool (Macon GA: Mercer University Press, 1999) 239-58.

[13]Gilkey, "Plurality and Its Theological Implications," 48-49.

[14]Ibid., 48.

[15]Ibid., 49.

content depends on the religious tradition and often the particular part of the tradition that one considers.

Several feminist thinkers have stressed the immanence of God over against transcendence because they believe the emphasis on distance between God and creatures radically devalues human beings and the world. Interestingly, some feminist thinkers have appropriated aspects of Tillich's theology to express God's immanence in human lives. For example, as we will show in chapter 6, section A, Mary Daly, in her early work, used the idea of power of being to express nonpatriarchal ultimacy and women's experience of immanence and transcendence as their consciousnesses develop.[16] Also, Sallie McFague makes favorable reference to Tillich's understanding of love as the moving power of life.[17]

Tillich calls the being of God "being-itself" to emphasize that God is not a being alongside or above other beings but rather the infinite power and meaning of being.[18] Unlike every ordinary being, being-itself does not participate in nonbeing, but being-itself is the ongoing power of being which resists nonbeing in everything that is.[19] Tillich maintains this tension in the concept of "being-itself"—unlike all other beings and yet immanently connected to all beings. He speaks of "an absolute break, an infinite jump," and yet "everything participates in the infinite power of being."[20]

God as "ground of being" might seem to maintain this tension of transcendence and immanence more than God as "power of being" because "ground" suggests source or cause or origin, all of which imply differentiation or distance. But Tillich collapses the tension when he says not only that God is the ground of the structure of being but also that God "*is* this structure."[21] The "structure of being" like the "power of being" emphasizes immanence more than transcendence.

Tillich's effort to maintain the tension between immanence and transcendence can be helpful in our effort to balance the feminist emphasis on the powerful immanence of God in feminist experience and the pluralist

---

[16]Mary Daly, *Beyond God the Father; Toward a Philosophy of Women's Liberation* (Boston: Beacon Press, 1973).

[17]McFague, *Models of God*, 102-103.

[18]ST 1:235.

[19]ST 1:236.

[20]ST 1:237.

[21]ST 1:238.

emphasis on the absolute which transcends and yet empowers ordinary religious phenomena.

God as Being-itself—Ontology and Theology. Yet another tension in Tillich's idea of ultimacy is between the ontological concept of being-itself and the theological symbol of God. There has been much discussion of Tillich's statement that "God is being-itself" is the most nonsymbolic statement possible.[22] Tillich adjusts this claim in the second volume of his *Systematic Theology* when he says that the nonsymbolic statement is that "everything we say about God is symbolic."[23] There he argues that "God is being-itself" is both rational and ecstatic expression, both nonsymbolic and symbolic.[24] And in yet another formulation, Tillich says that "the nonsymbolic element in all religious knowledge is the experience of the unconditioned as the boundary, ground, and abyss of everything conditioned."[25] Robert Scharlemann has shown that the seeming differences in these approaches are somewhat resolved when placed in the context of Tillich's whole theological system as a theonomous system of meaning.[26]

Tillich's statements show his concern to ground his system of symbols in something nonsymbolic and yet also retain the ultimacy of the ultimate which is inexpressible. But for our purposes, the tension in the effort to bring together symbol and concept, philosophy and theology, is important since the cross-cultural critique has moved most strongly philosophically and the feminist critique most strongly theologically. The cross-cultural critique has sometimes used the abstract concept to transcend specific symbols or metaphors while the feminist critique prefers new symbols and metaphors grounded in human experience. Tillich's efforts to bridge those differences can be important in formulating links between the two critiques and their resulting theories.

This same tension of ontology and theology comes out in Tillich's effort to show the relationship between the God of biblical religion and the god of

---

[22]ST 1:239.

[23]ST 2:9.

[24]ST 2:10.

[25]Paul Tillich, "Symbol and Knowledge," *Journal of Liberal Religion* 2/4 (1941): 203.

[26]Robert Scharlemann, "The Scope of Systematics: An Analysis of Tillich's Two Systems," *Journal of Religion* 48 (April 1968): 136-49.

the philosophers in *Biblical Religion and the Search for Ultimate Reality*.[27] In spite of their seeming opposition, Tillich claims that biblical religion and ontology "have an ultimate unity and a profound interdependence."[28] Through ontological analysis, the philosopher tries to show "the presence of being and its structures in the different realms of being" or the power of being resisting nonbeing in which things participate.[29] This description of ontology is comparable to the effort of cross-cultural philosophy of religion to show the basis of all religious traditions in the transcendent or ultimate.

But biblical religion offers a different approach for answering the ontological search: a personal god, who is experienced personally. Such an approach seems to treat God as a being, albeit a personal being, in contrast to the nonpersonal being-itself which empowers but yet is beyond all beings.[30] This effort is comparable to the feminist emphasis on personal transforming experience.

To affirm God as personal is to affirm a living relationship with God, a personal relationship, which like other personal relationships is not totally determined, is subject to change and interaction, is free and intimate.[31] But the ontological concept of being-itself suggests that which is beyond change. On the other hand, the relationship with being-itself is more intimate than the relationship with a personal god: "We speak *to* somebody, but we participate *in* something."[32] Biblical revelation suggests distance between the revealer and the people to whom revelation comes while ontology suggests the immanence of participation and tries to penetrate the power of being.[33] Yet biblical revelation posits a personal god while the god of ontology is impersonal. "Ontology generalizes, while biblical religion individualizes."[34] Similarly, cross-cultural philosophy of religion often generalizes ideas while feminist theology often individualizes experiences.

---

[27]Paul Tillich, *Biblical Religion and the Search for Ultimate Reality* (Chicago: University of Chicago Press, 1955).

[28]Ibid., 1.

[29]Ibid., 8.

[30]Ibid., 27-28.

[31]Ibid., 31.

[32]Ibid., 33.

[33]Ibid., 34.

[34]Ibid., 39.

Tillich finds the point of contact between biblical religion and ontology in the subjective side of each, more than the objective, doctrinal side. Both the person searching for ontological truth, threatened by nonbeing, and the believer who takes the risk of faith in the face of doubt share the "No" of doubt which is taken into the "Yes" of courage.[35] Both experiences involve final trust in the power of being and participation in particular experiences and symbols which give content to their experience, questions and answers.[36] Similarly, both the feminist and the pluralist have doubted traditional theological doctrines but move on to offer new concepts and symbols that cohere with their experiences of the world.

The person who speaks of ultimate reality ontologically has encountered it existentially, just as the person who speaks of God in faith.[37] "Religiously speaking, this means that our encounter with the God who is a person includes the encounter with the God who is the ground of everything personal and as such not *a* person."[38] Tillich concludes that faith includes itself and the doubt of itself. The tensions are not resolved but Tillich argues that when one lives courageously in the midst of these tensions, that one discovers "their ultimate unity in the depths of our own souls and the depth of the divine life."[39]

The tension between the abstract formulations and concrete, personal expressions in both pluralism and feminism may have to be handled similarly—recognized and affirmed, lived in courageously but not resolved. Religious pluralism attempts to develop an approach which will take seriously each of the diverse religious traditions but which will also allow for truth more broadly than within one tradition. The persons of the religious traditions and their specific views are valued, but at the same time, we are looking for an approach which includes the variety of such persons and their traditions. Feminism also is caught in this tension as it attempts to keep the ultimacy of God but avoid abstractions that hide patriarchal assumptions. One effort has been the use of metaphors which can be more experimental, imagistic, and pluralistic than traditional symbols.[40] Thus, for both pluralism

---

[35]Ibid., 63.

[36]Ibid.

[37]Ibid., 65.

[38]Ibid., 83.

[39]Ibid., 85.

[40]See McFague, *Models of God*, 37. McFague does express appreciation for

and feminism, we are caught in this same tension that Tillich describes. And perhaps we too are left with affirming and living courageously in the tension between the abstractions and the concrete, personal images.

The God above God. A similar tension in Tillich's understanding of ultimacy is between the contentless point of the God above God and the concrete symbols of God which can be doubted. Once again, we are confronted with the doubter who yet has faith and the faith which can be doubted. The doubter may doubt specific contents of meaning, such as the God of the divine-human encounter or the patriarchal, imperialist God. But if the doubter accepts meaninglessness and has the courage to face meaninglessness, that is a meaningful act. In *The Courage to Be*[41] Tillich interprets this meaningful act as an experience of meaning, based in the power of being-itself. The power to accept meaninglessness is not rooted in any concrete, meaningful content but rather in the contentless power or ground of being. Tillich calls the acceptance of this power absolute faith.[42]

Nonbeing threatens faith through doubt, but in absolute faith the power of being overcoming nonbeing is experienced. In *The Courage to Be*, being is defined as "the negation of the negation of being."[43] Negation as an active negation implies the character of power in being-itself. Nonbeing negates but has no character in and of itself; rather it gathers its qualities from the being that it negates, such as guilt in relation to moral being.[44] In absolute faith, the person experiences the negation of the negation of meaninglessness, but it is without content and therefore does not deny the ultimate meaninglessness of concrete meanings.

In this sense, being-itself or the power of being is a limit concept as well as a grounding concept for Tillich. That which is experienced as the limit of doubt, that which undergirds doubt and the courage of despair, is also the ground of all forms of courage.[45] Particular forms of courage that affirm more concrete meanings than the absolute faith which faces meaninglessness

---

Tillich's distinction between the symbol "God" and God as being-itself, but she sees her own metaphorical theology as more open and free than Tillich's.

[41]Paul Tillich, *The Courage to Be* (New Haven: Yale University Press, 1952).
[42]Ibid., 177.
[43]Ibid., 179.
[44]Ibid., 40-41.
[45]Ibid., 190.

are rooted in that same absolute faith, in being-itself as the ground and power of being and meaning.

Perhaps then we should look at the abstract direction of cross-cultural proposals as expressing limit and grounding concepts of ultimacy, with the traditional expressions as particular examples of contents. Any of the particular contents can be doubted, as we can see when we look at the critiques arising from pluralism and feminism. But both pluralism and feminism have not been content to rest on an abstract point of ultimacy beyond all concrete expressions. Rather, they have affirmed the relativism such a view implies and have moved on to constructing feminist metaphors or pluralist concepts of God and Christ.

The Ground of Being and Feminist Theology. Among particular contents in Tillich's own theology is his use of the ground of being as a symbolic concept for the ultimate. Tillich associates this use of ground of being with feminine aspects of divinity. In his discussion of the Trinity, Tillich notes the high status of the Virgin Mary in Roman Catholic devotion and asks whether there are any elements in Protestant symbolism that transcend the alternative male-female or which can be developed over against "the one-sided male-determined symbolism."[46] Tillich suggests that "ground of being" symbolically points to "the mother-quality of giving birth, carrying, and embracing, and at the same time, of calling back, resisting independence of the created, and swallowing it."[47] Tillich sees the rootedness of all in the ground and power of being as helping to balance out the male-dominated (patriarchal) symbols of divinity. The ground and power of being suggests a more intimate relationship between God and creatures than the father-image who demands of his children where God is one superior person among other persons.[48] Tillich has recognized the one-sidedness and implied oppression of the father symbolism that have more recently been critiqued by feminists.

This aspect of Tillich's thought has not been ignored by feminists. For example, McFague uses and agrees with Tillich's suggestion that the ground of being points to a mother-quality which both gives birth and calls all life back to reunification.[49] She also connects that mother quality with Tillich's

---

[46]ST 3:293.
[47]ST 3:294.
[48]ST 3:294.
[49]Sallie McFague, *Models of God*, 101-103.

emphasis on love as reuniting the separated. But whereas Tillich's discussion of this point almost reads as a divergence in his system, McFague makes these metaphors the center of her theology. The metaphors of God as Mother and Lover unfold more fully the meanings of life-giving and reuniting love expressed in Tillich's "ground of being."

Being—Nonbeing; Reality—Nothingness. Tillich also recognized some of the issues raised by the Christian theologian's encounter with non-Christian religious traditions. Focusing on ontological aspects of Tillich's approach to these issues, we once again find Tillich pointing to the important difference between the personal symbolism of the ultimate in Christianity and the transpersonal expression of the ultimate in Buddhism.[50] Tillich then points to the transpersonal expression of the ultimate as being-itself which indicates its nonidentity with particular existing things and thereby helps the Christian to understand the Buddhist expression of "absolute nothingness."[51] On the other hand, Tillich points out that some forms of Buddhism affirm the Buddha-spirit in many personal manifestations. Thus, there may be points of similarity, but these do not negate or transcend the important differences among the diverse traditions.

It is interesting that Tillich's encounter with diverse religious traditions, especially Japanese Buddhism, does not lead him to deeper discussions of the relation of being and nonbeing but rather to discussions of typologies of religion, the proposal of a method or attitude of approach to pluralism, and the positing of the religion of the concrete spirit as the ground and goal of religions. But as we have shown in chapter 2, Tillich's ontology does show some similarities to ideas of ultimacy in Japanese Buddhism.

The Christ as New Being. The focus on Christ as male and the focus on Christ as the unique savior, the final, one-and-only savior have been strongly critiqued by both feminism and pluralism. Just as Tillich's doctrine of God as being-itself opens up possibilities for advancing beyond patriarchal and imperialistic theology, so also does Tillich's doctrine of Christ as New Being.

By reducing the traditional emphasis on the historical Jesus of Nazareth and emphasizing the universal content in the Christ, Tillich's symbol of the New Being can be understood without gender and can be applied more

---

[50]Paul Tillich, *Christianity and the Encounter of the World Religions* (New York: Columbia University Press, 1963) 65-66.
[51]Ibid., 67.

broadly than Jesus of Nazareth. Although Tillich does not pursue all the implications of his theology of the New Being, others can and have. As discussed more fully in the next chapter, feminist Mary Daly has used the New Being to refer to the healing experiences of women whose consciousnesses have been raised.[52] She keeps Tillich's emphasis on the healing, reconciling aspects of the New Being while rejecting the identification with the male Jesus of Nazareth.

Similarly, talk of New Being expressed outside of Christianity opens up truth in non-Christian traditions. But this leads us to distinguish between a philosophy of religious pluralism that may not be rooted in a particular religious tradition and a theology of religious pluralism that is rooted in a particular tradition. Clearly, Tillich's approach to New Being is more helpful for the latter because Tillich continues to affirm the final revelation in Jesus as the Christ, the New Being (see chapter 1).

Perhaps "New Being" could be a neutral enough term that the ontological significance of reunion, reconciliation, and healing could cut across religious traditions. But that means opening it up far beyond Tillich's focus in the Christ. Even with that openness, one would have to see how such a concept or symbol works in interreligious dialogue or in feminist discussions, whether it can really be separated from its roots in Jesus as the Christ (or even whether finally it should be). In a discussion of religious pluralism, Tom Driver notes that some aspects of Tillich's own Christology could be judged negatively by his critique of idolatry. While Tillich did focus on the "self-emptying ultimacy" of the Christ (apart form specific content), Driver notes that Tillich found such ultimacy only in the crucified Christ, the center for all human history.[53] Of course, this is a most sensitive and complex area of application of the critique of idolatry.

Conclusions

Tillich's distinction between God and being-itself, between symbols and the unconditional itself, can be helpful for including both feminist and pluralist approaches. Such a distinction points to the relativity and imaginative construction of theological expression. Tillich's concern to provide a nonsymbolic basis of symbols and yet to relativize all theological conception

---

[52]Daly, *Beyond God the Father*, chap. 3.
[53]Driver, "The Case for Pluralism," *The Myth of Christian Uniqueness*, 215.

in relation to the ultimate causes him difficulty in his discussion of the relation between God and being-itself. But it is supported by the radical relativity demanded by both feminism and pluralism.

The lack of recognition of relativity in theological construction has created an idolatry of male expressions that feminism critiques and an idolatry of Christian forms of expression that pluralism critiques. Tillich's distinction between God and being-itself provides the basis for his guardian standpoint of ultimacy. The self-sacrificing aspects of the Protestant principle as criterion of religious truth is rooted in Tillich's focus on the crucified Jesus as the Christ. But the roots of that are in the guardian standpoint, distinguishing relative human expressions of ultimacy from ultimacy itself—symbols of God from being-itself.

But it is also the identification of God as being-itself that makes possible the symbolic expressions of ultimacy. Tillich recognized the importance of the interconnection and relatedness of symbols to that which they symbolize. Tillich's expression of God as the ground of being points to relatedness and yet separation while the power of being points to participation. It is God as ground and power of being that connects not only religious symbols to their object but also the symbol makers to their source and ongoing root.

In relation to idolatry, Tillich recognized not only the consequences for religious truth of idolatry but also its destructiveness for human lives. Whether one looks at the oppression of females or the imperialistic rejections of non-Christians, one can see the destructiveness of idolatry.

Tillich's emphasis on the dynamic interrelation of being and nonbeing can and has led to substantive dialogues between some Mahayana Buddhists and Tillich's thought. This is a particular application of Tillich's ontology which can be helpful in dialogue but may be too focused for any overall conclusions about cross-cultural religious truth (see chapter 2).

We conclude, then, that Tillich's ontological theology offers many possibilities for helping contemporary theology take account of the feminist and pluralist critiques; yet Tillich's own theology is limited by its ties to specific Christian symbols and events as final revelation. Today, such finality has been radically critiqued, but the symbols and concepts Tillich used to express his theology may still be helpful in a more radically relativized context and in interreligious dialogue, where participants affirm their roots in a particular tradition. The creative tensions within Tillich's own theological system continue outside his system in the tensions of pluralism and feminism as we build theology in and for our present situation.

Chapter 6

Tillich and Mary Daly's Feminist Theology

At first glance Mary Daly's feminist theology and Paul Tillich's philosophical theology may seem quite different. But further investigation shows the influence of Paul Tillich on Mary Daly's thought, especially in her *Beyond God the Father: Toward a Philosophy of Women's Liberation.*[1] In what follows I shall treat Tillich's influence on Daly in two ways. First, I shall analyze Daly's use of Tillich's theological ideas and show similarities and differences in their application of those ideas. Second, I shall use some of Tillich's ideas to critique Daly and to offer suggestions for future nonsexist theology.

In section A I will deal primarily with *Beyond God the Father* and not extensively with *The Church and the Second Sex* or Daly's later works for several reasons.[2] First, *Beyond God the Father* is the most systematically theological of all Daly's writings. Second, *Beyond God the Father* still deals with the principal doctrines of Christian theology, which makes comparative analysis in relation to other contemporary Christian thinkers possible. Daly's later books, *Gyn/Ecology* and *Pure Lust*, offer descriptions of the journeying of women and call for women to join that journey through exorcism of the patriarchal past to the ecstasy of a gynocentric future. In these later works, Daly sees herself moving beyond *Beyond God the Father* both in language and in content although she does not repudiate its contents. Finally, *Beyond God the Father*, in contrast to the later works,

---

[1]Mary Daly, *Beyond God the Father: Toward a Philosophy of Women's Liberation* (Boston: Beacon Press, 1973).

[2]Mary Daly, *The Church and the Second Sex*, with a "New Feminist Post-Christian Introduction" by the author (New York: Harper & Row, 1975)—original text of *The Church and the Second Sex* (1968). "Later works" refer to *Gyn/Ecology: The Metaethics of Radical Feminism* (Boston: Beacon Press, 1978) and *Pure Lust: Elemental Feminist Philosophy* (Boston: Beacon Press, 1984). These later works are discussed in sect. B of this chapter.

retains an androgynous ideal and does not close the door to women and men who want to deal seriously with the problem of sexism within Christian theology.

A. Application

In *Beyond God the Father* Daly offers a feminist philosophy that attempts to move beyond the patriarchal character of traditional theological language and doctrines. Her method is quite similar to Tillich's, as are several of her theological ideas. However, she limits the application and scope of these ideas primarily to the specific situation of women seeking liberation. Does such a limiting of scope constitute a misinterpretation, a misuse, or a mere particularization of Tillich's thought? I shall argue that Daly has not misinterpreted Tillich. Rather, sometimes she has merely particularized his ideas, and at other times she has developed them in ways that limit their full meaning or would be contrary to his thought. There is nothing inherently wrong in such development of another's thought, but I will show that her analysis would have benefited from a more careful following of some of Tillich's ideas.

In *Beyond God the Father* Daly makes explicit use of Tillich, but she does not consider Tillich's theology as adequate nonsexist theology in itself. She states that his theology is "potentially liberating in a very radical sense," but she sees his theology as too "detached" from the fact of sexual oppression and the situation of radical feminism.[3] Her criterion for acceptance or rejection of past theologies is this: "If God-language is even implicitly compatible with oppressiveness, failing to make clear the relation between intellection and liberation, then it will either have to be developed

---

[3]Daly, *The Church and the Second Sex*, 20-21. In earlier writings, Daly had argued for the value of Tillich's theology. She said that "his work provides a theoretical basis which can be extended and applied" (Mary Daly, "The Spiritual Revolution: Women's Liberation as Theological Reeducation," *Andover Newton Quarterly* 12 [March 1972]: 176n.9). In "After the Death of God the Father," *Commonweal* 94 (12 March 1971): 9, Daly says: "Tillich's way of speaking about God as ground and power of being would be very difficult to use for the legitimation of any sort of oppression." But in *Gyn/Ecology* Daly no longer sees Tillich as even potentially liberating (see 46, 377-78).

in such a way that it becomes explicitly relevant to the problem of sexism or else dismissed."[4]

A Comparison of Daly's and Tillich's Theological Methods

The Method of Correlation. In Tillich's method of correlation the contents of the Christian faith are explained through existential questions and theological answers that are mutually interdependent.[5] The analysis of existence that develops the existential questions is a philosophical task while the correlation of Christian answers with those questions is a theological task. In *Beyond God the Father* Daly engages both tasks while attempting to move beyond the traditional Christian symbols for answers. She says her method is not "an attempt to correlate with the existing cultural situation certain 'eternal truths' which are presumed to have been captured as adequately as possible in a fixed and limited set of symbols."[6] Nonetheless, in *Beyond God the Father* she chooses to develop several of these traditional symbols in a new direction. Daly does say that she finds Tillich's method less inadequate than other twentieth-century systematic theologians, yet it still does not offer a radical critique of patriarchal religion.[7]

In *Beyond God the Father* Daly's method is similar to Tillich's method of correlation in two ways.[8]

(1) Philosophical side. There is an analysis of the present situation, and out of that come several existential questions. Daly deals only indirectly with the situation of humankind as a whole; for women, the present situation is one of alienation from the patriarchal world. Examples: (a) The existential question of transcendence is asked by women in their efforts to go beyond the present situation and the traditional patriarchal meanings. (b) The

---

[4]Daly, *Beyond God the Father*, 21.

[5]Paul Tillich, *Systematic Theology* 3 vols. (Chicago: University of Chicago Press, 1951–1963) 1:60. (Hereafter, *Systematic Theology* is cited as ST, with volume and page numbers.)

[6]Daly, *Beyond God the Father*, 7.

[7]Ibid., 200n.10.

[8]In discussing Daly's method, I am using only *Beyond God the Father*. Her methods in *The Church and the Second Sex*, *Gyn/Ecology*, and *Pure Lust* are quite different. Even in *Beyond God the Father*, Daly says she is overcoming methodolatry by asking nonquestions and dealing with nondata; but a method is discernible.

existential question of the source of courage and hope is asked by women in their efforts to face alienation. (c) Also, in the face of alienation, women are seeking New Being.

(2) Theological side. Daly not only shows that spiritual/religious questions are asked in the women's revolution but also discusses religious values and meanings which answer those questions. In the "process of women becoming," the religious values and meanings of the power of being and New Being are experienced.

Daly argues that her philosophical and theological tasks are different from Tillich's philosophical and theological approaches because he still stayed within the bounds of patriarchal religion.[9] Yet the similarity of terms and the basic structure of Daly's system point to a Christian basis for her analysis in spite of her naming it a "post-Christian" philosophy.

Tillich distinguishes his method of correlation from a "naturalistic" method in which the Christian message derives from human existence. Daly's attempt to see the feminist experience as a prototype of religious experience is similar to the naturalistic method. Daly seems to set up the women's revolution and process of becoming as an absolute good and absolute meaning. She says: "The becoming of women in sisterhood is the countercultural phenomenon *par excellence* which can indicate the future course of human spiritual evolution."[10] She talks of the process of women becoming as meaning a "Fall *into* the sacred" and the "arrival of New Being."[11] Religious meanings are derived from women's basic process of becoming. Tillich criticized the liberal theology of the nineteenth century because it put questions and answers on the same level of human creativity.[12] Although Daly wants to avoid this mistake, at times she comes close to it.[13]

---

[9]Daly, *Beyond God the Father*, 11.

[10]Ibid. In an interview in 1971, Daly said: "Possibly the divine spark manifested in women, the image of God in themselves as they become humanized will be like a second incarnation" ("The Church and Women: An Interview with Mary Daly," *Theology Today* 28/3 [October 1971]: 349).

[11]*Beyond God the Father*, 67-68. In *Gyn/Ecology* Daly states that "the Journey is itself participation in Paradise," where paradise is seen as an open cosmic movement of the self (6-7).

[12]ST 1:65.

[13]In *Beyond God the Father* Daly does argue that the question of ultimate

Daly's method, then, bears important similarities to Tillich's method of correlation. Understandably, she wishes to move beyond the confines of patriarchal religious symbols and roles, but she still uses some of Tillich's terms, which are interpretations of those symbols. In interpreting these for women's experience, Daly needs to be careful not to identify women's experiences with religious meaning. Her method is similar to correlation, but her failure to follow it more closely leaves her open to the mistake of naturalism and an identification of the finite with the infinite.

Kairos. To what extent is Daly responding to a *kairos*, as Tillich has used that term? For Tillich, the *kairos* is a fulfilled, creative moment of time and a time of decision.[14] In his decision to become a religious socialist, Tillich saw something eternally important manifest in the creative possibilities of the time.[15] But Tillich also talked about the *kairos* more broadly when he spoke of knowledge as involving the *kairos*.[16] The historical period in which the knowledge is formed demands a decision in relation to the Unconditioned. A positive decision toward the Unconditioned and the *kairos* would be a decision to actualize the creative possibilities of the moment, as a negative decision would be a refusal of the same possibilities. In his *Systematic Theology*, Tillich says that individuals and groups reexperience the central *kairos*, the manifestation of the New Being in Jesus as the Christ, through relative *kairoi* in which the Kingdom of God is present in several particular manifestations. The central *kairos* is both the criterion and

---

transcendence implies an awareness of the limited, transitory character of finite goals and structure, etc. Also, in "The Spiritual Revolution: Women's Liberation as Theological Reeducation," Daly speaks of the danger of absolutizing the space for freedom set aside in the mind as part of the movement (171). But her interest in avoiding the placement of the women's movement and religious meaning on the same level is much less in *Gyn/Ecology*. There the absolute meaning is in the journeying of women beyond patriarchy in this life (e.g., 6-7, 423-24).

[14]See Paul Tillich, "Kairos und Logos," *Gesammelte Werke* 4 (Stuttgart: Evangelisches Verlagswerk, 1961) 46; Paul Tillich, "Beyond Religious Socialism," *Christian Century* 66 (15 June 1949): 732; Paul Tillich, "Nietzsche and the Bourgeois Spirit," *Journal of the History of Ideas* 6 (June 1945): 309; Paul Tillich, "Kairos," in *The Protestant Era*, trans. James Luther Adams (Chicago: University of Chicago Press, 1948): 33, 49; Tillich, "Historical and Nonhistorical Interpretations of History," *The Protestant Era*, 27.

[15]Tillich, "Ethics in a Changing World," *The Protestant Era*, 155.

[16]Tillich, "Kairos und Logos," 50, 56.

the source of power of all the relative *kairoi*.[17] This experience of *kairos* is an involved experience, not a detached analytical observation.

Daly does not use the term *kairos* to refer to the historical situation in which she is living and to which she is responding, but her description of that situation in *Beyond God the Father* has the characteristics given to the idea of *kairos* by Tillich. Consider her descriptions of the feminist situation:

> The women's revolution, insofar as it is true to its own essential dynamics, is an ontological, spiritual revolution, pointing beyond the idolatries of sexist society and sparking creative action in and toward transcendence. The becoming of women implies universal human becoming. It has everything to do with the search for ultimate meaning and reality, which some would call God. . . .

> As the women's movement begins to have its effect upon the fabric of society, transforming it from patriarchy into something that never existed before—into a diarchal situation that is radically new—it can become the greatest single challenge to the major religions of the world, Western and Eastern. Beliefs and values that have held sway for thousands of years will be questioned as never before. This revolution may well be also the greatest single hope for survival of spiritual consciousness on this planet. . . .

> What I am proposing is that the emergence of the communal voca-tional self-awareness of women is a *creative political ontophany*.[18]

These quotations express Daly's view that the present situation is a time for something new, a creative moment in history, a time for the development and fulfillment of spiritual consciousness, a time in which the ultimate, the sacred, is becoming manifest. Decision is demanded of all to become a part of the process or not. Moreover, Daly speaks of women as bearers of New Being. Her experience is an *involved* experience. The time is for her, in short, a *kairos*.

In *Gyn/Ecology* Daly continues to express the idea that the time is one of decision and that new spiritual meaning is being experienced. Women are

---

[17]ST 3:270.
[18]Daly, *Beyond God the Father*, 6, 14, and 34.

beginning to break through the patriarchal ideas and structures. "Within a culture possessed by the myth of feminine evil, the naming, describing, and theorizing about good and evil has constituted a maze/haze of deception. The journey of women becoming is breaking through this maze—springing into free space, which is an a-mazing process. Breaking through the Male Maze is both exorcism and ecstasy."[19] Consider also her description of Gyn/Ecology itself: "This is an extremist book, written in a situation of extremity, written on the edge of a culture that is killing itself and all of sentient life."[20] The present situation is a kairos.

But Daly rejects the male symbol of Christ as New Being and therefore would reject the idea of the manifestation of New Being in Christ as the central kairos, as the source and criterion of all other kairoi. Tillich argued that kairoi can be demonically distorted and also erroneous.[21] Because the kairos is a historical moment, it stands under historical destiny. "No situation envisaged as the result of a kairos ever came into being. But something happened to some people through the power of the Kingdom of God as it became manifest in history, and history has been changed ever since."[22] The implication is that all kairoi outside the central kairos are relative. The danger is in making a relative kairos an absolute, an idol. For Tillich, the Cross of the Christ is the absolute criterion of all kairoi. In a later section I shall discuss more fully what the Cross of Christ as criterion means. At this point, I would argue that sometimes Daly makes the present situation of feminists into an absolute norm.

The Development of a Theological Norm. For Tillich, a norm is a universal guiding principle made concrete for a particular situation.[23] It guides further creative activity with respect to the particular situation. The norm for a theological work is created by critically considering past norms

---

[19]Daly, Gyn/Ecology, 2.

[20]Ibid., 17. In The Church and the Second Sex, 1968, Daly had called for reform in the church with respect to women, but she had not yet seen the process of women becoming as a breaking-in of new spiritual meaning. In 1968, the time was not yet a kairos for her.

[21]ST 3:371.

[22]Ibid.

[23]See Paul Tillich, "Das System der Wissenschaften nach Gegenständen und Methoden," Gesammelte Werke 1 (Stuttgart: Evangelisches Verlagswerk, 1959) 220.

and present norms as well as the specific situation. Tillich followed this process in his *Systematic Theology* when he critically considered several past Catholic and Protestant norms in relation to the present human situation of despair and meaninglessness. His norm for the *Systematic Theology* is the New Being, which is manifest in Jesus as the Christ as ultimate concern.[24]

Daly too followed this process in developing her theology in *Beyond God the Father*. She critically considered past and present theologies in relation to the present situation of women. For example, she considered and rejected the popular patriarchal view of God, the patriarchal interpretation of the Fall, and the male symbol of the Christ. Her rejection is a rejection of anything even compatible with patriarchal structures or values. Her offering for now and for the future is a set of meanings and values which she sees as leading to an androgynous mode of living, to fulfillment of women as women, and thereby to a higher spiritual, social, and psychological stage for all persons. Her norm of thought, I would argue, is that the experience of women-becoming manifests ultimate meaning and reality and New Being. Instead of Tillich's norm of ultimate meaning and reality being manifest in Jesus as the Christ, Daly sees ultimate meaning and reality manifest in the feminist experience of becoming. The critical significance of that difference will be discussed later in this essay.

We have seen, then, that Daly's method and approach has been influenced by Tillich's theological method. The major difference between their approaches is Daly's tendency to absolutize the feminist experience of becoming in her move beyond patriarchal religion. With this discussion of method as background, we can move to an analysis of Daly's use of specific ideas from Tillich's theology, namely the power of being, courage and New Being.

Analysis of Daly's Use of Tillich's Theological Concepts

The Idea of God as the Power of Being. Both Daly and Tillich go beyond the "inadequate god of popular preaching" in their thought. For Tillich the move from the God of theism to the "God above the God of theism" is a necessary move in the experience of facing radical doubt about God.[25] For Daly, the move from the idea of the "Supreme Being" to a new

---

[24]ST 1:49-50.
[25]Paul Tillich, *The Courage to Be* (New Haven: Yale University Press, 1952)

understanding of God is a necessary move in the feminist experience of alienation from the God who is supreme patriarch.[26]

Tillich contended that theological theism that presents arguments for the "existence" of God and develops a doctrine of God as a reality independent of human beings must be transcended because it is bad theology. Tillich argued that not only do the theologians make God into an object (as a being) but that God as a subject makes the person into a mere object.[27]

> He deprives me of my subjectivity because he is all-powerful and all-knowing. I revolt and try to make him into an object, but the revolt fails and becomes desperate. God appears as the invincible tyrant, the being in contrast with whom all other beings are without freedom and subjectivity. He is equated with the recent tyrants who with the help of terror try to transform everything into a mere object, a thing among things, a cog in the machine they control.[28]

Daly's discussion of the feminist rejection of the patriarchal Supreme Being is strikingly similar to Tillich's discussion of why the above theological theism is bad theology. "The widespread conception of the 'Supreme Being' as an entity distinct from this world but controlling it according to plan and keeping human beings in a state of infantile subjection has been a not-too-subtle mask of the divine patriarch."[29] Daly argues that the women's movement may be the most likely effort to overthrow the oppressive elements in such theism, not because the women's movement attacks the patriarchal God but because it leaves "him" behind. Thus, Daly, like Tillich, rejects the popular conception of God as a Supreme Being who reduces his subjects to mere powerless objects.

Again following Tillich, Daly moves beyond the idea of a patriarchal Supreme Being to the idea of God as the power of being.[30] For Daly, God

---

182-90. "The content of absolute faith is the 'God above God.' Absolute faith and its consequence, the courage that takes the radical doubt, the doubt about God, into itself, transcends the theistic idea of God" (182).

[26]Daly, *Beyond God the Father*, 16-22.

[27]Tillich, *The Courage to Be*, 184-85.

[28]Ibid., 185.

[29]Daly, *Beyond God the Father*, 18.

[30]In *Gyn/Ecology* Daly moves beyond *Beyond God the Father* and consequently moves further away from Tillich's conceptions in her thinking. In *Gyn/Ecology*

as the power of being is the root of the experience of transcendence, courage, and hope which all can have. Although open to all, this experience of transcendence and hope comes particularly in women's experience of facing alienation from the androcentric world.[31] For Tillich, God as the power of being is the source of the courage to be, which is operable for all who are able to take their anxiety upon themselves. There is similarity in the two discussions of the "power of being," but Daly asserts that Tillich's discussion is inadequate because "the specific relevance of 'power of being' to the fact of sexual oppression is not indicated."[32]

God as the power of being offers a view of God as dynamic and active rather than as a static entity. For Tillich, the dynamic character of God as the power of being is expressed in the idea of being eternally overcoming nonbeing.[33] Daly argues that God should be understood as a dynamic Verb rather than a static noun.[34] Again for Daly, particularly women perceive this dynamism in their experience of self-affirmation, which is rooted in participation in the power of being over against nonbeing.[35]

Tillich's treatment of God as the power of being is more universal than Daly's use of that idea. While it may be true that the idea of power of being is significant for women's struggle for liberation, Daly must be careful not to limit the experience of the power of being to women's experience alone. But for both thinkers, God as the power of being is understood in relation to courage and the process of being overcoming nonbeing.

Courage as Revelatory in the Confrontation with Nonbeing. Courage, for Tillich and Daly, is existential courage—courage that enables persons to face the threats of nonbeing (Tillich), "to confront the experience of nothingness."[36] Tillich discussed courage in relation to the existential anxiety that stems from the threats of nonbeing in the forms of fate and

---

she no longer uses the word God, but she continues to use "be-ing." In place of God she speaks of Goddess who "affirms the life-loving be-ing of women and nature" (xi). She also speaks of a sense of power, not of the "wholly other," but of the "Self's be-ing" (49).

[31]Daly, *Beyond God the Father*, 28, 32.

[32]Ibid., 20-21.

[33]Tillich, *The Courage to Be*, 34, 180-81; see also ST 1:272.

[34]Daly, *Beyond God the Father*, 33.

[35]Ibid., 34, 43.

[36]Ibid., 23.

death, emptiness, and meaninglessness, and guilt and condemnation. To affirm oneself in spite of the fact of nonbeing is an act of courage.[37]

Tillich argued that because courage is grounded in the power of being-itself, it has a religious basis, whether recognized by all persons or not.[38] Courage is revelatory because it shows the nature of being and can make the person aware of the power of being.[39] Not all persons will be conscious of the source of their courage, but they can still accept the power of being and participate in it. Their very acts of courage are possible, because of their participation in the power of being, and therefore they show the power of being.

Daly basically uses Tillich's understanding of courage but does not find his treatment totally adequate for her purposes because he does not show any awareness of how his analysis might be relevant to women's struggle with patriarchal structures of evil.[40] In Daly's view, "at this point in history women are in a unique sense called to be the bearers of existential courage in society."[41] Women are experiencing and showing existential courage in their attempts to liberate themselves from the patriarchal structures of the world, in their facing alienation from the present world because of its open or implied subordination of women, and in their efforts to develop new religious meanings that are free from sexism.[42] Women today confront the threats of nonbeing in such things as loss of jobs or friends (fate), guilt over not following what society has demanded for the woman's role, and loss of traditional religious and social meanings because the forms of those meanings seem to exclude women.[43]

---

[37]Tillich, *The Courage to Be*, 155.

[38]Ibid., 156, 181.

[39]Ibid., 178-81.

[40]Daly, *Beyond God the Father*, 23. In *Gyn/Ecology* Daly attacks Tillich's understanding of courage and self-acceptance because it does not portray courage "in the full sense of accepting responsibility for one's process" (377). Daly believes Tillich left persons with the sense that they are unacceptable and guilty, but ultimately forgiven by a loving God. For Daly in *Gyn/Ecology*, the courage of self-acceptance means "recognizing the Divine Spark in the Self and other Selves and *accepting* this Spark" (377). It means refusing self-sacrifice.

[41]Daly, *Beyond God the Father*, 23; see also *Gyn/Ecology*, 21.

[42]Daly, *Beyond God the Father*, 23-24.

[43]Ibid., 24.

Daly contends that women's experience of courage in confronting these threats of nonbeing is revelatory. The experience makes women aware that the structures are finite—human products rather than absolute structures—and it pushes women's consciousness beyond despair with the present finite world to a transcendent hope for the future.[44] Women's courage and hope not only show their self-affirmation for the present moment but also reveal the power of being; indeed, their courage and hope are rooted in it.[45]

Thus, for both Tillich and Daly, existential courage involves self-affirmation in the face of threats of nonbeing and is rooted in the power of being. Because of that grounding in the power of being, courage can reveal the power of being. Daly focuses on the feminist experience of courage while Tillich discusses what he sees as universal human experience.

The Fall and Original Sin. Tillich's influence on Daly's thinking is more apparent in her discussions of the power of being and courage than in her discussion of the Fall and original sin, but a brief comparison of their viewpoints on this topic is necessary before discussing their understandings of the New Being.

Tillich partially demythologizes the story of the Fall by discussing the "transition from essence to existence."[46] As a result of this transition, every existing being is separated and alienated from the ground of its being, other beings, and its own essential being.[47] Daly rejects Tillich's understanding of the Fall as existential estrangement because it does not deal with the man-woman relationship in the story and because it is compatible with the traditional images of the Fall that have supported sexist structures in society.[48] Daly claims that because there is a destructive image of women in

---

[44]Ibid., 24-27.

[45]For Daly, it is the feminist experience that points to God as dynamic, as Verb, as Be-ing. "The anthropomorphic symbols for God may be intended to convey personality, but they fail to convey that God is Be-ing. Women now who are experiencing the shock of nonbeing and the surge of self-affirmation against this are inclined to perceive transcendence as the Verb in which we participate—live, move, and have our being (*Beyond God the Father*, 33-34). In *Gyn/Ecology* Daly speaks of the feminist process of becoming and journeying as "be-ing in the Triple Goddess, who is, and is not yet" (14).

[46]ST 2:29.

[47]ST 2:44.

[48]Daly, *Beyond God the Father*, 44-45. Earlier in *The Church and the Second Sex* Daly used Tillich to bolster her argument against literal belief in the

the biblical story of the Fall, ignoring the male-female element and sexist aspects of the story implies that sexism is neither an important aspect of the story nor a problem in our society.[49]

Daly's interpretation of the Fall is that the biblical story expresses the nature of original sin as the "projection of guilt upon women" by men.[50] The original sin of women has been the internalization of guilt and self-hatred, a sin that has been passed on through socialization.[51] Yet the Fall can have a positive meaning for the future; in the feminist revolution a "fall" into the sacred and into freedom for all is occurring.[52] Women are coming to a new nonpatriarchal knowledge of human beings, and as they share it with men, they can move to a better society, free from the alienation of patriarchy.

Although Daly states that she has rejected Tillich's understanding of the Fall, both reject a literalist reading of the biblical story of the Fall, and both see the Fall as resulting in a situation of estrangement or alienation.[53] Tillich talks of estrangement from one's essential self, from one's true being—while Daly speaks of women's internalization of guilt, which certainly involves estrangement of the woman from her true self and the woman from the man. Daly's view of original sin can be seen as a particular example of Tillich's discussion of existential estrangement and its effects. Yet her vision of a "fall" into the sacred that will bring about a better society, free from patriarchy, abandons the estrangement and ambiguity Tillich accepts as part of human life.

The Idea of Christ as the New Being. For Tillich, the New Being is the answer to the predicament of existential estrangement; it has the power to reunite what has been estranged. Every person can participate in the New Being, and this participation means that one experiences the power of the

---

story of the Fall (185).

[49]Daly, *Beyond God the Father*, 45.

[50]Ibid., 47.

[51]Ibid., 48-49.

[52]Ibid., 67. See also her "New Feminist Post-Christian Introduction" to the second edition of *The Church and the Second Sex*, 39.

[53]Judith Plaskow offers a more in-depth critique of Tillich's doctrine of sin and grace than does Mary Daly. See Plaskow, *Sex, Sin, and Grace: Women's Experience and the Theologies of Reinhold Niebuhr and Paul Tillich* (Lanham MD: University Press of America, 1980) esp. 109-20, 135-75.

New Being which has overcome estrangement not only for the New Being itself but for all who participate in the New Being. This participation in the New Being does not mean a total conquering of estrangement; salvation is fragmentary and incomplete.[54]

Tillich sees Jesus as the Christ as the bearer of the New Being, but he also believes that the power of the New Being can be present apart from Jesus of Nazareth.[55] There can be healing and saving power throughout history, but Jesus as the Christ is the "ultimate criterion of every healing and saving process."[56] Experiences of the saving power of the New Being throughout all human history must be judged by the power of the New Being in Jesus as the Christ because in him that power is complete and unlimited. There may be other manifestations of New Being, but they will not supersede the New Being in Jesus as the Christ.

Daly follows Tillich's understanding of the New Being as a healing power which overcomes alienation and self-estrangement, a healing power which brings a new meeting with the sacred. She agrees with Tillich that people are seeking New Being, and she uses his idea that there may be other manifestations of New Being than Jesus as the Christ. But she does not think Tillich's analysis of Jesus as the Christ as the New Being takes adequate account of the oppression that has stemmed from the male symbol of the Christ.[57] A male symbol for the New Being implicitly and inevitably reinforces existing sexist structures. Daly argues that the bearers of New Being are "the primordial aliens: women."[58] Because Daly sees original sin as the male projection of guilt upon women and the female internalization of that guilt, she affirms that in the situation of patriarchy a male symbol of New Being *cannot* liberate the human race from those sins. A male symbol "is one-sided, as far as sexual identity is concerned, and it is precisely on the wrong side, since it fails to counter sexism and functions to glorify

---

[54]ST 2:167-68.
[55]ST 2:101, 121, 166-68.
[56]ST 2:168.
[57]Daly, *Beyond God the Father*, 72.
[58]Ibid.

maleness."[59] Daly does not deal with the fact that a female embodiment of New Being is also one-sided.

In suggesting that women are the bearers of New Being, Daly is not choosing one person as the bearer of New Being. Rather New Being is present in the process of women becoming more whole persons by transcending sexist structures.[60] The manifestation of New Being is communal rather than centered in one person or symbol.[61] Daly does not say that women are Christs but rather that this process of women becoming is the Antichrist, a spiritual awakening bringing people "beyond Christolatry into a fuller stage of conscious participation in the *living* God."[62] This "arrival" of women can free Jesus from his role as scapegoat and savior.[63]

It may seem as though Daly's discussion has come a long way from Tillich's conception of the New Being as present in Jesus as the Christ. But Daly is following Tillich on the function of New Being as a healing power, the idea of New Being as possibly manifest outside of Jesus of Nazareth and the idea of ordinary persons as participating in the power of the New Being. Yet because of her rejection of anything that may be implicitly patriarchal, Daly also rejects the idea of Christ as criterion for other manifestations of New Being. It is the use of Christ as criterion which provides the most damaging critique of Daly's theology.

---

[59]Ibid. In "A Short Essay on Hearing and on the Qualitative Leap of Radical Feminism," *Horizons* 2 (Spring 1975): 121, Daly says, "Since the Christ symbol is a uniquely male symbol for divinity, it is oppressive. It says: 'For men only.' " It is important to remember that Daly sees her writings past 1973 as post-Christian. Earlier, in *The Church and the Second Sex*, Daly had argued that emphasis on the maleness of Christ was a distorted understanding of the meaning of Christ (199). But in her "New Feminist Post-Christian Introduction" in the second edition of that book, she says that that earlier view was Daly's misunderstanding. "She was trying to transcend the untranscendable, that is the message of male supremacy contained in the symbolic medium itself" (43).

[60]In *Gyn/Ecology* Daly speaks of women discovering their own new be-ing in their journey of becoming (14). The term "new being" is no longer capitalized, thereby seemingly separating it more clearly from Tillich and any implicit connections with the male Christ.

[61]Daly, *Beyond God the Father*, 72, 139, 152.

[62]Ibid., 96.

[63]Ibid.

A Critique of Daly
Using the Protestant Principle and the Absolute Paradox
Expressed in the Symbol of the Cross of Christ

In this section Tillich's ideas of the "Protestant Principle" and the absolute paradox expressed in the symbol of the Cross of Christ will be used to more fully develop a critique of Daly's theology in *Beyond God the Father*. Here the main question will be to what extent Daly makes the feminist experience of women-becoming into an absolute or an idol.

Through his use of the Protestant Principle, Tillich pushes the idea that there can be no visible realization of the holy in the context of existence; all existence is ambiguous over against the ultimate.[64] All human knowledge and truth are conditioned and ambiguous over against the Unconditioned, as are all human movements and institutions. In "The Two Types of Philosophy of Religion" Tillich said: "It is the danger of every embodiment of the unconditional element, religious and secular, that it elevates something conditioned, a symbol, an institution, a movement as such to ultimacy."[65] Daly has recognized this danger but not always surmounted it.

Since the ultimate is always expressed through existence, that which expresses the ultimate should not be made into an absolute. In *Dynamics of Faith* Tillich expresses the criterion this way: "The criterion of the truth of faith, therefore, is that it implies an element of self-negation. That symbol is most adequate which expresses not only the ultimate but also its own lack of ultimacy."[66] A theological statement or norm should not make itself or a finite movement or institution into an absolute. A statement or reality that really expresses or manifests the ultimate will also deny its own ultimacy. As we have seen earlier (in chapters 1, 4, and 5), for Tillich, the symbol that satisfies the above criterion and that serves as the criterion for all other religious symbols is the Cross of the Christ. The form of the symbol of the

---

[64]Tillich, "Kairos und Logos," 75.

[65]Paul Tillich, "The Two Types of Philosophy of Religion," *Union Seminary Quarterly Review* 1 (May 1946): 29.

[66]Paul Tillich, *Dynamics of Faith* (New York: Harper & Row, 1957) 97. In his *Systematic Theology* Tillich says that "a revelation is final if it has the power of negating itself without losing itself" (1:133).

Cross is the "absolute paradox," which is the unity of the Unconditioned and the conditioned.[67]

Daly is aware of the problem of idolatry[68] and argues that the meaning of the question of God should be in acting openly toward the future that is really ultimate. The awareness of participation in ultimate reality as the source of all authentic power enables one "to be free of idolatry even in regard to one's own cause, since it tells us that all presently envisaged goals, lifestyles, symbols, and societal structures may be transitory."[69] Daly does not want present feminist concern to be idolatrous about limited objectives but to have a vision of the future that is open to the ultimate (and a vision of the ultimate that is open to the future).

But Daly's awareness of the problem of idolatry does not mean that she avoids it in developing her theology. Does Daly's claim of ultimate meaning and reality manifest in the feminist experience of becoming follow the Protestant Principle? Does it show the form of the absolute paradox? Or does she make the feminist experience itself into an absolute? I shall show that at times she attempts to keep the ultimate as ultimate over against the finite; however, at other times she identifies the feminist experience with the ultimate.

In Daly's discussion of the power of being, which gives power, courage, and hope to women in their struggle against patriarchal structures, she does not equate the experience itself with the ultimate. For example, she says that "the unfolding of the woman-consciousness is an *intimation* of the

---

[67]The absolute paradox is discussed by Paul Tillich in an unpublished typescript, 1919, entitled "Rechtfertigung und Zweifel." This "Rechtfertigung und Zweifel" of 1919 is quite different from the 1924 essay of the same title that is published in the *Gesammelte Werke* 8 (Stuttgart: Evangelisches Verlagswerk, 1970). Also, see Tillich's discussion of paradox and Christ in ST 2:90-92.

[68]In Daly's earlier writings, she discusses the Protestant Principle and the problem of idolatry. For example, in 1970, discussing the question of what one change in the church she would make, Daly said: "The evil to be eradicated is idolatry. I take idolatry to mean treating a finite reality as if it were ultimate. In this case one fixes one's ultimate concern upon something limited in itself" (Mary Daly, "If You Could Make One Change in the Church, What Would It Be?" *Commonweal* 92 [1 May 1970]: 161). See also "Return of the Protestant Principle," *Commonweal* 90 (6 June 1969): 338-41, in which she calls for using the Protestant Principle as "an attitude of protest against all false securities" (338).

[69]Daly, *Beyond God the Father*, 29.

endless unfolding of God."[70] The term "intimation" protects against an idolatrous statement. The idea that religious meaning and value are present in the feminist experience does not make an idol of feminist experience.

But even though Daly does not directly state that the feminist experience of becoming is the ultimate, she does make an absolute of it by often forgetting the ambiguity within the experience. In her discussion of original sin and the Fall, Daly talks about a "fall" into the sacred and sees women's new nonpatriarchal knowledge of human beings as that "fall." As women share that with men, they can move to a better society; women are the bearers of New Being. Women's experience of self-affirmation and pride not only frees themselves but also men, and even the memory of Jesus. In other passages dealing with topics which we have not discussed in the first part of the essay, Daly pushes more and more for the idea that the feminist experience of becoming will be the salvation for women and eventually the world. For example, Daly speaks of sisterhood as cosmic covenant and Antichurch.[71] The cause of the women's revolution is seen as "the final cause: the cause of causes."[72]

> In this sense, our cause can function as "the final cause," that is, by incarnating the desire to break out of the circle and communicating that desire, awakening women and consequently men to become ourselves. The final cause is the beginning, not the end, of becoming. It is the first cause, giving the motivation to act. The feminist movement is potentially the source of real movement in the other revolutionary movements (such as Black Liberation and the Peace Movement), for it is the catalyst that enables women and men to break out of the prison of self destructive dichotomies perpetuated by the institutional fathers. Radical feminism can accomplish this breakthrough precisely because it gives rise to an intuition of androgynous existence.[73]

---

[70]Ibid., 36; italics mine.

[71]"Sisterhood implies the recognition that the bonding of women is the only hope for universal human becoming. It involves a steadfast refusal to sell ourselves short in the name of a delusory instant 'human liberation' " (Daly, "A Short Essay on Hearing and on the Qualitative Leap of Radical Feminism," 123).

[72]Daly, *Beyond God the Father*, 179ff.

[73]Ibid., 190.

The ambiguity of the women's movement seems to be ignored or forgotten. The becoming of women is seen as changing attitudes about the environment, war, and other movements against oppression. Daly does see the source of power as Be-ing, but still women are the bearers of that Be-ing on earth, in a way that other human beings are not and cannot be.

Daly's affirmation of the feminist movement is even stronger and more idolatrous in *Gyn/Ecology*. The feminist movement is now described as metapatriarchal movement in which women can *dis-cover* Life and participate in Paradise.[74]

> We use the visitation of demons to come more deeply into touch with our own powers/virtues. Unweaving their deceptions, we name our Truth. Defying their professions we dis-cover our Female Pride, our Sinister Wisdom. Escaping their possession we find our Enspiriting Selves. . . . Refusing their assimilation we experience our Autonomy and Strength. Avoiding their elimination we find our Original Be-ing. Mending their imposed fragmentation we Spin our Original Integrity.[75]

Nevertheless, Daly tempers that adulation of feminist journeying when she speaks of "be-ing" in the Triple Goddess, who is, and is not yet."[76] That phrasing can suggest ultimacy and transcendence beyond the finite woman's process of becoming. Daly also speaks of the divine Spark in the feminist Self, but it is the woman who acknowledges the Spark and accepts it as her own. The woman knows that *only she* can judge her Self.[77]

To affirm any finite movement as so good, so true, so revelatory, and so ultimate is to come close to idolizing it.[78] The Protestant Principle needs to be followed more carefully by Daly. By not following through on it, her

---

[74]Daly, *Gyn/Ecology*, 6-7.
[75]Ibid., 423.
[76]Ibid., 14.
[77]Ibid., 378; italics mine.
[78]In a book review of *Beyond God the Father*, Ruether criticizes Daly's moral naiveté about women, particularly Daly's implication that woman is responsible for evil only insofar as she has cooperated with male evil (Rosemary Radford Ruether, *Journal of Religious Thought* 30/2 [1973]: 73).

arguments and analysis are hurt. Good ideas lose significance because the claims for her feminist philosophy are so extreme.

Daly's analysis is also inadequate because she often limits the manifestation of the ultimate to feminist experience. For example, she says that "at this point in history women are in a *unique* sense called to be the bearers of existential courage in society."[79] At this time, can only women be the bearers of this courage? Daly says that men too are invited to confront the nothingness that women confront,[80] but that nothingness is identified with patriarchal structures. Are nothingness or nonbeing present apart from or outside of patriarchal structures? The experience of the new participation in the power of being becomes available for men when women move to the boundary of patriarchal institutions and structures.[81] We now have a reversal of the view that women's experience of God or relation to the image of God is dependent on men's.[82] A male symbol cannot liberate the human race from the patriarchal sins; only women can have that role. Women's experience has become normative and absolute. This view is expressed even more strongly in *Gyn/Ecology*. There Daly makes it clear that she is speaking gynomorphically rather than anthropomorphically.[83] She does not want to settle for the simple label of "antimale" but emphasizes that her book is "Furiously and Finally Female."[84] The Journey of Women becoming and affirming Selves no longer involves androgyny, and it is not seen as an invitation to men but rather to women's Selves.[85]

With respect to the absolute paradox, it might be argued that the women's movement expresses it to some extent because the women involved in it are negating their "old nonbeing" in becoming new beings. The new self is found in negation of the old self. But that is still different

---

[79]Daly, *Beyond God the Father*, 23; italics mine.

[80]Ibid., 42.

[81]Ibid., 40-42.

[82]It is interesting to note that earlier Daly saw the women's movement as more open to men (e.g. "Church and Women: An Interview with Mary Daly," 351). Elisabeth Schüssler Fiorenza argues that Daly does not want to absolutize women but that her attempt to overcome the sex stereotyping of patriarchy ends up involving scapegoating and castrating the "other," i.e., placing women over men (*Horizons* 2 [Spring 1975]: 117-18).

[83]Daly, *Gyn/Ecology*, xi-xii.

[84]Ibid., 29.

[85]Ibid, xii.

from the negation of the New (that is, for Jesus, the New is the Christ) still holding the new as truth. To say that Jesus is not the Christ is to affirm in some sense that he is the Christ. To deny that women are new beings does not affirm their new being.

Daly has raised an important issue for contemporary theology in describing past and present sexism and showing the need to move beyond the patriarchal viewpoint. Contemporary theology needs to consider the following questions. Is theology that assumes or pushes for patriarchal understandings of God, Jesus, sin, and so forth, and for male dominance adequate for the present American cultural situation? Should God be symbolized with mostly male symbols? Should the maleness of Jesus as the Christ be emphasized? As women and men become more aware of the symbolic and real cultural effects of language on our living, and as our common language begins to incorporate more nonsexist words, theology also needs to be communicated in nonsexist language. But has Daly really provided a nonsexist theology? No, she has developed a feminist theology that has token statements for men but is primarily for women only. She seems to have reversed patriarchalism and substituted a matriarchalism.[86]

When Daly says that women's experience of becoming manifests ultimate meaning and reality, she needs to acknowledge that it does not do this totally or in all aspects of the experience. Much more recognition of the ambiguity in the women's movement, more stringent application of the Protestant Principle and more awareness of paradox in expression of the ultimate is needed in Daly's theology. Daly should not just affirm radical feminism as revelatory but should also show how it is an inadequate expression of the ultimate and of New Being. If affirmation and negation of the presence of ultimacy is not found in a movement or appraisal of a movement, then the finite movement is made into an idol.

Daly's application of Tillich's ideas for the present women's movement is helpful for providing a theoretical base for understanding radical feminism. A major problem is that she does not use the universal application of those ideas for all human beings. Daly often criticizes Tillich for being too universal

---

[86]It is interesting to observe that in earlier writings Daly rejected the idea of making a matriarchal society in place of the present patriarchal society. See "Church and Women: An Interview with Mary Daly," 349. But in Gyn/Ecology Daly is interested in renewing connections with the goddesses of the past, many of whom were viewed as mother-goddesses. For example, see Gyn/Ecology, 111.

and for not applying his ideas to the problem of sexism. In turn, she is criticized for narrowing the application and significance of the ideas to one movement and ignoring their universal significance. That women were often left out of or were subordinated by traditional theologies of the past does not make it right or true to do the same to men today. Daly needs to incorporate the Protestant Principle, the fact of ambiguity, and the paradoxical expression of the ultimate.

Suggestions for Future Nonsexist Theology

It is not mere chance that Daly and some other women theologians have been influenced by Tillich's theology.[87] Tillich's ontological theology is not overtly patriarchal. His discussions of power of being, New Being, being-itself, and Spirit for the most part avoid sexist connotations. Moreover, his theological method provides for responding to the present situation and not just resting on the traditional terms of our theological past. In conclusion, I shall briefly outline how several of Tillich's ideas can be useful for future nonsexist theology.

With respect to method, we can use Tillich's ideas of the *kairos* and correlation as a basis for responding to the present feminist situation. This understanding of theological method means that we do not rest with past theologies, including Tillich's, as adequate for all time, but rather that we continue to analyze the present situation and *develop* past ideas, thereby creating new ideas for the present. For some, the present feminist situation is a *kairos*, demanding creative decision and response. Theological ideas need to be correlated with our analysis of the present situation. If we do see the present historical moment as a *kairos*, then we must remember that our response should be to the Unconditioned which breaks into the moment and not just to the political, psychological, and cultural needs of the present.

This leads to a second set of Tillich's ideas important for developing nonsexist theology. The Protestant Principle should continue to remind all religious thinkers of the finitude and ambiguity of their present situation, their present concerns and causes, and their theological ideas. Feminists must be careful not to see human works or a human movement as saving

---

[87]Joan Arnold Romero points this out in "The Protestant Principle: A Woman's Eye View of Barth and Tillich," *Religion and Sexism: Images of Woman in the Jewish and Christian Traditions*, ed. Rosemary Radford Ruether (New York: Simon and Schuster, 1974) 336.

in themselves. To see women as more holy or more ethical or more good than men is not only to reverse the sexism of the past but also to forget the faults, ambiguity, and finitude that are our common existential situation. I am *not* arguing that we should ignore the feminist problems, situation, or movement, but rather that in responding to that we should not make them absolute or idolatrous. Similarly, the idea of the absolute paradox is a reminder that the manifestation of the ultimate in our world includes affirmation and negation of its presence.

Third, we need to work to overcome our patriarchal past in theology by developing a theology that is equally open to women and men and that allows for an androgynous understanding of all persons. The specific ideas can arise from the present situation of feminists, or some past theological ideas can be applied to the feminist situation, but the ideas should be open to all. For example, Tillich's ideas of God as ground and power of being or being-itself, Christ as New Being, finite being, existential being and alienation, and life as ambiguous are theological ideas that are applicable to the feminist situation and that can help free theology from its negative patriarchal connotations and implications.

Tillich himself was aware that some of his theological terms reduce the male element in traditional Christian symbols. In his discussion of the Trinity, he pointed to the "power of being" as decreasing the male element and to the "ground of being" as expressing female elements, specifically "the mother-quality of giving birth, carrying, and embracing, and, at the same time, of calling back, resisting independence of the created, and swallowing it."[88] He argued that the essential meanings of the second and third persons of the Trinity transcend the alternative of male or female. In Jesus as the Christ, the symbol of self-sacrifice does not belong exclusively to either male or female. The Spiritual Presence involves ecstasy that transcends both male and female symbolism of the Holy Spirit.[89]

In the midst of the feminist situation, we need to develop nonsexist theology that seeks neither male dominance nor female dominance. Our future is best helped by critically developing ideas from the past (without totally rejecting all the past) and creating new ideas in a way that they are meaningful for the present and open to the future. If we are too caught up in the present, we can lose some of the good of the past and be unprepared

---

[88]ST 3:294.
[89]Ibid.

for future changes. Worst of all, we can make the present the norm for all time, an absolute, which has lost the ongoing critique of the ultimate.

Tillich's influence on Daly's *Beyond God the Father* is extensive, although at times we wish it had been even greater. In *Gyn/Ecology*, Daly needed to remember even more Tillich's ideas of the Protestant Principle, ambiguity, and paradox. It is my hope that Tillich's influence on feminist theology will continue and that his greatest impact on it will be his understanding of the Protestant Principle, the ongoing critique of finite ideas and movements by the ultimate.

B. Rejection

This section B extends Tillich's critique of idolatry to show its ethical significance for developing a criterion against injustice. The theme of idolatry provides a critical perspective for considering religious approaches to sexual roles. Specifically, the critique is then applied to two examples: (1) the Roman Catholic position barring women from the priesthood and (2) Mary Daly's radical feminist positions in *Gyn/Ecology* and *Pure Lust*.

Early feminist work in Religious Studies on the social roles of men and women often focused on the inequality and injustice suffered by women for much of Western history.[90] Later studies concentrated on bringing forth the stories of women from our past and searching for positive alternatives to sexist theologies, ethics, and social roles.[91] My discussion in this section combines these two efforts by suggesting a criterion of religious and ethical truth that can be applied to past sexist traditions but can also be a norm for future development of religious symbols and ethics.

---

[90]Examples include Daly, *The Church and the Second Sex*; Ruether, ed., *Religion and Sexism*; Julia O'Faolain and Lauro Martines, eds., *Not in God's Image* (New York: Harper & Row, 1973); and Vern Bullough, *The Subordinate Sex* (New York: Penguin, 1974).

[91]Examples include Patricia Wilson-Kastner, *Faith, Feminism, and the Christ* (Philadelphia: Fortress Press, 1983); Elisabeth Moltmann-Wendel, *The Women around Jesus* (New York: Crossroad, 1982); Elisabeth Schüssler Fiorenza, *In Memory of Her* (New York: Crossroad, 1983).

Paul Tillich's Paradoxical Criterion against Idolatry

Tillich defines idolatry as "the elevation of a preliminary concern to ultimacy. Something essentially conditioned is taken as unconditional, something essentially partial is boosted into universality, and something essentially finite is given infinite significance."[92] Idolatry involves understanding something finite *as* ultimate and treating it as absolute in itself. Tillich often uses the example of nationalism, where the nation is taken as absolute in itself. Here, we shall focus on treating gender as an ultimate and absolute quality rather than as a finite characteristic.

The problem of idolatry is tied to the nature of revelation and the nature of religious language. Revelation is the manifestation of something ultimate and transcendent in and through finite experience. That ultimacy which is beyond finite being is experienced and known in the context of the human world, with finite, conditioned realities as the bearers of infinite reality. Tillich argues that any reality can be a medium of revelation. This possibility does not result from a special quality inherent in such a reality but from the relationship of participation that all reality has with the source of reality which Tillich has called "being-itself" or the "ground of being."[93]

Because anything finite can become a vehicle of the ultimate, there is a paradoxical character to revelation itself. The finite entity which bears revelation is both finite and infinite. In describing the structure of sacred experience in diverse religious traditions, Mircea Eliade points to this paradox of the manifestation of the sacred. "By manifesting the sacred, any object becomes *something else*, yet it continues to remain *itself*, for it continues to participate in its surrounding cosmic milieu."[94] For example, the Bible conveys the Word of God to some people and yet is also a finite book like any other book. Or an image that is experienced as a sacred image is yet an ordinary, finite statue. Thus, the very structure of revelation ties together finite and infinite in a paradoxical relationship—that something is both infinite and yet finite.

---

[92]ST 1:137.
[93]ST 1:118.
[94]Mircea Eliade, *The Sacred and the Profane* (New York: Harcourt, Brace, and World, 1959) 12.

In idolatry the ongoing finitude of the revelatory object is ignored, and the finite, conditioned object comes to be seen as ultimate and unconditioned in itself. The paradoxical relationship of revelation is broken. For example, the image is seen as *the sacred* or the Bible is worshiped as unconditioned in itself rather than as a vehicle of the Word of God. Or people may make something finite into an ultimate concern around which their lives revolve and for which they will sacrifice and even die. They may not recognize that they have attached ultimacy to something finite, such as nation, money, or ideology, but their lives attest to it.

So idolatry, like revelation, has a subjective and objective side. The objective side of revelation is the manifestation of the ultimate itself; the subjective side is the response of people to that manifestation. When a concern is experienced as ultimate, it demands the surrender of the person to it, and the person surrenders in the hope of fulfillment from it.[95] This can mean that other claims of ultimacy are often rejected in the name of one's ultimate concern; one's ultimate concern centers one's life and overshadows other concerns.[96] This structure holds true whether one's concern is true revelation or idolatry. One perceives ultimacy and responds to it with one's whole self in the hope of fulfillment. But as we shall see, idolatrous concerns can be destructive and dehumanizing rather than ultimately fulfilling.

On the objective side, if anything can be a bearer of ultimacy and revelation, then presumably either male or female beings could be vehicles of divine revelation. In the history of religions, including the history of Christianity, we can find both. But if one understands ultimacy as beyond maleness and femaleness and sees gender as a finite characteristic, then the maleness or femaleness of the revelatory vehicle is not absolute and unconditioned. When either maleness or femaleness *exclusively* is seen as an essential element of divine revelation, we have idolatry. The finite distinction between male and female becomes absolutized with focus on the gender of the bearer of divine revelation. In idolatry the paradox of finite and infinite in revelation is resolved in an idolatrous identification of the finite and infinite.

Religious language attempts to describe experiences of the ultimate and to express the ultimate in such a way that the listener or reader will be directed toward the ultimate. Religious language, then, can be a bearer of

---

[95]Tillich, *Dynamics of Faith*, 1.
[96]Ibid., 1-2.

divine revelation, and as such uses symbolic language that points beyond its character as finite, conditioned language to the ultimate itself which is beyond the direct form and content of the language. But, as with the structure of divine revelation, the paradox can be lost if people come to use the finite, conditioned symbols as absolute forms of expression. The language then loses its symbolic and pointing qualities, with the focus on the finite expression itself. Such a loss occurs for many people with the use of exclusive religious language, whether it is patriarchal or matriarchal.

Like the structure of divine revelation, the structure of religious language has both an objective and a subjective side.[97] The objective side, the "content," focuses on the ability of the language to point beyond itself to the ultimate. The subjective side, the "response," focuses on the ability of the language to make the ultimate understandable, to elicit response, and to be accepted by people as really expressing the ultimate, offering meaning and truth.

As the history of religions shows us, religious symbols change with varying historical and personal situations. This change can come when a person or a group of people no longer finds a particular language or set of symbols effective expressions of the ultimate. In fact, their critique may be a critique of idolatry. One could look at the changing language of the Protestant Reformation in this light. More recently, many people have questioned the ability of gender-specific language to express the ultimate. God as Father, God as He, Lord, King, etc. are male symbols which were at one time effective symbols of God but no longer are for many people because of their patriarchal origin. The finite, conditioned element no longer points beyond itself but has brought focus to itself. The ongoing use of that language and the insistence that only patriarchal language is acceptable are idolatrous responses, taking the finite male element as essential. The critique of such language should call us back to the paradoxical structure of revelation and religious language.

Tillich's critique of idolatry on the objective side focuses on the paradoxical character of the expression of ultimacy in theological symbols and

---

[97]For more on Tillich's theory of symbols as related to paradox, see my discussions in "Paul Tillich's Theory of Theological Norms and the Problems of Relativism and Subjectivism," *Journal of Religion* 62/4 (October 1982): 359-75, and in "The Significance of Paradox for Theological Verification: Difficulties and Possibilities," *International Journal for Philosophy of Religion* 14 (1983): 171-82.

statements. Tillich offers this criterion for avoiding idolatry in religious expression: "The criterion of the truth of faith, therefore, is that it implies an element of self-negation. That symbol is most adequate which expresses not only the ultimate but also its own lack of ultimacy."[98] In the paradoxical structure of revelation, the finite medium is negated as finite, becoming "transparent" to the ultimate, but also the finite conditioned medium is maintained in itself. Thus, the paradoxical structure of revelation is taken as normative for judging expressions of religious truth. For Tillich, the Cross of Christ fulfills the paradoxical criterion. Tillich is not just pointing to the paradoxical unity of divinity and humanity in the person Jesus. Tillich sees a deeper paradox in the Cross itself. For it is through his death and sacrifice on the Cross that Jesus is the Christ: Jesus *negates* himself as Jesus on the Cross; yet Jesus the resurrected Lord *is* the Christ because of the Cross. "Jesus could not have been the Christ without sacrificing himself as Jesus to himself as the Christ."[99] Tillich realizes that the people can weaken the paradox of the Cross by focusing on one side—the resurrected Lord, and he calls such a forgetting of the Cross "idolatry."

Idolatry is not just an issue of truth but also of ethics. The demonic distortion of the finite taken as absolute can cause disruption to persons' lives. In *Dynamics of Faith* Tillich suggests that idolatry can destroy the self in the object of idolatrous faith. In all forms of faith, the person centers his or her self in the object or concern which is seen as absolute and infinite. Ideally, the commitment of self in faith can bring a unified relationship between the person or subject and the object of faith. But in idolatrous faith the finite object cannot really transcend the split between subject and object. The finite concern remains a finite object which can be approached with ordinary knowledge and action.[100] Consequently, there is always the possibility that the subject will recognize the limitations of the object or concern, pull back from his/her allegiance and thereby lose the center, causing a disruption to the personality of the subject.[101]

Such a process can be seen in the feminist critique of patriarchal theology. Many people who had used patriarchal expressions as proper symbols of God became increasingly aware of the maleness of those

---

[98]Tillich, *Dynamics of Faith*, 97; also see ST 1:133.
[99]Tillich, *Dynamics of Faith*, 97-98.
[100]Ibid., 11.
[101]Ibid., 12.

symbols. Those patriarchal symbols could no longer effectively express the ultimate or center their lives. Feminist writings in religion show anger at the absolutizing of patriarchal images, anguish at the loss of traditional understandings, now seen as conditioned and finite, and longing for new expressions of faith to center their lives. In Tillich's terms, the traditional faith had idolatrous elements, which had come to be recognized as no longer worthy of allegiance. This disruption has sometimes led to rejection of all forms of faith, the loss of one's central concern and a slow but painful search for a replacement that is truly ultimate.

On a broader scale, Tillich suggests that existential disappointments that stem from idolatry can lead to "individual and social diseases and catastrophes" such as cynicism, widespread indifference, fanaticism, and tyranny.[102] With the loss of a traditional center of faith, persons may pull away from commitment, fearing a similar loss once again. Others may turn to a fanatical commitment, a new idolatry, and cling to it for fear of losing certainty. This fanaticism can be seen in some radical feminists who substitute the female for the male in expression and devotion. Persons going through either type of response are open to the abuse of tyranny—either because they are indifferent to claims around them or because they need the certainty that tyranny provides.

Tillich connects the critique of idolatry with the issue of justice. When something finite claims holiness and sacredness for itself, it implies the nonholiness and inferiority of other finite beings under its power. In the name of the sacred powers, laws and structures of life are produced. Injustice, then, is not only legitimated by divine claim, but the unjust structures often are seen as divine in themselves. Justice then becomes "the criterion which judges idolatrous holiness."[103]

Critiques of unjust laws and structures are often perceived as attacking God or the sacredness itself. Yet these critiques do not really attack holiness. They protect it or liberate it from demonic and idolatrous identification with the finite. For example, feminist critiques of theology or ecclesiastical structures are often rejected as trying to destroy the essence of the Church or of Christian faith. But they are really pointing to the idolatrous identi-

---

[102]ST 3:355.
[103]ST 1:216.

fication of the male gender with the essence of God, Christian faith, and church.

If idolatry can lead to injustice and destruction of people's lives, then it is immoral as well as false. Idolatrous truth claims lead to dehumanizing ethics—ethics that work out the idolatry in everyday living. There are many examples out of the past—in the divine right of rulers and the absolute superiority of one race, the rationalization of slavery. Our present concern is the absolutizing of one sex over the other. Thus, the critique of idolatry should lead to improved ethics; a criterion for testing idolatry becomes important not only for issues of religious truth but also for issues of human rights and ethical values.

Applications of the Critique of Idolatry

The Roman Catholic Position against the Ordination of Women. In spite of some Church statements affirming the equality and dignity of women,[104] the Roman Catholic position against the ordination of women has been unchangeable. The Church has tried to argue that the affirmation of equality and the denial of the priesthood to women do not really conflict. The 1977 Vatican "Declaration on the Question of the Admission of Women to the Ministerial Priesthood" argues that "equality is in no way identity, for the church is a differentiated body, in which each individual has his or her role. The roles are distinct, and must not be confused; they do not favor the superiority of some vis-à-vis the others."[105]

But to argue that the ordination of males only does not favor the superiority of some over others is to ignore reality. Throughout its history, the Roman Catholic Church has consistently required the control of religious movements and religious orders through its ordained hierarchy. Positions of real power in that church have been controlled extensively by males. For centuries, important ministries of sacraments have been reserved to males alone. The words of equality and dignity seem empty in the face of such a history.

The Declaration begins with historical arguments to show that the exclusion of women from the ordained priesthood has been the constant

---

[104]For example, see "The Church Today," (*Gaudium et Spes*) *The Documents of Vatican II* (New York: America Press, 1966) 227-28.

[105]The Vatican Declaration: "Women in the Ministerial Priesthood," *Origins* 6/33 (1977): 523.

tradition of the church from Jesus, the apostles, Paul, and the early church both East and West up to the present. But these historical arguments are sealed with arguments based upon symbolic representation, and it is here that the idolatry of the male is especially clear.

It is argued that the priest represents Christ in his ministry, "to the point of being his very image,"[106] particularly in the celebration of the Eucharist. The community is supposed to be able to recognize easily that image of Christ in the priest. The Declaration asserts the importance of the "natural resemblance" that must exist between Christ and his minister and argues that this natural resemblance would be lost if that role were taken by a female.[107] Basically, the Vatican is arguing that because Jesus was a male, the representation of Christ in the ordained priest must be a male.

Such a view means that the *maleness* of Jesus is taken as an absolute element of the ministry of Christ and the ongoing representation and imaging of Christ. But maleness is a characteristic that belongs to the finite human world. To focus on the maleness of Christ as absolute is to elevate that finite human distinction to infinite significance and thereby to create an idolatry. Such idolatry skews the full paradox of Christ as divine and human and as sacrificing himself in being the Christ.

The absolutization of the maleness of the priesthood damages the symbolic representation of the Christ as fully divine and fully human. The priest is said to represent the person of Christ, with the understanding of personhood focussing on his maleness. The tradition of the church has not required moral purity or even spiritual superiority in order to represent Christ more fully. It is his maleness which sets the criterion of representation. While the finite, human character of the priest himself is recognized, his maleness is seen as absolute. That constitutes an idolatry of the male aspect of the bearer of revelation.

In light of our earlier discussion of Tillich's view of the effects of idolatry, we would expect dehumanizing and destructive attitudes and ethics for other humans to result. Several teachings and practices of the Roman Catholic Church bear that out. Accompanying the elevation of the male in church matters has been a restriction of the female to primarily nurturing roles and a corresponding exclusion from leadership. Women could rise to leadership within female religious orders, but most such leaders were under the control

---

[106]"Women in the Ministerial Priesthood," 522.
[107]Ibid.

and rule of a male hierarchy. Women were respected as mothers and teachers and occasionally as saints, but such roles were seen as quite distinct from and less powerful than the role of the ordained priest. The biology of woman was seen as having a direct bearing on her possible social roles, especially within the church itself. A religious woman was to "hide" her sexuality; a married woman could use her sexuality to produce and nurture children. The Church's position on birth control further accentuated the role of the woman as babymaker and homemaker.

Some changes have been brought about in particular churches, with the movement of women into some visible public roles in worship and into some leadership roles in committees and commissions. But those changes have not reduced the exclusivity of males in real power and in major decision-making roles in the Church as a whole. Documents concerning the family, birth control, the role of women in the church and in society, the priesthood, and so forth are still set forth by ordained males. They now usually provide forums for women to speak, but the final authority and leadership does not rest in any women. The idolatry of the male that allows only males to be ordained has produced a structure of power in the Church that denies women the right to full, equal participation in decisions and actions.

Furthermore, numerous Catholic women experience the estrangement and loss of personal center that Tillich describes as part of the reaction when idolatry is recognized. For many, the Church had been a part of the center of their lives. The maleness of the priests had not been recognized as idolatry, but now that questions of discrimination and proper symbolic representation of Christ have been raised, the maleness of the priests and the exclusion of females is recognized as the absolutization of a finite characteristic. The criticism of the past and the call for a reformed future that will allow all people regardless of gender to live out their full human capabilities is part of the process of finding a new center. Some are impatient, some have given up, and some keep hoping that their pleas will be heard. Many are deeply disturbed by the effects of male idolatry on individual lives, especially those females who want and are denied an ordained ministry, and on the life of the church, which they believe will benefit from the gifts of both men and women.

Mary Daly's Views. The reaction to the male idolatry of the past has led some women to call for a reversal of order. Male idolatry has sometimes been replaced with a form of female idolatry. Mary Daly's *Gyn/Ecology* and *Pure Lust* are written with feminist symbols and metaphors as a corrective to the patriarchalism of the Christian tradition. But if Tillich's analysis of idolatry holds true, female idolatry would also produce dehumanizing and destructive ethics.

Daly points out the idolatry of patriarchy and the destructive tendencies of it in *Gyn/Ecology*. She describes the symbolic import of patriarchal religion, where women are seen as threats to men's meaningful world and therefore oppressed.[108] But she misdirects her critique in focusing on males and failing to identify the problem as that of idolatry. Daly says that women must "go past the obvious level of male-made reversals and find the underlying Lie."[109] Yet I question whether her discussion surpasses a male-made reversal from patriarchy to matriarchy. Daly makes it clear that her goal is not androgyny since she understands that as another form of male deception.[110]

For Daly, the process of moving out of the patriarchal limitations involves a new Self-creation by women.[111] This new Self-creation involves being acceptable to one's Self rather than letting others judge. Only the woman can judge her Self. The courage to accept her Self does not involve self-sacrifice but affirmation of the divine Spark in her Self.[112] Daly then describes the ecstasy of the woman's discovery of Self:

> Demystifying/demythifying their obsessions we re-member our Woman-loving Love. Refusing their assimilation we experience our Autonomy and Strength. Avoiding their elimination we find our Original Be-ing. Mending their imposed fragmentation we Spin our Original Integrity.[113]

---

[108]Daly, *Gyn/Ecology*, 39.

[109]Ibid., 60.

[110]Ibid., 68.

[111]"To the degree that the Female Self has been possessed by the spirit of patriarchy, she has been slowly expiring. She has become dispirited, that is, depressed, downcast, lacking independent vigor and forcefulness. . . . As she creates her Self she creates new space: semantic, cognitive, symbolic, psychic, physical spaces. She moves into these spaces and finds room to breathe, to breathe forth further space" (ibid., 340).

[112]Ibid., 378.

[113]Ibid., 423.

This description suggests that Daly takes the feminist experience of consciousness raising as a primary place for the disclosure of Be-ing.

In *Pure Lust*, Daly talks about the function of symbols and metaphors to express this deep experience of women. Daly agrees with Tillich that symbols develop out of particular situations and will change or die as situations change. These symbols "open up levels of reality otherwise closed to us."[114] Metaphors are like symbols but evoke more action and change than symbols. Therefore, Daly sees metaphors as essential to Elemental feminist philosophy which is itself transformation of woman's experience.[115] She uses the metaphor of "Arch-Image" to evoke memories of the Goddess symbol in women's consciousness and the awareness of the Self-affirming be-ing of women.[116] Daly has substituted female for male symbols and metaphors, absolutizing feminist women's experience. The focus is on the female and feminist aspects of the symbols and metaphors, with no concern for their appropriateness for all humans. Such a movement might be appropriate as part of the expression of a finite movement's experiences.[117] But when Daly relates that experience to Being itself and to the experience and expression of the Divine spark, then she has moved into the theological arena of expression of the ultimate and is susceptible to the critique of idolatry.

Much of *Gyn/Ecology* is devoted to analyzing various cultural practices that harm, mutilate, or destroy women living in patriarchal systems—from Chinese footbinding to American gynecology and psychiatry. She argues that patriarchy has led women into destructive and dehumanizing ethics, social structures, and patterns of thought for women.[118] Patriarchally controlled

---

[114]Daly, *Pure Lust*, 25.

[115]Ibid., 26.

[116]Ibid., 98.

[117]Some see Mary Daly's language and arguments as political effort, perhaps more than theology or philosophy. For example, see Michel Dion, *Liberation feministe et salut chretien: Mary Daly et Paul Tillich* (Quebec: Editions Bellarmin, 1995).

[118]"Just as footbinding was required by the men of China, so is mindbinding a universal demand of patriarchal males, who want their women to be empty so that they will be forced to suck male projections/ejections, becoming preoccupied, prepossessed" (Daly, *Gyn/Ecology*, 254). Daly also describes the terror and horrors of torture, political imprisonment, mental hospitals, nuclear weapons, etc. as forms of sadomasochism, stemming from the structures of patriarchy (ibid., 95-96).

consciousness is described as "brokenhearted" and fragmenting being.[119] Much of the evil in the world is not seen as humanly created evil but as *male*-created evil.

Daly implies a dichotomy of good and evil related to women and men respectively. For example, she is somewhat critical of women who side with the patriarchal powers and structures, but she also excuses them as really acting out of *man*made guilt and understanding rather than out of their female be-ing.[120] Really transformed women would not betray or mislead other women; their destructive actions must stem from and be blamed on males.

New structures and understandings for women focus on their experience in this world. In rejecting the male understanding of happiness as attainable only after death, Daly posits happiness as a "life of activity," including artistic, political, spiritual, and athletic activities.[121] She offers the example of writing a book of feminist philosophy as a Metaphor of her Journey into Metabeing.[122] Underlying this activity is a kind of telic or intentional force which is connected with the desire to experience one's "ontological connectedness with all that is Elemental" in reality.[123] Part of this process of experiencing connectedness includes women Be-Friending other women, creating "a context in which women can Realize our Self-transforming, metapatterning participation in Be-ing."[124] Thus, women's feminist experiences reveal and participate in ultimate Being.

Daly says that she does not conceive of a system that simply substitutes the oppression of the male for the oppression of the female. Rather she conceives of a creative context beyond the dichotomy of justice and injustice.[125] But in fact her proposals focus only on women's experience and women relating to other women. For example, women are to Take Heart and Give Heart to other women.[126] Daly does not explicitly say that men are excluded from the spiritual and creative transformations that she describes,

---

[119]Ibid., 386.
[120]Daly, *Pure Lust*, 215.
[121]Ibid., 340.
[122]Ibid., 343.
[123]Ibid., 354.
[124]Ibid., 374.
[125]Ibid., 278.
[126]Ibid., 282.

but she clearly is talking to women about women's experience and identifying the evil structures as male. She does not talk about friendship with people but rather with women. She attributes the evils of political power, military efforts, and sexual exploitation to males and male structures. To free oneself from them is to begin transforming one's Self and to create new possibilities of Be-ing. But these new possibilities of Be-ing do not really seem open to men.[127]

Some of Daly's descriptions of the feminist process of becoming do hold true to feminist experience. But her focus on women alone and her absolutization of their experience is a new form of idolatry that advances little beyond the patriarchal form of idolatry which she herself has so strongly criticized. To leave out the male element of humanity in presenting her philosophy and ethics is as potentially dehumanizing and destructive as the subordination of females in patriarchal theology and ethics.

Possible Contributions of the Critique of Idolatry

The critique of idolatry calls us to develop a theology that recognizes the ultimate as absolute and our finite forms as limited. The present situation calls for recognizing sexist idolatry where it occurs and working to remove it through nonsexist or inclusive language and religious symbols.

With the critique of idolatry as background, we can understand why nonsexist language is less threatening to both sexes than either type of sexist language. Patriarchal language offends the feminist, and feminist matriarchal language offends males and nonfeminists—at least in part because one is offended by religious language that limits the ultimate to one finite aspect of being. Inclusive language does not offend because it allows the ultimate to be expressed through it, without absolutizing the gender of the expression.

The critique of idolatry is significant for ethics because it is tied to issues of justice. Social structures, such as an all-male priesthood, which live out the idolatry, need to be judged and changed by the critique of idolatry. Idolatrous structures offer limited social roles to the persons who are excluded. These social structures, especially in religious traditions, cannot be changed without recognizing the idolatry inherent in them. When we remove the idolatry of gender and open up structures to both males and females, we

---

[127]Her criticism of academic administrations that refuse to let some Women's Studies courses be for "women only" suggests this exclusion of males (*Pure Lust*, 372).

will allow people to focus on the quality and the expression of the role rather than on the gender of the person fulfilling that role. This is particularly important where the role itself is supposed to be symbolic of God or a divine mediator.

The critique of idolatry can help us understand the response of Daly and other similar feminists as the result of the destructive consequences of idolatry that Tillich outlined in *Dynamics of Faith* and *Systematic Theology*. But a new form of idolatry will only lead to further destructive consequences. We must work for language and structures that express ultimacy through them without absolutizing their finite forms. Specifically, we must develop inclusive language and symbols to express the ultimate and work for just social structures that allow equal opportunities for both sexes.

Finally, the critique of idolatry need not be tied to the Christian tradition but can be applicable interreligiously and cross-culturally, as we have shown in earlier chapters. Although clearly for Tillich the critique of idolatry was tied to the symbol of the Cross of Christ, the critique can be related to the very structure of religious expression. Following Eliade, we have suggested that all religious expression has a paradoxical form. But we have also seen that that paradoxical form can be broken with absolutization of the finite form itself. The critique then is not tied to the Cross but to the paradoxical form. The connection of the critique of idolatry to justice is similarly applicable across religious traditions. If the consequences of idolatry are destructive and dehumanizing, then the critique of idolatry can be important not only in theological judgments of truth within various religious traditions but also in ethical judgments of structures and roles within those same traditions.

Chapter 7

Feminist Critique
of Roman Catholic Theology

Roman Catholic feminists have challenged the patriarchy in traditional theology and in religious and social structures as idolatrous and unjust. Rooted in these critiques of patriarchy, feminists are developing new theologies of liberation. Can the thought of Paul Tillich, a male theologian who himself was rooted in patriarchy, be useful in forming feminist theologies? Historically, Tillich's thought has been applied by some feminists in critiquing patriarchy and in formulating new theological approaches.[1] In this essay, I will first explore the relevance of Tillich's ideas to feminist critiques of idolatry and injustice and then suggest ways in which his thought is relevant to constructing feminist theology.

Feminist Critiques of Idolatry and Injustice

Critique of Idolatrous Symbols. In arguing that the pervasive patriarchal character of theological language and church structures is idolatrous, several Roman Catholic feminist theologians have used Tillich's critique of idolatry. For example, as we have seen in the previous chapter, in her early critiques of the Roman Catholic Church, theologian Mary Daly called for using the Protestant Principle as a protest against false securities[2] and named idolatry as the primary evil to be eradicated from the Church.[3] Going

---

[1]In *New Catholic Women* (San Francisco: Harper & Row, 1986), Mary Jo Weaver describes Roman Catholic feminist theology as "to some extent indebted to the profound insights of Paul Tillich" (146). Weaver especially notes Tillich's influence on Mary Daly (153-54) and Anne Carr (157).

[2]Mary Daly, "Return of the Protestant Principle," *Commonweal* 90 (6 June 1969): 338.

[3]Mary Daly, "If You Could Make One Change in the Church, What Would It Be?" *Commonweal* 92 (1 May 1970): 161.

beyond idolatry toward the really ultimate is a major purpose of Daly's highly influential book *Beyond God the Father*.[4]

Like the early Daly, feminist theologian Anne Carr sees Tillich's critique of idolatry as a resource for feminist theology.[5] Carr uses Tillich's theory of religious symbols because it takes account of both positive and negative interpretations of symbols, both the element of participation in unconditioned reality and the conditioned nature of the symbol itself.[6] Applying Tillich's approach to feminist issues, Carr argues: "In criticizing the functions of the symbols of God and Christ, feminist theology exposes the idolatry that occurs when preliminary or conditional concerns are elevated to unconditional significance; something finite (maleness) is lifted to the level of the infinite."[7]

Although these women theologians use elements of Tillich's theology to critique the extensive patriarchy in theology and the church, we have argued in earlier chapters how Tillich's use of the criterion of paradox connected with the critique of idolatry can be helpful in feminist theology. Applying this to patriarchy, the tendency of people to absolutize the maleness of symbols for God or Christ breaks the paradox and is rejected as idolatrous. This critique can also be applied to some feminist efforts to absolutize femaleness and assert the superiority of women over men, as shown in the last chapter. As with symbols rooted in male experience, symbols rooted in female experience can be authentic expressions of experiences of ultimacy but they need to be continually relativized in relation to ultimacy itself. It is this "guardian standpoint"[8] of ultimacy that allows for and demands ongoing critique of religious symbols.

---

[4]Mary Daly, *Beyond God the Father* (Boston: Beacon Press, 1973) 6: "For my purpose is to show that the women's revolution, insofar as it is true to its own essential dynamics, is an ontological, spiritual revolution, pointing beyond the idolatries of sexist society and sparking creative action in and toward transcendence."

[5]Anne Carr, *Transforming Grace* (San Francisco: Harper & Row, 1988) 101-102.

[6]Carr, *Transforming Grace*, 101-102, 140, 167.

[7]Ibid., 102.

[8]Tillich discusses the "guardian standpoint" in "Kairos und Logos," *Gesammelte Werke* 4 (Stuttgart: Evangelisches Verlagswerk, 1961) 74.

Such continuing criticism of traditional religious symbols is often rejected as threatening to the sacred elements of traditional theology. But that rejection is rooted in the failure to distinguish the finite expressions of ultimacy and ultimacy itself. Human formulations about God, Christ, and the church are just that—human and finite. Critiques of idolatry are aimed at penetrating human formulations to recover the divine depth that the symbols were trying to convey.

Existential Disappointment and Injustice. Idolatry can have destructive consequences for an individual's faith experience, as shown in the previous chapter. Many women find themselves deeply disillusioned by the patriarchy in traditional Roman Catholic theologies and liturgies. Some withdraw painfully from their church while others continue to be involved in spite of their loss of meaning.

Idolatrous identification also can lead to injustice. "Justice is the criterion which judges idolatrous holiness."[9] Tillich defines justice as "that side of love which affirms the independent right of object and subject within the love relation."[10] In *Love, Power, and Justice*,[11] Tillich asserts that structures of justice should fit the needs of people, treat all people as equal persons with inner freedom, and offer political and cultural self-determination. When religious symbols are made into idols, there are social and cultural effects that violate these principles of justice.

The identification of something finite as holy gives absolute power to that finite symbol, object, person, or movement. Those people who are associated with that sacred center take on the holiness and absoluteness also. It is clearly implied that other finite beings who are not intimately connected with that sacred center are profane and inferior. Using the authority of such sacred power, social and religious structures are established that delineate who has more of this sacred power and who is left outside of it. Unjust structures and the treatment of others as inferior becomes divinely legitimated; idolatry leads to injustice, with a violation of the principles of justice.

---

[9]Paul Tillich, *Systematic Theology*, 3 vols. (Chicago: University of Chicago Press, 1951–1963), 1:216. (Hereafter, *Systematic Theology* is cited as ST, with volume and page numbers.)

[10]ST 1:282.

[11]Paul Tillich, *Love, Power, and Justice* (New York: Oxford University Press, 1960) 57-62.

When maleness is seen as a necessary element of religious symbols for God and Christ, it is not surprising to find women excluded from social, political, and religious power structures. Maleness (a quality of finite being) has been absolutized, creating an idol and legitimating injustice toward females. As analyzed in the previous chapter, the Roman Catholic position on the ordination of women, as set forward in the 1977 Vatican "Declaration on the Question of the Admission of Women to the Ministerial Priesthood" offers an example of such idolatry and injustice (see chapter 6, section B).

Critiques of patriarchy are threatening because the idolatry is tied up with social-political structures. Those who benefit from the idolatry are likely to defend traditional symbols and structures. They do not experience the injustice and are threatened by the possibility of their own existential disappointment if their objects of ultimate concern are revealed to be less than infinite. Thus, we have an ongoing tension in the Roman Catholic church between those who call for more just church structures and more adequate religious symbols and those who want to hang on to the theological and social-political security of traditional symbols and structures.

Dominating Power versus Empowerment. Implicit in this discussion of justice and injustice is the issue of power. In general use and in Christian theology, the concept of power contains an ambiguity: power as dominating and power as empowering. Women and other oppressed groups have been victims of dominating power used to keep them subordinate and often backed up with claims of divine power. An important element of the feminist critique of traditional theology has been the rejection of images and structures of dominating power and the affirmation of empowerment in symbolizing God and in positing new social and religious structures. Traditional hierarchical structures have been seen as unjust because they left women and other minorities with little or no public power. The extent to which patriarchal hierarchy (husband, wife, children, servants/slaves) has continued to influence our social structures today is an example of such injustice.

Tillich's discussion of hierarchy is not helpful to feminist critiques of dominating power. He continued to defend hierarchy as a necessary or natural social structure even in egalitarian groups.[12] While Tillich is correct that groups do center power in leaders, it is also true that leaders can

---

[12]Ibid., 44-45, 94.

empower rather than dominate the members of the group. Decision making and political, social power can be shared. Feminist theologies have emphasized the mutual power relations of friendship rather than hierarchy.[13] Such a model takes seriously each individual human person as a whole self, capable of self-determination and mutual interaction with others. This model of mutuality fits Tillich's own criteria for structures of justice better than the hierarchy he supports.

Part of the process of women's affirmation of themselves as full human persons switches the image of power from being dominated to being empowered. For those who experience the process as spiritual, the image of God also changes from overpowering to empowering. Tillich's understanding of the power of being participating in all being and empowering all forms of courage can be useful.

What we see in these critiques of patriarchy is that Tillich's critique of idolatry and his analysis of justice can be helpful. But we also recognize that Tillich's patriarchal approach prevented him from seeing the implications of his analysis for male-female power in theology or in society, a task engaged in by feminist students of his theology.

Constructive Efforts in Feminist Theology

The Role of Female Experiences in Theology. A basic root of feminist theology is women's experience. Although traditional theology claimed to be universal, it often left women invisible except where sexual roles and procreation were discussed. The patriarchal language of theology and church liturgies (man, men, he, brothers, sons) is an example of such invisibility.[14] The power structures of church and society that give final decision making to men leave women out. Women who have experienced a new sense of themselves as full persons with autonomy yearn to have that experience integrated with their spiritual life, their church life, and their work for

---

[13]For example, see Sallie McFague, *Models of God* (Philadelphia: Fortress Press, 1987) chap. 6; Carr, *Transforming Grace*, 143-51; Carter Heyward, *The Redemption of God; A Theology of Mutual Relation* (Lanham MD: University Press of America, 1982) 149-78; and Mary E. Hunt, *Fierce Tenderness; A Feminist Theology of Friendship* (New York: Crossroad, 1992).

[14]Rita Burns, "Breaking the Grand Silence: A Diocesan Practice," *Women in the Church*, ed. Madonna Kolbenschlag (Washington: Pastoral Press, 1987) 1:183.

liberation of all oppressed peoples. Theology as well as the structures of church and society need to include women's experiences while avoiding past stereotypes.

The American Roman Catholic bishops attempted to take account of women's experiences in the early drafts of their pastoral on women's concerns, but the final draft and vote were produced by men, once again setting forward what the proper stance and roles of women in the Roman Catholic Church can be. The early process of listening to women was replaced in the end by a process of men deciding about women.

Because of their own sense of having been left out of past writings about women, feminist writers emphasize women's experiences. Wary of earlier claims of "universality" that ignored women, these thinkers are sensitive to the diversity of women's experiences and do not claim a universality for their own approaches.[15] Instead, they speak of setting forward their own perspectives and call on other women to do the same. Yet there has been general agreement on women's experiences of patriarchy and sexism and the injustice of structures that contribute to such experiences.[16] Based on these experiences, the best of feminist theology works to project images that do not subordinate any group but rather serve to liberate all people.

Tillich certainly acknowledged the important role of experience in developing theology.[17] Experience is not only important as a source of theological reflection but also as the connector to, and practical verifier of, theology. The norms of theology should be rooted in the present situation, and one test of their adequacy is the ability to affirm and express people's religious experiences.[18]

While Tillich sees his theology speaking to universal human experience in his own time, that "universality" prevents his theology from being a liberation theology. His categories serve more to analyze the present situation than to criticize and transform it. But when his categories are

---

[15]Carr, *Transforming Grace*, 118.

[16]Ibid., 118, 123.

[17]ST 1:40-46.

[18]For a fuller discussion of Tillich's theory of theological norms, see Mary Ann Stenger, "Paul Tillich's Theory of Theological Norms and the Problems of Relativism and Subjectivism," *Journal of Religion* 62 (October 1982): 359-75.

brought into a particular context of oppression, such as contemporary women's experiences, they can be used as part of a liberating effort.

It was such an effort that engaged Daly in *Beyond God the Father* (see chapter 6, section A). Unlike many other theological writings of the mid-twentieth century, Tillich's theology used terms that were not immediately recognizable as patriarchal. Their abstract nature transcended gender, making them more palatable to budding feminists. Daly found Tillich's concepts useful also because of their dynamic quality and their existential roots. Yet she argues that Tillich's theology cannot be fully liberating because he does not discuss the "relevance of God-language to the struggle against demonic power structures,"[19] such as sexual oppression.

Given the extensive use of Tillich's terms in *Beyond God the Father* and the broad impact of that work on religious feminists, one might expect other feminist theologians to appropriate some of Tillich's terms. That does not happen, in part because some writers stress the patriarchy hidden in abstract concepts.[20] Although Daly criticizes Tillich in her later works, *Gyn/Ecology* and *Pure Lust*, as we saw in the last chapter, she does argue that Tillich's work "is worth studying and criticizing by those who would embark upon the adventure of dis-covering Elemental philosophy (provided, of course, that we employ his writings only as springboards for our own original analysis)."[21]

Religious Symbols. To the extent that abstract concepts are suspected of latent patriarchy, some feminists have been exploring more concrete images as symbols and metaphors. They do not aim at the universality of abstract concepts, but they do hope that others will respond positively to such images. Most feminists intentionally focus on symbols from women's experiences that have been ignored in traditional theology.

It is interesting to note that Tillich recognized the lack of female symbolism in Protestant theology, particularly its rejection of the image of the Virgin Mary.[22] He did not expect the image of the Virgin Mary to be

---

[19]Daly, *Beyond God the Father*, 43.

[20]See, e.g., Rosemary Radford Ruether's discussion in *Sexism and God-Talk: Toward a Feminist Theology* (Boston: Beacon Press, 1983) 67. Ruether argues that "abstractions often conceal androcentric assumptions and prevent the shattering of the male monopoly on God-language."

[21]Daly, *Pure Lust*, 29.

[22]ST 3:293.

reinstated in Protestant circles, but he asked "whether there are elements in genuine Protestant symbolism which transcend the alternative male-female and which are capable of being developed over against a one-sided male-determined symbolism."[23] His suggestion was to recognize female qualities in the "ground of being." The symbolic aspects of "the ground of being" point to "the mother-quality of giving birth, carrying, and embracing, and, at the same time, of calling back, resisting independence of the created, and swallowing it."[24] Some might object to this description of female symbolism as stereotyping females, but some feminist theologians also have suggested imaging God with the qualities of mother.[25]

It is significant that Tillich was concerned to develop language that reduces male dominance and transcends the alternative male-female in symbols of the divine.[26] Yet as Daly asserts, Tillich did not recognize the connection between male-dominated symbolism and actual oppression of females. While Tillich did want balance, he did not see the pervasive male symbolism as idolatrous, an application that could have pointed to the injustice of patriarchal imagery.

Similarly, feminists have to be careful in assuming that use of female symbolism will be tied to a better power situation for women. A study of female symbolism in diverse cultures and faith traditions will destroy that assumption. One can have strong goddess imagery (such as the Hindu goddesses or the Sun Goddess of Japan) and still maintain a strongly patriarchal society and oppressive structures for women. Roman Catholic feminist Rosemary Radford Ruether cites Tillich's critique of the Protestant rejection of the image of the Virgin Mary, but then points out that "it is churches with a high Mariology which are most negative to women. It is the Protestant churches without Mariology which ordain women. . . . Mariology, as it is used by the clergy, seems antithetical to the liberation of women."[27] Recognition of the importance of female symbolism by itself does not challenge patriarchal structures of church or society. The key issue, once again, is the use and abuse of power. What is needed is theological language

---

[23]ST 3:293.

[24]ST 3:294.

[25]McFague, *Models of God*, 97-123.

[26]ST 3:294.

[27]Rosemary Radford Ruether, *New Woman, New Earth* (New York: Seabury Press, 1975) 37.

for a new spirituality that emphasizes empowerment rather than dominating power, and mutuality rather than hierarchy.

New Spirituality. Because the issue of power is tied to reformulating theological and spiritual language, some critics might argue that feminist theologians derive their theological answers from the human situation rather than from revelation. But most feminists would not quarrel with Tillich's method of correlation where the theological answers to life's questions "are 'spoken' to human existence from beyond it," not derived from the analysis of human existence itself.[28] Feminist thinkers would respond to their critics that they have indeed encountered new spiritual meaning, that the sacred is being experienced and acknowledged in new modes.

For several feminist theologians, the new spirituality emphasizes the interconnectedness of all beings, humans with humans and nonhumans, rooted in an underlying divine unity. The interconnectedness is not just mystically experienced but also leads one to political efforts to eradicate sexism, racism, and classism.[29] Carr describes feminist spirituality as keeping the feminist critique of patriarchy and affirming feminist sisterhood but also as envisioning "noncompetitive, nonhierarchical, nondominating modes of relationship among all human beings and in relation to nature."[30] In *New Woman, New Earth*, Ruether calls for a "prophetic vision to shape a new world on earth," a vision that includes inferiority but also a strong sense of reciprocal interdependence with all humanity and the earth.[31] Theologian Madonna Kolbenschlag describes the new spirituality as a spirituality of passion with a mission of solidarity.[32] This passion is a passion for life, which includes all aspects of life (physical, sexual, emotional, religious, social, political) and all of life (human and nonhuman) and includes resistance to traditional structures as well as creative imagination to envisage new structures of solidarity.[33] Although Daly definitely sees her work as post-Christian, she tries to express the spirituality of feminist women. In *Beyond God the Father*, she speaks of "sisterhood as cosmic covenant," a relation-

---

[28]ST 1:64.

[29]Carr, *Transforming Grace*, 209.

[30]Ibid., 207.

[31]Ruether, *New Woman, New Earth*, 211.

[32]Madonna Kolbenschlag, "Spirituality: Finding Our True Home," *Women in the Church* 1:198.

[33]Ibid., 206-11.

ship and a process that renames the cosmos, involves charismatic gifts of healing and prophecy, builds nonhierarchical, nondogmatic community, and embraces the earth as part of the sisterhood.[34]

These efforts to express a new spirituality are directed toward other feminists who are in the process of transforming their whole selves to full human persons independent of patriarchal structures. The focus is the liberation of women, but the struggle for liberation is extended to all dominated beings, human and nonhuman. Liberation and its spirituality are not limited to women but can be seen as gifts of transforming power to the whole church.[35]

Part of the power of these liberating efforts comes from the sense of newness many women experience in their spiritual self-development. Even when we turn to past sources, whether biblical or theological, we read them with "new eyes" and capture new insights. Sometimes these insights reveal patriarchy to be criticized; at other times we find empowering images or concepts. But the key of acceptance is the ability of those concepts and images to broaden empowerment to all humans and to help us create more just social structures and models of interdependence with our whole world (social and natural).

Feminist Appropriation of Tillich's Major Symbols. Tillich's theology on its own terms cannot provide the liberating spirituality envisioned by feminist theologians. But reinterpretations and applications of aspects of his theology can be part of a theological base for the new spirituality. For this purpose, three of his nongendered theological concepts will be explored here: power of being, New Being, and Spiritual Presence. Although these terms are abstract, the application of the symbol is more concrete and potentially liberating.

The dynamic and immanent qualities of symbolizing God as "power of being" are very helpful to a feminist spirituality. Daly emphasizes the dynamic quality by imaging God as Verb, but I think it is important to maintain the focus on "power." Many women reject patriarchal power as overpowering and dominating others. Yet these same women feel themselves to be empowered in a new way and experience that empowerment as spiritual and not just social. God as the power of being participating in

---

[34]Daly, *Beyond God the Father*, chap. 6.
[35]See Carr, *Transforming Grace*, 214.

the struggles of life, as the root of our courage to face threats of nonbeing,[36] can express that experience of ongoing empowerment to meet and resist injustices. That power is experienced in the midst of life, as part of life, and yet it is greater and deeper than an individual's human power. In *The Courage to Be*, Tillich speaks of the power of being as the God above the God of theism, "the God who appears when God has disappeared in the anxiety of doubt."[37] For the feminist, the anxiety of doubt may be experienced, but more central is an anxiety that Tillich did not name individually—the anxiety of injustice and oppression.[38] The courage to face this anxiety is also rooted in the God who appears when ordinary human power has been squelched and oppressed—a spiritual power of being that empowers people to continue their efforts for justice.

The symbol of the power of being can also image the underlying unity of all beings, working well with the feminist emphasis on the interconnectedness of reality. Everything that is participates in the power of being and yet "the power of being is the power of everything that is, insofar as it *is*."[39] The power of being, then, is the root of our unity with all of reality, from the earth to God. What Tillich does not develop adequately is a more horizontal image of the interactive nature of the power of being.[40] For Tillich, "the power of being must transcend every being that participates in it."[41] But we also experience and can be empowered through other beings, both human and nonhuman. The experience of the power of being is not always a direct or more vertical experience of the ground of being or the God above God. How we treat other people, nature, and objects and how

---

[36]Tillich, *The Courage to Be* (New Haven CT: Yale University Press, 1952) 178-81.

[37]Ibid., 190.

[38]Franklin Sherman made this suggestion of a fourth anxiety of injustice and oppression in a discussion of *The Courage to Be* for the North American Paul Tillich Society meeting in Anaheim, California, November 1985.

[39]ST 1:231.

[40]Tillich does analyze the ontological unity of love and power in *Love, Power, and Justice*, 48-53. He speaks of every self as a power structure (53) and emphasizes that love involves reunion of those who are separated (48-49). He also speaks of love being united with power to destroy what is against love. But he speaks of the necessity of compulsory power rather than the radiating power of love which empowers individuals.

[41]ST 1:231.

we are treated by them involves dynamics of power, and these experiences often mediate the spiritual, ultimate power of being.

Tillich's symbol of the New Being as saving, reconciling power can express the exciting, new energy that comes out of the feminist experience of overcoming self-estrangement and alienation. Daly broadens Tillich's term from its focus on Jesus as the Christ to describe women as the bearers of New Being as they struggle for justice in the midst of patriarchy.[42] At one point, Tillich hints at a broader application of the term than Daly's focus on women, suggesting that the universe is "open for possible divine manifestations in other areas or periods of being."[43] But if one takes seriously the feminist interest in a spirituality of interconnectedness, then the symbol of the New Being can be reinterpreted to speak of moments of reconciliation between people or between people and nonhuman beings. Certainly, Christians will see Jesus as the Christ as the one who best embodies that reconciling power, but other faith traditions and other religious approaches may name another.

Perhaps the least developed and yet potentially most effective of Tillich's symbols for feminism is "Spiritual Presence," the symbol that unites elements of meaning from the symbols of the power of being and the New Being.[44] Spiritual Presence expresses the experience of ecstatic moments when the normal ambiguity of life, the mixture of positive and negative (essential and existential), is transcended. Such moments involve the empowerment of the power of being and the reconciliation of the New Being, but Spiritual Presence expresses the underlying unity of such moments, the experience of transcendence or depth that momentarily eliminates the divisions between being and the limitations of life. People can experience Spiritual Presence through anyone or anything. Tillich connects the symbol of Spiritual Presence, with its implications of immanence and ongoing process, to people's experiences of faith, love, unity with others,

---

[42]Daly, *Beyond God the Father*, 72.

[43]ST 2:96.

[44]This unity is not surprising when one contemplates the structure of Tillich's system. The power of being as one symbol of being-itself is the theological answer to the questions implied in essential being; the New Being is the theological answer to the questions implied in existential being. But life involves a mixture of essential and existential elements, giving us ambiguity (ST 3:12, 32). Spiritual Presence is the theological answer to the questions arising from the ambiguities of life.

and aesthetic, cognitive, or moral theonomy. The mystical quality or element of participation and unity connecting individuals and all dimensions of life with Spiritual Presence has great potential for grounding a spirituality of interconnectedness. Given the current interest in ecology, it would be helpful to add the dimension of nature to Tillich's discussion. It is important that Tillich continues to see Spiritual Presence as a guard against demonic power or idolatry or heteronomy. When ultimacy is connected with ordinary life, it is all too easy to absolutize the ordinary.

As feminists develop the symbol of Spiritual Presence, they will want to emphasize more fully than Tillich its implications for individual self-realization, interdependence and community, the struggle for justice for all peoples, and our ecological unity. Spiritual Presence can empower us through a kind of mystical participation that momentarily releases us from the ambiguities and anxieties of life. But that Spiritual Presence can also give us the courage to build community, to make others aware of our interdependence, to work for justice in the church and in our global society, and to balance our relationship with the earth. That courage stems from the interpenetration and ongoing process of Spiritual Presence in all of reality and in all dimensions of life. Tillich's description of ecstatic moments of unambiguous life fit well with the moments of truth, beauty, justice, and unity that we all experience in life. His recognition of the multidimensional unity of life and his rejection of a hierarchy of levels of life (such as spirit over matter) can be expanded upon by feminists who are working for new theological models of mutuality. Future development of feminist spirituality can be enhanced by critically expanding the symbolism of Spiritual Presence.

Conclusion

Paul Tillich's theology has been and still can be a significant resource for feminist Roman Catholic theology, not only in its critique of traditional, patriarchal Roman Catholic theology, but also in the development of new theological approaches that seek to empower all humans and express the interdependence of all creation. Tillich and his theology lived under patriarchy and although his thought was "new" for his time, it still retained elements of that old patriarchal structure. But as we search for "new" spiritual depths that can empower us in the struggle for justice and harmony, we must build on the insights of the "old" and move beyond those insights to new modes of expression that address our current situation. This is not just a matter of "cleaning up" patriarchal language but producing other language that can continue to express the Spiritual Presence, the participation of the Eternal in our lives. Feminists must critically build upon the insights in earlier theologies while directing their theologies to present and future possibilities.

In *The Shaking of the Foundations* Tillich expresses the relation of the old and the new to the experience of the power of the Eternal:

> Its saving power is the power of the Eternal within it. It is new, really new, in the degree to which it is beyond old and new, in the degree to which it is eternal. And it remains new so long as the eternal power of the Eternal is manifest within it, so long as the light of the Eternal shines through it. For that power may become weaker; that light may become darker; and that which was truly a new thing may become old itself.[45]

As always, we stand under ambiguity and the critique of idolatry, tools Tillich gives us, tools that can be applied to patriarchal theology (including Tillich's) and eventually also to our own new theological efforts.

---

[45]Paul Tillich, "Behold, I Am Doing a New Thing," *The Shaking of the Foundations* (New York: Charles Scribner's Sons, 1948) 185-86.

Part III

Religion and Society

Chapter 8

On the Boundary: Protestantism and Marxism[1]

Paul Tillich was born a Protestant, grew into a critical Marxist-Christian, and in the end fulfilled his life as a dominant Protestant theologian. He was born into that most Protestant of all social institutions—a pastor's family. Catholicism spurned the entanglement of family for its clergy and religious spiritual leaders. Eastern Orthodoxy relegated the family to second-class status with its requirements that bishops be monks. Among Christians, only Protestants permitted and in reality insisted—until recently—that church leadership be married clergymen. Tillich's early life and existence until World War I was patriarchal-Prussian-Lutheran existence as a pastor's son. In his education, he prepared to follow in his father's footsteps in the learned-Brandenburg ministry.

Two artifacts I found symbolize the shocks that drove Tillich into his adult, lifelong conversation with Marxism. The first is from my grandfather's attic in Humboldt, Iowa, and the second is from the Paul Tillich archives at Harvard.

As a young boy, it became necessary at my grandfather's death to clean out the family home. In the attic we found a German helmet from World War I, which had a crest reading—in German of course—*For Fatherland with God and King*. The helmet had been picked up on the Western front and its loss had probably cost some German-Christian soldier his head. I often remembered that helmet when I was working on the Tillich paper in the Harvard Archives.

---

[1]The general ideas of Paul Tillich on religious socialism and Marxism are covered in many studies and I did not want to repeat the work of my *Paul Tillich's Radical Social Thought* (Atlanta: John Knox Press, 1980) or other essays, so I have chosen selectively some areas of recent interest. This essay, presented at the North American Paul Tillich Society's centenary celebration of the birth of Paul Tillich at Emory University in 1982, was revised for this volume.

Tillich had left his boyhood home of dreaming innocence, his pastoral work in Berlin, and his patriarchical home with everything in place, to go to war. He had his Ph.D. in theology, he was married, and his family represented the learned German clergy. His father had served as chaplain to the emperor on a trip to Jerusalem. It was a world of patriarchical capitalism, with the empire and Lutheranism in a symbiotic relationship. He went to war in a surge of patriotism and without clear political convictions.

By the end of the war Tillich had suffered nervous collapses repeatedly; he had helped bury the cream of the German officer corps; his wife had become pregnant by his friend; and the empire had been defeated and thrown into revolution.

His first course in Berlin, "Christianity and the Social Problems of the Present," indicated the new social passions of the young Privatdozent. There are two cultural artifacts from this period in the Harvard Archives. The first is a flyer calling for a meeting to organize a new church. The program was summarized in four points:

(1) renew religious motifs in culture;
(2) support the new republic and socialism;
(3) align the church with the international peace movement; and
(4) institute parliamentary control of the church.

The second is a red poster with a hammer-and-sickle symbol announcing that Paul Tillich will speak to a rally of Independent Social Democrats (ISD). Pastors Richard Wegener and Paul Tillich were called upon to justify their participation in the ISD rally. They wrote a paper for the Brandenburg consistory justifying their position. They argued that

(1) the personal encounter of the person and God is beyond any economic or social form;
(2) Christianity is inevitably involved with society;
(3) Christianity has greater affinity with socialism than with capitalism; and
(4) socialism had no essential fight with Christianity.

The reaction of the church hierarchy was hostile and they were ordered not to speak at any more ISD rallies.

Tillich's socialism alienated him from the church of his father, but the socialism developed in small religious discussion groups. He understood his form of religious socialism not to be a movement for the whole church, but to be a small nonpolitical movement which would reflect the development of the ideas rooted in social reality. Even as he led in various discussion circles he learned from others and depended on others for political-economic concepts. The groups lived on the boundary between socialism and religion.

Paul Tillich's special place on the boundary was the engagement of the early Karl Marx with Lutheranism. He could not stand the tendencies toward legalism and biblicism that he found in Calvinism; the economics of *Das Kapital* and the determinist-scientific Marxist writers held little interest for him. But a trained economist with a passion for analyzing Calvinism influenced his methodological approach to the encounter with Marxist critique of bourgeois society.

The Use of Max Weber

Max Weber haunts the socialist writing of Paul Tillich. Basic concepts are taken over, utilized, and usually not acknowledged. I want to suggest that the importance of this is that Paul Tillich had already integrated Max Weber into his socialism by an early date. At least by 1926 the socialist presentation of Tillich was shaped by Weber. Weber had reshaped his own writing on religion and economics during the First World War, so the work was relatively fresh.

The central concept of Tillich's *Die religiöse Lage der Gegenwart*, published in 1926 (ET: *The Religious Situation*, 1932), is "The Capitalist Spirit." It does not differ from Weber's concept "The Spirit of Capitalism." The explanation of the use of term makes use of Weber's ideal type methodology. Tillich writes: "It is rather a symbol for an ultimate, fundamental attitude toward the world."[2] The purpose of the book is to show that the dominance of the spirit of capitalism is receiving significant challenges.

The economic organization of modernity arose on grounds of autonomy and the overthrow of superior powers. The economic influence dominates the selves that develop within the system. "The spirit of a finitude which lives within itself is, for our time, the spirit of capitalist society."[3] The awe and mystery of the world have been replaced by control of finite reality by

---

[2]Paul Tillich, *The Religious Situation*, trans. H. R. Niebuhr (New York: Henry Holt & Co., 1932) xxv.
[3]Ibid., 71.

humanity. Personality is freed from mystery and pressed into the bondage of living within a system of rational, calculating manipulation of reality. The economic function comes to control life.

> This is one of the weightiest characteristics of the capitalist time. The goad of unlimited desire does not allow the spirit time for anything which does not serve time itself. It drives the spirit about within the inescapable and unending circle of the finite.[4]

The personality of early twentieth-century humanity is portrayed by Tillich as living in Max Weber's iron cage.

In 1926, Tillich had moved beyond the early romantic socialism of revolutionary enthusiasm. His 1926 book did not show the full movement into and transformation of socialist categories that his 1932 work, "Die Sozialistische Entscheidung" (much later translated as *The Socialist Decision*, 1977), would exhibit. The 1926 study is more a critique of the culture while hoping for a religious change, by 1932 he is proposing a program for changing society and calling for socialist change.

The Religious Situation showed how completely sectarian Christianity and Calvinism had merged in North America with capitalism. Christianity and capitalism reinforced each other in a way that appeared impregnable to Tillich. Neither Catholicism nor Lutheranism revealed a social program fit to the crisis. In prophetic critique and precapitalist Catholic religiosity he saw some hope for a religious orientation against the capitalist spirit of "the ideal of a self-sufficient finitude."[5] He saw Protestantism bereft of an independent culture, so the resistance to capitalism will come from its greatest source of strength, its theological work. Still *The Religious Situation* is basically an analysis of the way things are and whence they have come and it does not show the goals or power of transformation.

A few years later (in 1929) Tillich explicitly referred to his use of these broad concepts as ideal types. The proletariat was described as a class dependent upon the sale of their labor under market conditions. He said the concept was not entirely an empirical concept but a representative or typological one.[6]

---

[4]Ibid., 75.
[5]Ibid., 117.
[6]See *Political Expectation*, ed. James Luther Adams (New York: Harper &

The next year (1930) he used the term *principal* "to refer to the summarizing characterization of a political group."[7] Principal was a way to avoid the endless empirical particularities and to refer to the dynamics of a movement or to its spirit. Principal also emphasized the decision or existentialist character of identifying a group with its central powerful idea. So with the term *principal* he can carry forward the typological, descriptive-critical work of *The Socialist Decision*.

The utilization of Weber's method to describe Marxist ideas began to transform Marxism for Tillich. Religion could never be only a by-product of the substructure of the society.

Economic materialism as taught by some Marxists is excluded by method from the system. Metaphysical materialism is overthrown by a descriptive method forged to demonstrate the relative significance of religious-intellectual phenomena. Historical materialism remains a possibility and over against a historical idealism Tillich affirms materialism but most of this affirmation is making use of unacknowledged Weberian-ideal types. Furthermore, Marxism is a term used to describe the growing self-realization of the proletariat in overcoming their alienated situation. The equation of Marxism with this growing consciousness meant it was not primarily an idea, but the power of a movement. It also meant that if the power faded, so did Marxism.

The Socialist Decision

In 1929 when Tillich joined the Social Democratic Party (Sozialdemokratische Partei Deutschlands, SPD), it was to strengthen the party now out of power for a return to power to oppose groups bearing other ideas. He tried to join religion and social democracy, calling on both religion and social democracy to reform. Their separation and antagonism reflected the human estrangement. Their union would have given the possibility of a theonomous political movement.

The ideas of reform, planning, criticism of social democracy were reinforced by ideas within Protestantism. Protestantism's reform and critique

---

Row, 1971; repr.: ROSE 1, Macon GA: Mercer University Press, 1981).

[7]Paul Tillich, *The Socialist Decision*, trans. Franklin Sherman (New York: Harper & Row, 1977) 9. (Original: *Die sozialistische Entscheidung* [Potsdam: A. Protte, 1933].)

needed to be reinforced by myths of origin or catholicity while socialism needed the principle of expectation which could best be grasped in religious terms. But neither enough Socialists nor enough Christians could be persuaded to join both these historically antagonistic movements. Tillich tried to unite conceptually those which historically were opposed.

The Socialist Decision is Tillich's most creative political philosophy. It was written under pressure. He was warned by Max Horkheimer that certain sentences in the manuscript could cost him his life. Two months after its publication he was suspended from his university position in Frankfurt. But it was not only inspired by the pressure, he had a program: the reform of socialism so that it could resist Nazism.

The Socialist Decision expresses his deeply speculative mind as it organizes the fruit of fourteen years of socialist conversations and previous lectures. It also represents Tillich the fighter, who fought as a philosopher could best fight by criticizing Nazi claims to truth, by explaining, criticizing, and relativizing Nazi thought. The hope for the success of his program rested in the variable of moving revolutionary support away from the political romanticism of Nazism to the critical politics of social democracy.

The introduction to the volume of two types of political philosophy was translated and published in the *Interpretation of History*.[8] (The remainder of *The Socialist Decision* awaited the publication in 1977 of Franklin Sherman's translation.) The two types of political philosophy are those founded in myths of origin and those originating in prophetic criticism of those myths. Other political movements bearing political ideas can be analyzed fruitfully in terms of expansions of these concepts. Hence Nazism is analyzed as a revolutionary form of political romanticism as it attacks the present in terms of a radical reading of myths of origin, that is, blood, soil, nation. The spirit of Judaism rooted in prophetic criticism is essentially opposed to political romanticism.

Other sections of the book move beyond the analysis of political romanticism to analyze Western capitalism as akin to Western socialism in sharing the critique of the myths of origin. Western capitalism's progressiv-

---

[8]*The Interpretation of History*, trans. N. A. Rasetzki and Elsa L. Talmey (New York/London: Charles Scribner's Sons, 1936). (This volume was composed of several of Tillich's philosophical, political, and theological essays, including an autobiographical sketch written especially for this publication.)

ism depended upon the myth of harmony, that is, "the invisible hand" of Adam Smith, and that myth too is dissolved in socialist criticism.

Socialism in its turn is criticized in several areas of its unresolved problems as socialist hopes seemed to outrun socialist possibilities. Socialism reflected the powers of origin in the realities of the anguish of its proletarian population, it criticized the belief in harmony, and it demanded change. The demand for change remained heteronomous without the concept of *expectation*. Expectation, the worldly eschatology of prophetic religion is necessary if the tensions of socialism are to be resolved. It is the prophetic expectation that the *new* can emerge. Expectation indicates that the demands of ethics of critical consciousness are supported by the powers of origin. Hence there is hope. There may be chaos and barbarism, but the powers of change reflect the powers of origin so they can be trusted. The religious roots of socialism are seen in this concept of expectation. Despite his valiant tries in the volume to avoid utopianism, the sense of expectation that religious people and socialists could ally in 1933 in a political movement seems utopian. Tillich saw the possibility of defeat, and he could predict and did predict barbarism, war, and chaos if political romanticism prevailed.

Shortly before the Nazi electoral gains he had a dream of sheep grazing in the deserted yards of the center of government in Berlin's Potzdammer Platz. After the war he saw in a New York newspaper a picture of sheep grazing in Potzdammer Platz. It was only a short walk from the deserted, boarded-up buildings of the "Thousand Year Reich" to the Kaiser Wilhelm Memorial Church. Here the ruined remains of imperial Germany are now united in their bombed-out form with the new church structure. I like to think that this was the church where in 1933 Hannah had to restrain Paul's curses and obscene gestures when they exited from a Nazi-dominated church meeting. Cursing the sick culture and prostituted church of Germany in 1933 was appropriate. Heinrich Heine (1797–1856)—German poet, literary and social critic, and a Jew—many years before (1834–1835) had prophesied correctly that the cathedrals were doomed.

> Christianity—and this is its fairest merit—subdued to a certain extent the brutal warrior ardour of the Germans, but it could not entirely quench it; and when the cross, that restraining talisman, falls to pieces, then will break forth again the ferocity of the old combatants, the frantic Berserker rage whereof Northern poets have said and sung so much. The talisman has become rotten, and the day

will come when it will pitifully crumble to dust. The old stone gods will arise then from the forgotten ruins and wipe from their eyes the dust of centuries, and Thor with his giant hammer will arise again, and he will shatter the Gothic cathedrals.[9]

Concept of Humanity

In 1935, Tillich wrote a report on "The Christian and the Marxist View of Man" for the Universal Christian Council for Life and Work Research Department.[10] It continues the anthropological explorations in *The Socialist Decision* and makes the analogies between his Protestantism and Marxism quite clear. Part of the report is still in outline form and many of the sources of Tillich's thought are referred to only by name and their specific contributions left undeveloped. A second edition of the paper was developed in 1959 and that is the version of the paper in the Harvard Tillich Archive. The report is complete enough to be a prospectus for a major study, perhaps a small book. It is not surprising that Tillich was still in 1959 engaged at a deep level with Marxism. He continued publishing on Marxism in the United States through the 1930s, 1940s, and 1950s, and in Germany and Japan in 1960. The evidence of these later works of Tillich belies the assertion by Weisskopf in *The Thought of Paul Tillich* that "Tillich's socialist writings stem from the time before his emigration to the U.S. and therefore do not cover events after 1933."[11]

Tillich's 1935 report, outline, prospectus, or whatever it is, is a reminder that the lifelong, primary-dialogue partner to Paul Tillich's Protestantism was Marxism. John Stumme has dated the origins of this dialogue of his work in "Inner Mission" and "Church Apologetics" to the

---

[9]Quoted by Beate von Oppen, in *Religion and Resistance to Nazism* (Princeton NJ: Princeton University Center of International Studies, 1971) 9.

[10]Paul Tillich, "The Christian and the Marxist View of Man" (Universal Christian Council for Life and Work, December 1935, 2nd ed., 1959; Harvard Tillich Archive). The 1959 2nd ed. is referred to here.

[11]*The Thought of Paul Tillich*, ed. James L. Adams, Wilhelm Pauck, and Roger L. Shinn (San Francisco: Harper & Row, 1985) 76.

proletariat which led to a debate on 12 December 1913 with Karl Liebknecht who later organized the German Communist Party.[12]

The first section of the paper shows that neither Marxism nor some tendencies in Protestantism have an "articulate anthropology." Their refusal to articulate anthropology in both cases was rooted in their negative evaluation of historical existence. However, within both Protestantism and Marxism developments have produced anthropologies that try to unite radically critical attitudes with anthropology capable of supporting hope for healing. Their convergent trends reveal their common prophetic heritage and make comparisons possible.

The second section of the paper is an outline presentation of the basic ideas of Protestant anthropology. The result of the presentation is to show that there are

> seven problems of equal importance to Christianity and Marxism: humanity's original true nature, the transition to a state of contradiction, the character of this contradiction, existence in contradiction, the overcoming of the contradiction, the goal of the perfection of humanity.[13]

The exploration of the seven problems in the third section demonstrates that there are structural analogies between prophetic Christianity and Marxism especially in its original form in Marx himself. He does not intend to argue for identity of ideas but to show typologically certain analogies. As the second section had begun with "The galvanizing point of view of Christian-Protestant anthropology is the relation of man to God," the third section begins with "The controlling viewpoint of all socialist-Marxist anthropology is man's position within society."[14] Then the analogies in the seven areas are presented.

The fourth and final section of the paper shows the contradictions between Christianity and Marxism in the areas where structural analogies were found. In each case the fundamental antithesis is one of immanence and transcendence. Christian anthropology is related to God and Marxist

---

[12]John R. Stumme, *Socialism in Theological Perspective*, (Missoula MT: Scholars Press, 1978) 55.

[13]Tillich, "The Christian and the Marxist View of Man," 5.

[14]Ibid., 5 and 9.

anthropology to society. All of the fundamental oppositions can be seen to be an expression of the transcendence-immanence issue.

Marxism is seen as adopting one element, that of the critical-prophetic motif, while Christianity also preserves the possibilities of mysticism and a certain inward existence distinct from social contradictions. Conditions of the relationship between Marxism and Christianity depend on whether the relationship is exclusive or particular; the first possibility of interpretation leads to life-and-death struggle. The second interpretation, which was that of religious socialism, would understand Marxism as the critical-prophetic-immanent tendency of Christianity's own life. Such an interpretation would then regard it as the task of the church to "search for a way of receiving it again into itself."

This tightly outlined and argued paper then ends with this plea for reunion of the separated, and the return of the prophetic elements to their religious roots.

Near the End

The existentialist's notes become louder in Tillich's 1960 essay "On the Boundary" published for *The Christian Century* in the "How My Mind Has Changed" series. He admits the reasons for his lessened political interest.[15] It was a time of prevailing trends and not of decisive actions. Political decisions were confined to small power groups which excluded wide general influence on significant decisions. The neurotic conditions of the world were seen in neurotic individuals. As a German-born American it wasn't a time for his own expressions of German religious socialism. He did not really understand American politics. But then as always much of his work was in response to requests. Harvard asked him to lecture on German philosophy and on religion and culture. Not many were asking for fresh work on religious socialism in the United States. Tillich of course was never a pure existentialist. Those years at Harvard saw the essentialism emphasized in volume 3 of his *Systematic Theology* and in the Harvard courses. However, the existentialism appeared in his focus on the individual.

Here his Lutheranism emerges dominant. He had always known of the more radical place for the individual in Christian faith, but in these final

---

[15]Paul Tillich, "How My Mind Has Changed," *The Christian Century* 77 (7 December 1960): 1435-37.

years it becomes dominant in his preaching and particularly in his emphasis on psychology and mental health. In 1935 he had written that

> The transcendential foundation offers Christianity the possibility of disassociating to a certain existence the inward existence of the individual from among the structural framework of the objective contradiction. This is the ground of the possibility of the care of individual souls and of mysticism within Christianity. In Marxism, however, such a disengagement of the interior existence of the individual is made impossible by the purely social interpretation of the contradiction.[16]

By 1960 this possibility of the care of individual souls had become dominant in his own work. He now tended to lecture on religion and society and not often on religious socialism. He rooted his social action in fighting the demonic, not in the expectation of victory in society.

John Stumme has summarized well the approach of his closing years: "There was for him no going 'beyond religious socialism.' "[17] Religious socialism had been his venture from the end of World War I to the end of World War II; pragmatic, reform politics were in order after World War II. The church had to wait passionately and actively for signs of a new theonomy. The doctrine of the Kairos, even if sometimes romantic, had always meant there were periods without the Kairos.

During the spring quarter of 1962–1963 at the Divinity School of the University of Chicago, Tillich made a remark in his lectures on the history of Christian thought that is a clue as to the importance of Karl Marx for his thought. The remark needs to be taken seriously as a clue to the importance of Marx for Tillich's ongoing thought.

> What I will do now is perhaps surprising to you. I want to give you here the theology of the most successful of all theologians since the Reformation, namely, Karl Marx. I will consider him as a theologian. And I will show you that without doing this, it is impossible to understand the history of the twentieth century and large sections of the late nineteenth century. If you consider him only as a political

---

[16]"The Christian and the Marxist View of Man," 16.
[17]Stumme, Socialism in Theological Perspective, 255.

leader or as a great economist, which he also was, or as a great sociologist, which he was even more, then you cannot understand from what sources the power came which transformed the whole world and conquered nearly half of it in the twentieth century.[18]

Stages of Socialism

Appropriate political action always accounts for the cultural possibilities. To act without recognizing the cultural limits is utopian. Politics for Tillich, however, is not just adjusting to culture, it may mean opposition to the dominant culture. The drive to oppose culture arises from ethics and the ability to discern possibilities for change.

Ethics is the understanding of practical activity toward the realization of the unconditioned. Ethics won't realize the ideal community, but by expressing action guides in transcendent symbols it affects the community's action. Despite the complexity of the biographical formulation of Tillich's ethic and the wide range of sources from which it is drawn, the form of this ethic is clear and consistent.

The structure is threefold: first, the ultimate principle of Christian ethics is *agape* which is known as the law of human nature; second, human wisdom is represented in laws, moral principles, guidelines; third is the concrete situation in which the actor takes upon himself the risk of moral decision. This pattern of love, law, and situation is present in most of Tillich's writing on ethics.

Agape is the one universal element of the human moral situation. Occasionally, he describes the universal element as "the human itself." The seeming ambivalence in his ethics, of course, derives from his claim that a properly conducted analysis of human nature reveals love as the essence of life. Though in much of his writing it would rather seem that the experience of love is the starting point of the analysis: "In man's experience of love the nature of life becomes manifest."[19]

---

[18]Paul Tillich, *A History of Christian Thought*, ed. Carl E. Braaten (New York: Simon & Schuster, 1968) 476.

[19]Paul Tillich, *Love, Power, and Justice* (New York/London: Oxford University Press, 1954) 25.

The second level of the theory accepts the relativity of all moral principles unless they are alternative formulations of *agape* which in itself includes justice and the honoring of a person as a person. Moral principles or middle axioms are not despised, but they are thoroughly relativized. They are useful as guidelines. If they are embodied *agape* and if they meet the situation, they are what the moral decision maker acts upon.

The third level, that of the situation, requires loving listening. It is at this level that the tools of the social and psychological sciences are most important for Tillich. His antimoralism demands that as many of the particulars of the situation be understood as possible. There is no security, but only the risk of moral decision and the comfort that trust in the power of forgiveness gives.

Love as the absolute is the principle of justice that keeps it creative. Justice forms the society in a relationship that allows development of human beings in community. Being under conditions of human life can express itself in a form encouraging unity and growth.

It seemed to Tillich in 1919 that religious socialism expressed the absolute, was appropriate to the principles of human wisdom, and was the decision to be made. I think that by 1932 religious socialism was for him a less direct expression of the absolute, but it was still an appropriate action to be taken even at the risk of career and life as it expressed the best human option. By 1965 when it seemed that religious socialism was no longer an expression of the absolute for many societies, it was still for him the best human option available, and it could not find a place in the American soil to flourish.

Marxism had remained a dialogue partner of Tillich's from the German revolution after World War I until his death in 1965. His lecture on Karl Marx in the academic year 1962–1963 at the University of Chicago repeated what he himself found of enduring value in the thought of Karl Marx.

1. *Historical materialism.* After Marx, it was no longer possible to think of isolated individuals who were independent of society. Human life was dependent upon the social-economic realities.
2. *Alienation.* The Marxist theories of society contributed to human understanding the thesis that in historical life all human existence is estranged from its true meaning and that its creations reflect and continue this estrangement.
3. *Ideology.* Marxist analysis revealed how ideas and—particularly important for Tillich—religions and philosophic ideas could

reflect false consciousness as they justified or protected unfair aspects of human relations. Much of religion did actually reflect the self-interests of the dominant classes.

4. *Critique of religion*. Marxist critique revealed the church's need for self-correction and the overcoming of the estrangement between the working classes and the religious establishment.

For Tillich, the Marxist critique failed and turned into totalitarianism because it rejected God and lost principles of internal critique. The group of the vanguard or remnant itself became self-righteous and blind to its own idolatrous ideology because it suppressed the reference to the Ultimate.[20] So for Tillich, Marxist atheism defeated itself. Religious socialism, which could have preserved the best of social reform and social revolution, was too sophisticated. The masses would support religion or socialism, but not the required synthesis. The dialogue of his Protestantism and Marxism occupied his mind, but the social reality eluded him.

---

[20]*A History of Christian Thought*, 476-87.

Chapter 9

Conversations
in Religious-Socialist Circles

From 1975 to 1990, I wrestled with Paul Tillich's commitment to religious socialism. This search to understand why a realist would commit himself to a utopian cause occupied my mind in many diverse ways. Beyond Tillich, I was attracted to the revolutionary possibilities of religious socialism for Latin America in the movement of liberation theology. It too failed. My own movement has taken me to a Christian-democratic, mixed-economy version of what could be a religiously based, fair America. The conclusion is not that different from Tillich's except he did not ever surrender the vision of a religious socialism.

This process of inquiry into the roots of Tillich's religious-socialist commitments revealed that these were communal commitments. His insights, conclusions, and decisions were formed in conversation with others who were struggling to articulate a vision of reform for their societies. He was never without these partners in conversation, and the specific economic dimensions of his hopes were particularly dependent upon experienced economists. He would often lead in the philosophy of history and religious conceptual discussions while others like Eduard Heimann or Reinhold Niebuhr would lead in the economic or political dimensions of the discussion. The discussions occupied him from 1918 to 1965, but three specific groups can be isolated as the most important for his search: the Kairos Circle, the Frankfurt School, and the Fellowship of Socialist Christians.

A. The Kairos Circle

The Kairos Circle, also known as "the Berlin Circle," the "circle around Tillich and Mennicke," or "the circle around the *Blätter für religiösen Sozialismus*," met every week or so in a restaurant or a home for discussion. It had evolved under the leadership of Carl Mennicke, Günther Dehn, and Paul Tillich as they had moved out of the *Soziale Arbeitsgemeinschaft*. Günther Dehn, a member until about 1923, wrote that it never grew to more than ten or twelve members. Various commentators list different participants. Eberhard Amelung's list[1] combined with the list from John Stumme[2] produces the following names: Günther Dehn, Eduard Heimann, Adolf Löwe, William Löwe, Hans Hartmann, Carl Mennicke, Trude Mennicke, Gustav Radbruch, August Rathmann, Hugo Sinzheimer, Karl Ludwig Schmidt, Hans Simmons, Paul Tillich, and Arnold Wolfers, giving a maximum number of fourteen.[3] The group functioned for Tillich from 1920 until 1924, when he moved to Marburg. Some members assembled several times later and they kept in touch by correspondence, conferences, and so forth, but for Tillich the Kairos Circle as it originally functioned concluded with his departure from Berlin. The ideas developed there continued to appear in his thought, and Carl Mennicke and Adolf Löwe shared his company and influenced his thought through Frankfurt, and in New York he reunited with Eduard Heimann and Adolf Löwe. Mennicke survived the war in concentration camps.

My reading of the Kairos Circle supports the conclusion of Stumme's critique of Amelung. The circle was not dominated totally by Tillich's ideas; most of the members were not intellectuals to be dominated. The circle did not have the same ideas, but they shared some of the same problems upon which they reflected. The circle was as broad as Christian and atheist, socialist and communist. The journal of the circle attained about 500 in circulation and was published from 1920 to 1927. The group had only minimal commitments to either church or party, an alienation out of which Tillich could conjure up the virtue of finding a new way. They maintained some contact with other religious socialist groups, but did not merge with them.

Mennicke summarized the group's conversations as having four major concerns: (1) Barth's theology, (2) Marxism, (3) the proletariat, and (4) the shape of the future socialist society.[4] But they were united in their conversations as much by the heady political climate and pressures of their day as they were by ideology.

---

[1]Eberhard Amelung, "Religious Socialism as an Ideology: A Study of the Kairos Circle in Germany between 1919 and 1933" (Ph.D. diss., Harvard University, 1962) 6.

[2]John R Stumme, *Socialism in Theological Perspective: A Study of Paul Tillich, 1918–1933* (Missoula MT: Scholars Press, 1978) 35.

[3]Ibid., 62.

[4]Ibid., 34.

The Political Context

The years 1919–1924 were the turbulent, chaotic, years of the Weimar Republic. By 1925 some semblance of stability had come to the Republic. Tillich lived in Berlin until spring of 1924; and while sympathetic to the radical Independents to whose rally he had spoken, his primary political education was in the discussion groups of socialist intellectuals that came to be known as the Kairos Circle. Tillich's essay of 1922, "Kairos," explains the centrality of this concept to the group's philosophy of history. His essay of 1923, "Grundlinien des religiösen Sozialismus" ("Basic Principles of Religious Socialism"—see at note 12, below) expresses the outlines of his political philosophy at that time. Not all of the Kairos Circle would accept the total thought of either of these two essay, but they represent Tillich's contributions to the group. His concepts of Kairos and Religious Socialism were shaped by the political life that impacted on all who lived in Berlin.

The 1919 German national elections witnessed the overwhelming victory of the Social Democrats. They polled 11.5 million votes; their nearest rival was the Catholic Center Party with almost 6 million votes. The Liberal Democrats polled approximately 5.5 million. The governing coalition was formed from the three parties and Philipp Scheidemann presided over the coalition cabinet. Friedrich Ebert, the president, promised to rule for all Germans while not forsaking his working-class origins and his socialist principles. The National Constitutional Assembly had met in Weimar partly because of the continuing disorder in Berlin. By August of 1919 it was becoming clear that the Independents and the Communists were not to share power and that the socialist measures of the new Weimar Coalition would be moderate.

Democracy was assailed by both the extreme right and the extreme left. The crippling pressures came from the victorious allies, however, as they forced the German government to accept the stringent terms of the Versailles Peace Treaty. The coalition broke over the acceptance of the new borders, the loss of colonies, the economic reparations, and the insults to the German nation. A new government was formed; but in accepting the Treaty, the Social Democrats were damned from all sides in Germany. The bold new experience in democracy was being strangled by the victorious democratic nations who seemed unaware that the empire they had opposed in the war had been transformed into a struggling democracy. The Treaty of Versailles officially ending the war also lost the peace. The theory spread that a proud Germany had not lost the war on the battlefield, but by domestic betrayal. Those who reluctantly were forced to support the Treaty were seen as the traitors.

A constitution was promulgated in August 1919, and in September the government moved to Berlin. The Weimar Constitution was a mixture of socialist and liberal principles reflecting the alliance of Social Democrats, Democrats, and Center interests. It was written in the midst of civil disorder, even civil war, and immense powers for the protection of social order were given to the president. The Independents and Nationalists opposed the Constitution. The hatred between the Independents and the Social Democrats reached a new intensity in January of 1920 when rioting before the Reichstag resulted in forty-two persons being killed by troops. The Social Democrats' hold on the workers weakened, and hostility to the government from the left deepened.

Political life in Germany stumbled from one crisis into another. Resisting allied demands for the reduction of the army, rightist leaders moved against the government. A brigade occupied Berlin; the government fled and Wolf-gang Kapp was installed as head of the revolutionary government. The Social Democrat appeal for a general strike was honored by the unions, and much of German industry stopped. The ineptness of the conspirators, the resistance to the putsch by the proletariat, and the steadfast unity of the constitutional government caused the conspirators to surrender their positions.

In the Ruhr, utopian socialists launched a counterattack which left them in control of several key industrial cities. The French retaliated by occupying Frankfurt on 6 April 1920. The newly formed Müller government, again a coalition of Center, Democrat, and Social Democrat, was able to secure the withdrawal of France in middle May. The social disorder was accompanied by the decline in the value of the currency and widespread lawlessness which shook the authority of the government.

The elections of 1920 saw the sharp decline of the voting strength of both the Democrats and the Social Democrats. The center was weakened while both rightist parties and the Independents on the left scored substantial gains. The Independents attracted 4,895,317 votes, only slightly behind the Social Democrats' 5,614,456. These elections revealed the trends that were to dominate the Weimar Republic: the eroding of the center and the rise of the extreme parties.

The refusal of the Independents to join a moderate government with the Social Democrats permitted a new coalition to emerge and the SPD was out of power in 1920, only two years after the formation of the new government. The process of socialization of the economy was set back further.

The growth of fighting groups on both sides of the political spectrum increased the instability of the society. Walter Rathenau, the liberal Jewish foreign minister, was assassinated by rightwing nationalists on 24 June 1922. "Organization C," the refuge of supporters of the Kapp putsch, were responsible. The murderers were caught, but the government as usual was unable to enforce stiff penalties against conspirators from the right.

Throughout 1923 strikes and moves for the secession of areas of the Ruhr and Bavaria kept Germany in turmoil. The Hitler-Ludendorf attempted putsch in 1923 in Munich was suppressed and the importance of Hitler was unappreciated. In the elections of December 1924, the Nazis were so soundly defeated that they appeared to be of no political significance.

The foundations of the world order seemed to be shaking. The death throes of the old empire prevented the emergence of a new order, and the forces for the new order were divided among bourgeois, fascist, and radical groups. The political issue explicated in the concept of Tillich's Kairos group was: How can we affirm action for decisive change without surrendering to the enthusiasms of the activists? Or, how can we mediate between the determinists and the romantic activists? Experience taught that action or praxis was vital to social change, but action had to be in accord with the objective social conditions. In religious terms the question around the Kairos Circle was: How does the eternal relate to the temporal? To combine the religious and the political question meant to ask: When are moments of historical action eternally significant?

Tillich's essay "Kairos" is a call to a consciousness of history that is grounded in the "depth of the unconditional."[5] The unconditional is expressed as a quality of experience which is absolute or ultimate. It is captured in "the greatest and first commandment": "Thou shalt love the Lord thy God with all thy heart. . . . " It is a philosophy of history set against all forms of understanding history that deny it meaning.

The concept of *kairos* has its origins in the New Testament as "right time" rather than *chronos* or "formal time." The demands and opportunities of each time vary. The moments of absolute demand are the moments of

---

[5]Paul Tillich, "Kairos," in *The Protestant Era* (Chicago: University or Chicago Press, 1948) 32.

kairos.[6] The idea that particular times are filled with significance is contrasted both to Eastern mystical tendencies which would deny the significance of history and to Western mechanistic thinking which would obscure the significance of history.

The danger of the crisis theology of Karl Barth was that the significance of the present might be eclipsed. Barth was correct to relativize all historical creations. There is no absolute church or absolute state. But Tillich insists when an old order is passing and a new order is emerging, the new order is *en kairos*. The new order is subject to judgment and change, but its coming is the content of history. For Tillich, obviously, the new socialist order was in the right time in the early Weimar Republic.

The philosophy of history represented by kairos is a form of dialectical interpretation of history. There is no final stage in the kairos interpretation. The "age of the Holy Spirit" (Joachim of Fiore/Flora) or the "classless society" (Marx) are not to be thought of as final stages; they, too, are subject to criticism and transformation. The concept of kairos tries to retain the idea of classical history that each moment is significant and also the progressive conviction of progress in the appearance of the new in history. The dialectical interpretation united the above two, and the addition of the kairos doctrine amended the dialectical interpretation.

Tillich settles for a paradox. In the moment of kairos the absolute is expressed, but yet it is not an absolute. Judgment and further transformation await every realization. The proper response in such a situation is to refrain from trying to capture the absolute, rather one should surrender to it. Christ as the one who surrenders the self is clearly the norm for life in moments of kairos. As Christ reveals the individual surrendering to the universal, so in moments of personal kairos or social kairos the particular is to be surrendered to the universal. Clearly, Tillich is using his Christology as a formulation for philosophy of history, but for him the secular images of "the third epoch of world history" or the "Kingdom of God" can express the same reality.[7]

A time of kairos was confronting the Western world. Religious socialism was the theological interpretation of socialism in light of the kairos philosophy. Here in 1922 the rudimentary ideas that were to be expressed in *The Religious Situation* of 1926 and *The Socialist Decision* of 1932

---

[6]Ibid., 33.
[7]Ibid., 43.

are present. The task of religious socialism was the theoretical task of reminding socialism of its roots in the unconditional. Religious socialism had to attempt to free socialism from its bourgeois loyalties. Tillich rejected the attempts to unite socialism with the churches for the alliance would only strengthen them, whereas both needed to be thoroughly criticized and transformed.

In 1951 he returned to Berlin and lectured at the *Deutsche Hochschule für Politik* with which many of the original members of the Kairos Circle had been associated. His lectures were on Utopia, but he returned to the doctrine of the kairos. He expressed the concept of kairos as a way of saying both yes and no at the moment of decision. Yes could be said to the demand for absolute action. However, no was said to the demand for idolatry. New orders can be born and are in history; but they, too, will be transformed. Fulfillment, he said, is found in the vertical dimension of history; on the horizontal level fulfillment is always fragmentary.[8] Looking back on history since the end of World War I, he concluded that the interwar reflections on kairos were correct.

The final part of *Systematic Theology* returned to the theme of kairos and acknowledged the emergence of the term in the context of religious socialism.[9] In part the kairos that was expected had been fulfilled, in part it had not arrived, and in part it was betrayed by the Nazis. "Awareness of a kairos is a matter of vision."[10] It is the surrendering to the spirit which is doing something new. It is a full affirmation of what is happening beyond calculation and analysis. Such affirmation is, of course, subject to error. Against theologians or philosophers who supported the Nazis, Tillich argued the "Cross of the Christ was and is the absolute criterion."[11] Moments of kairos are rare, and, as for Tillich himself, he regarded the interwar period as a time of kairos and thought that a future kairos for Western civilization was postponed until the rather distant future.

---

[8]Paul Tillich, *Political Expectation*, ed. James Luther Adams (New York: Harper & Row, 1971; repr.: Reprints of Scholarly Excellence (ROSE) 1, Macon GA: Mercer University Press, 1981) 179.

[9]Paul Tillich, *Systematic Theology*, vol. 3 (Chicago: University of Chicago Press, 1963) 369-72.

[10]Ibid., 370.

[11]Ibid., 371.

Religious Socialism

In 1923 Tillich published a lengthy essay, "Grundlinien des Religiösen Sozialismus" ("Guidelines of Religious Socialism"), in the journal of the Kairos Circle, *Blätter für religiösen Sozialismus*.[12] The essay incorporates work from *Das System der Wissenschaften* (*The System of the Sciences*), published the same year, which he had been working on since his days on the Western Front.[13] Some of the concepts of the essay are also found in a more developed form in his "Religionsphilosophie" ("Philosophy of Religion") published in 1925.[14] The work also suggests ideas that are more fully developed in his 1933 *Die sozialistische Entscheidung* (*The Socialist Decision*).[15]

Religious socialism as a movement is identified with neither a church nor a political party. It is a community of those who are grasped by the kairos of a new time and who are hoping that the emerging order can be religious and socialist. It joins in the socialist political struggles, but it does not want to bless them with religious sanction. The tactics of the socialist parties do not express the fullness of the socialist idea.[16]

Religious socialism, according to Tillich, is an attempt to reunite the sacramental basis of society with historical critical consciousness. In religion such a union would be represented by a synthesis of Catholic substance and Protestant critique. In society the union is a meaningful society utilizing modern technique.

The goal of religious socialism is nothing less than theonomy. Theonomy means the sovereignty of God or "God is all in all." Tillich distinguishes

---

[12]Translated by James Luther Adams and Victor Nuovo as "Basic Principles of Religious Socialism," in *Political Expectation*, 58-88.

[13]*Das System der Wissenschaften nach Gegenständen und Methoden: ein Entwurf* (Göttingen: Vandenhoeck & Ruprecht, 1923); repr. in GW 1 (1959); translated as *The System of the Sciences according to Objects and Methods*, trans. Paul Wiebe (Lewisburg PA: Bucknell University Press, 1981).

[14]"Religionsphilosophie," in *Lehrbuch der Philosophie*, 2 vols., ed. Max Dessoir (Berlin: Ullstein, 1925) 2:765-835.

[15]*Die sozialistische Entscheidung* (Potsdam: A. Protte, 1933); ET: *The Socialist Decision*, trans. Franklin Sherman (New York: Harper & Row, 1977).

[16]"Basic Principles of Religious Socialism," 88.

theonomy from both otherworldly utopianism and this-worldly utopianism.[17] Theonomy preserves the "yes" of religion to socialism as well as the religious reservation of religion to socialism. Similarly, the religion that negates itself is most open to what the spirit is doing in society. Expressed in terms of social ethics, theonomy is the right and the just. Concretely, it is seen in its opposition to demonic distortions of humanity's life.

In the area of economy, Tillich argues that the modern, rational economy denies personality as fully as did the ancient order. He looks for a restoration of an eros relationship between person and thing. The meaning is not clear, but it seems that his intention was not that different from the young Marx, that is, the overcoming of the person's alienation from product. There is explicit rejection of the criticism of machines; rather the need is to find a new scheme of meaning that will allow people to participate meaningfully in a "mythos of technology."[18] The pattern is a familiar one for Tillich, the critique of modern autonomous society, and the seeking of a new basis for it.

The rational, capitalist society is organized demonically in that its foundation is the war of all against all in competition. The class struggle reveals the disharmony underlying the capitalist order. The reduction of all relationships of power and eros to economic terms denies the individual his subjective rights and leaves only objective dependent relationships. In the new society envisaged by Tillich, there is a return to some models associated with feudal society; but, of course, without power to pass on privilege to descendants or to hold to possession after the action's significance for the whole community has passed. He mentions the idea of "fief," whereby one has disposition of goods in relationship to the needs of the community. The society has a certain hierarchy of function as determined by those of the whole. Ideas of property through fief and representative property replace both state ownership and private ownership in his understanding of religious socialism.[19]

At the present time, the state is the defender of justice. Justice is upheld by power. Religious socialism rejects various forms of anarchism and accepts the present reality of the state while combating nationalism, particularly in its idolatrous forms. As Tillich hopes for an aristocracy to emerge that will

---

[17]Ibid., 62.
[18]Ibid., 76.
[19]Ibid., 79.

represent the struggle for a theonomous society, so in international affairs he hopes "the strongest bearers of the theonomous idea of humanity should constitute the leadership of nations."[20] There is a religious reservation about force. Tolstoy symbolizes such a reservation, but religious socialism cannot abandon the power that will sustain justice. The particular expressions of the theonomous society were for Tillich provisional. Meanwhile, religious socialists were to struggle to overthrow the demonic in education, state, and culture while awaiting the breakthrough to the new society.[21]

Tillich's writing on religious socialism in the turmoil of Berlin expressed the spirit of utopianism more than it did belief-ful realism. His awareness of the class struggle kept him from endorsing the SPD, but he could not give himself enthusiastically to the Independents either. The idea of kairos would remain central to his philosophy of society, but later reflection on the class struggle and a continuing discussion with social philosophers would in Dresden and Frankfurt produce a more realistic political outlook. From Frankfurt in 1930 Tillich reflected on those earlier years of excitement in Berlin:

> That was the spiritual situation in the five years after the Revolution, full of passion and power, full of despair and consciousness of death, full of the mood of doom and yearning. We still feel it in our blood, but we also know that something different has come into existence since then. All who had been broken and not built anew in those years experience a remarkable surprise; under closer examination that which they had created anew often very much resembled that which they had destroyed. The power of the old proved stronger than the five years of crisis had foreshadowed. Everywhere a reaction set in.[22]

Socialism had both universal and particular aspects. Its particular aspect depended on its being borne by the historical movement of the proletariat. To the extent that the Kairos Circle connected socialism and the proletariat

---

[20]Ibid., 82.

[21]Ibid., 88.

[22]"Die Geisteslage der Gegenwart," Tillich, *Gesammelte Werke* 10:116. (*Gesammelte Werke* hereafter will be cited as GW, with volume and page numbers.)

it risked its analysis upon the consciousness of the proletariat. Heimann had
seen the danger:

> If labor would cease to be socialistic, if it would agree to be
> accepted in socialism due to some sociopolitical and some bour-
> geois concessions, then it would no longer make sense to be a
> socialist; we intellectual socialists of bourgeois descent would then
> be unmasked as ideologists and romanticists; we would be like fish
> in a stream that is dried up.[23]

B. The Social Context of the Frankfurt School

As professor of Philosophy at the University of Frankfurt (1929–1933),
Paul Tillich was closely associated with the membership of the Institut für
Sozialforschung from the time of his arrival in Frankfurt. According to Horst
Bögeholz, his appointment to the university was opposed by some of the
philosophers. By the time of his expulsion in 1933, he was dean of the
faculty. The Institut was dedicated to social research and the development
of a critical theory of society. The membership of the Institut was left-
Hegelian or humanist-Marxist in inspiration, and left of the Social Democrats
of the Weimar Republic in politics.

Tillich's relationship to the Institut für Sozialforschung is important to an
understanding of his social philosophy. His support and encouragement of
the critical theory of the Institut für Sozialforschung indicates the type of
social theory and research that interested him. Furthermore, Tillich's social
theory had been a social product since Berlin. He worked his ideas out in
discussion and he wrote in loyalty to those with whom he talked. He
brought Adolph Löwe and Eduard Heimann from Berlin into the intimate
discussion group he shared with members of the Institut. His help to
Horkheimer in acquiring the chairmanship of the Institut shifted the Institut
from Marxist economics to a much broader social critique.

The Institut's wrestling with the theory-praxis question and the Institut's
conclusion of seeking truth in theory characterized Tillich's struggles. His
own final relative withdrawal from praxis to write his (German) "Systematic

---

[23]Eduard Heimann, *Kapitalismus and Sozialismus* (Potsdam: Alfred Protte,
1931) 189.

Theology" was a decision understandable in light of the Institut's social reality. The movement from Marxist social philosophy to Freudian psychoanalysis was a movement not of a solitary Tillich, but of a social group seeking a synthesis. Tillich's characteristic ways of addressing the issues of utopian thought, anti-Semitism, and economic theory were molded by his discussions with the members of the Institut and their associates. Reflection upon the social reality of the Institut is one avenue for understanding the Germanic origins of this immigrant's philosophy of culture and religion and its impact upon North America.

Tillich was close friends of three leaders of the Institut: Max Horkheimer, director from 1929, Leo Lowenthal, and Friedrich Pollock. Together with Karl Mannheim, Kurt Riezler, Adolph Löwe, and Karl Mennicke, these friends formed a Kränzchen, or intimate discussion group.[24] The group, which was of importance to Tillich's thought, was often hosted by him, first in Frankfurt and later in exile in New York City.

The Institut was independently endowed, though it cooperated with the University of Frankfurt. The independence of the Institut from state, university, and private capital enabled it to proceed in its own fashion to develop its critical theory. Those attracted to the Institut after 1929 were in large measure Marxists who could support neither the Communist line as practiced in Russia nor the socialism of the Weimar Republic in its diluted trade unionist and practical political form.[25] Rather they undertook to reform the intellectual roots of Marxism, and sought their inspiration in empirical research, cultural criticism, and the philosophy of the young Marx.

Independence from outside contact was, on the other hand, alienation from responsibility for society. Tillich was more involved in active socialist politics than were most members of the Institut. Most members were distant from the push and shove of responsible politics. They were closer to Max Weber's "ethic of absolute ends" than to the ethic of responsibility. However, they understood themselves as critical scholars of politics, not as politicians.[26]

---

[24]Martin Jay, *The Dialectical Imagination: A History of the Frankfurt School and the Institute of Social Research, 1923–1950* (Boston: Little, Brown and Co., 1973) 24.

[25]Peter Gay, "Weimar Culture: The Outsider as Insider," *Perspectives in American History* 2 (1968): 36.

[26]Ibid.

Tillich was at the height of his German academic career as professor of Philosophy in Frankfurt. At forty-three years of age his influence was widely felt, and he and Hannah Tillich lived a brilliant and exciting life in Frankfurt.[27] Part of this life was the frequent dinners and parties and the continuous discussion around the social situation with Karl Mannheim, Erich Fromm, Herbert Marcuse, and Max Horkheimer joining the debate. After 1930 the shadows began to deepen and cultural expressions turned more to nihilism. Aryan-Semitic disputes began to fracture the University. The Tillichs' friendships were largely among the Jewish intellectual circles.[28] Their families and friends came to divide among those supporting the Nazis and those allied with either the Communists or the Socialists. While attending a Nazi rally, Tillich perceived the demonic in Hitler. Then he began his critique of politics, *Die sozialistische Entscheidung* (*The Socialist Decision*), which was published in January 1933, and then suppressed.

With the political deterioration of 1932, panic ensued among the Frankfurt circle. The endowment of the Institut had been established abroad in 1931 to provide for its possible continuation in exile. The pace of life became faster as if all of life had to be lived before the end. Paul Tillich was among the first university professors to be dismissed in 1933 by the Nazi regime. Of the twelve dismissed at Frankfurt one was Tillich and the other eleven were Jewish. He considered the underground; friends advised him against it. Max Horkheimer feared that Tillich's hopes for a change in the German situation would cause him to linger too long and result in his death. In fact, in February 1933, Horkheimer read Tillich a line from one of his writings and told him that "if he would not leave Germany, it would cost him his life."[29] Tillich toured the country pondering his decision. In Dresden he missed arrest by the Gestapo only by a friend's forewarning.

The Tillichs prepared to leave Germany, but still he hesitated. Finally, realizing that no academic appointment was possible without recantation of his work, he had a final interview with the Nazi secretary of education. The secretary's responses to Tillich's queries about the Jews and modern culture

---

[27]Hannah Tillich, "Frankfurt," *From Time to Time* (New York: Stein and Day, 1973) 141-56.

[28]Ibid., 149.

[29]Max Horkheimer, "Erinnerungen An Paul Tillich," *Werk and Wirken Paul Tillichs* (Stuttgart: Evangelisches Verlagswerk, 1967) 17.

were unsatisfying. The secretary suggested Tillich leave Germany.[30] The decision was made.

Tillich's years at Frankfurt came to an end as an act of political power. The power that dismissed him was the power he had analyzed and resisted. Friends in New York, particularly Horace Friess of Columbia University and Reinhold Niebuhr of Union Theological Seminary, had seen the danger, and upon his dismissal from Frankfurt secured him an academic appointment at Union. Horace Friess met the Tillichs when their ship docked. Ursula Niebuhr helped them settle into their first apartment in Knox Hall, part of the Union Seminary quadrangle on 122nd Street near the corner of Broadway. Soon the Institut für Sozialforschung was to join them in exile in its new home at Columbia University just across Broadway.

Tillich made many contributions to the Institut. He helped found a chair of social philosophy for Max Horkheimer to fill when he assumed the directorship.[31] He assisted Theodore Adorno in securing his first position at Frankfurt. He shared with Mannheim, Horkheimer, and Sinzheimer the dismissal from the university on 13 April 1933. He urged the Institut's reestablishment in Frankfurt in June 1949, hoping to renew social research and modern social science in Germany.[32]

The Institut, through its research, publication, and conversation, created a model of social reality which is reflected in several areas of Tillich's thought. The model reflected the personalities and minds of the members of the Institut. The model can be seen in (1) the critical distance of philosophy from practical politics; (2) the combination of Freud and Marx; (3) the problem of utopian reflection; and (4) the economic theory.

In intellectual heritage and sociological position at Frankfurt, Tillich shared the position of the leading members of the Institut. This location in the broad spectrum of left-Hegelian, young-Marxist thought, and the academic elite of Frankfurt, kept most of them from active commitment to political parties. In the 1930s the proletariat was not behaving according to Marxist philosophy, and the wrath of the petit bourgeoisie was about to make the location of the Institut in Germany impossible. They were the alienated intellectuals. Tillich would vote socialist, and in 1929 he joined the Social Democratic Party, but the compromises of the socialist party kept him

---

[30]Hannah Tillich, "Frankfurt," 155.

[31]Horkheimer, "Erinnerungen an Paul Tillich," 16.

[32]Jay, *Dialectical Imagination*.

from enthusiastically endorsing it. The communist awkwardness kept him out of their circles. When he published his major work in politics, *The Socialist Decision*, it called for sophisticated reforms in socialism that the socialist leaders were intellectually and sociologically incapable of making. Its economics reflected the thought of Löwe more than it did the earlier Marxism of the Institut.

Critical theory as represented by Horkheimer, Adorno, and Marcuse, was suspicious of finished political-philosophical systems. The work of the school was in large part a critique of the intellectual tradition. Tillich shared the suspicion of existing systems, but he labored to produce a new synthesis. These synthetic attempts in Germany were largely unnoticed. His *System of the Sciences* received very few reviews. *The Socialist Decision* was consumed by the Nazi holocaust. The first volume of his German "Systematic Theology" announced for 1927 did not appear until after his death. His American *Systematic Theology* of three volumes began appearing in 1951, but it lacked the thorough analysis of religious symbol and political philosophy that had been promised in the announcement for the 1927 volume. Fromm and Marcuse were to contribute their works of synthesis in the United States in their unification of Freudian and Marxian perspectives. Tillich's work in the United States was to incorporate the Freudian perspective more and more into his theological synthesis, while playing down the Marxian elements; but with the gradual discrediting in his mind of Neo-Marxist philosophy, his final synthetic works of philosophical theology were not to have a totally integrated political philosophy. The critical transcendence that characterized the Frankfurt school's politics while Tillich was there, from 1929 to 1933, was finally dominant in his major work.

Tillich's closest friends in the Institut—Adorno, Horkheimer, and Marcuse—were all involved in psychoanalysis and/or the relationship of sociological theory to Freudian theory. In the early 1930s it was intellectually radical, almost academically taboo, to relate Marxism and Freudianism. Neither Communism nor the psychoanalytic movement would touch the synthesis. Nevertheless, the Institut went ahead, merging Freud and Marx. Some problems with Marxism seemed insolvable without new resources. Horkheimer received appreciative letters from Freud for his work in getting the Frankfurt Psychoanalytic Institute tied to the University of Frankfurt.[33]

---

[33]Jay, *Dialectical Imagination*, 88.

Erich Fromm gradually moved from his synthetic work at the Institut to reject crucial components of Freud's theory, including aspects of the concept of libido.[34] Marx came to play a much larger role in his thought. He opted for Marx's view of possible human reconciliation and gradually shook off Freudian pessimism. As a result, he was dismissed by the International Psychoanalytic Association and regarded as a revisionist.

Adorno, Fromm, Horkheimer, and Marcuse's differences about Freud did not become apparent until emigration. In America, Horkheimer attacked Fromm's revisionist form of Freudianism. He argued that Freud's sociological setting in bourgeois Vienna was not necessarily detrimental to the theory. Freud was correct that psychology was intended to focus on the individual, not society. The libido was a necessary concept. Reconciliation could not precede social reconstruction. Theory could not be complete until social contradictions were resolved.[35]

Marcuse's use of Freud to correct Marx followed his disappointment over the purges of Stalin and the cruelties of the Spanish Civil War.[36] In *Eros and Civilization*,[37] Marcuse presented Freud as a revolutionary utopian. Fromm's critique was thoroughgoing. The debate between the two ranged over issues of exegesis of Freud, the character of civilization, the possibility of integrated personalities, the nature of love, and the meaning of tolerance. The issues of the Institut of the 1930s were to continue to boil over into the United States of the 1960s and 1970s.

There is a book still to be written on Tillich's use of psychoanalytic categories and on the scores of lectures on mental health that he delivered in the 1950s and 1960s in the United States.[38] This chapter does not attempt

---

[34]Ibid., 90.

[35]Ibid., 102-103.

[36]Ibid., 107.

[37]Herbert Marcuse, *Eros and Civilization* (Boston: Beacon Press, 1955).

[38]Guyton B. Hammond has contributed a very valuable volume, *Man in Estrangement: A Comparison of the Thought of Paul Tillich and Erich Fromm* (Nashville: Vanderbilt University Press, 1965). Hammond's later work has contributed to understanding the intricacies of Tillich's relationship to critical theory as formulated in the Institut. Guyton B. Hammond, "Tillich and the Frankfurt Debates about Patriarchy and the Family," in *Theonomy and Autonomy*, ed. John J. Carey (Macon GA: Mercer University Press, 1984) 89-110; idem, "Tillich and the Frankfurt School on Protestantism and the Bourgeois Spirit," *Religion et Culture*, ed. Jean Richard (Quebec: Les Presses de L'universite Laval, 1987) 327-38; idem,

to analyze his psychoanalytic theory, but only argues that the move from Marx toward Freud was a move within a community of scholars. It was not simply a retreat from politics, but a way of becoming more "critical" of politics. It should also be noted that Tillich, like most other intellectuals, would respond to an invitation to lecture on a subject that was within his range of interest and competence. The fact that he used more Freudian terminology and lectured on psychology is in large part due to American disinterest in Marxian terminology and social revolution. Herbert Marcuse, in his preface to *Eros and Civilization*, indicated his indebtedness to Max Horkheimer and the Institut for his theoretical position and began: "This essay employs psychological categories because they have become political categories." This insight of the Institut was shared in Tillich's thought.

Fromm's thought contained progressive utopian elements which distinguished his work from the critical, negative character of the work of the Institut. Others associated with the Institut, especially Benjamin, Horkheimer, and Adorno, used their utopian visions as principles of critique of the present, not as plans for the future. There was a deep note of pessimism in their work, which Tillich shared.

Utopian hopes kept history moving, and negated the need for a mythological glorification of the present. Utopia, related to the prophetic spirit, confronted the "is" with an "ought." Tillich died in 1965, so we do not know his reaction to the Neo-Marxist activism of the late 1960s. However, he had opposed similar activism in the 1930s, looking for a middle way. Adorno expressed his dismay that much of the ideological fervor of the activists came from the theoretical work of the Institut. Martin Jay argued that Adorno's regrets pointed to "a fundamental conclusion of the theory itself: negation could never be truly negated."[39] With the dissolution of the proletariat, utopia had only a critical function.

For Tillich, finally "it is the spirit of utopia that conquers utopia."[40] This means that utopia is distinguished from the Kingdom of God. It contains the idea that there are particularly significant times in history in which much can

---

"Why Did Westerners Become Fascists? Fromm, Tillich, and Horkheimer on Character Types," *Papers from the Annual Meeting of the North American Paul Tillich Society* (September 1990) 8-12. See also Paul Tillich, *Meaning of Health*, ed. Perry LeFevre (Chicago: Exploration Press, 1984).

[39]Jay, *The Dialectical Imagination*, 279.

[40]Tillich, "The Political Meaning of Utopia," in *Political Expectation*, 180.

be accomplished. It also and most forcefully means that the freedom of the human spirit is such that no form of human organization will fulfill it. The human spirit is truly led to strive beyond its present boundaries, but while the Kingdom of God may be realized momentarily in human history as the vertical dimension intersects the horizontal dimension, fulfillment is never complete. Life continues as a tragic-ironic existence in which the critical function must be practiced.

Quite clearly, Tillich's theological affirmations were not shared by the secular Jews who dominated the Institut. Some of the members moved more toward religious affirmations in later life. Paul Tillich's influence on Eduard Heimann leading even to his eventual baptism is a particular case in point. Terence O'Keeffe is quite correct in stressing that in Frankfurt, Tillich as a theologian was quite distinct from the Institut. But I do not think he is correct in de-emphasizing the influence of the members of the Institut on Tillich's thought.[41]

Economics was never of independent, isolated concern to Tillich. The discipline was of importance as related to humanistic needs, and the ethical and psychological implications of economics interested Tillich. Tillich stood in debt to both Marx and Freud and, like his friend Herbert Marcuse, these perspectives were synthesized into his own. An example of the tensions in thought produced by this synthesizing is available for examination in *The Protestant Era*.[42] On one page, he wrote:

> The economic sphere is the most important historical factor—not in all times, as some dogmatic Marxists assert—but certainly within bourgeois capitalism.[43]

However, on the very next page, his psychological interest became apparent:

---

[41]For a perspective critical of the work of John Stumme, Guy Hammond, and myself on the Institut influence on Tillich see Terence O'Keeffe, "Tillich and the Frankfurt School," in *Theonomy and Autonomy*, ed. John J. Carey (Macon GA: Mercer University Press, 1984) 67-87.

[42]The references are to the original edition of *The Protestant Era* (Chicago: University of Chicago Press, 1948). The later edition was abridged, and in the process, the last three chapters, the most limited to the immediate postwar scene and the most socialist, were eliminated.

[43]Ibid., 239.

But more important than the immediate economic consequences of the monopolistic stage of liberal economy are its psychological effects on the masses.[44]

The two claims for importance do not contradict each other, but they show the tension between a Marxist claim for the centrality of economics and a tendency to focus on the psychological state of the masses. He writes: "These effects have created a revolutionary situation in the whole Western world." This bearing of the tension between psychological and economic sources of political change is characteristic of Tillich and his friends associated with the critical theory of the Frankfurt School. It is not necessarily an anti-Marxist move in scholarship, since some today would regard it as a proper development of Marx's own insights. But such work, before the views of Fromm and Marcuse were widely known, was quite radical and controversial.

In response to Clark A. Kucheman's critical essay on Tillich's socialism from a capitalist perspective, Tillich again indicated the subordination of economics to humanist concerns in his thought:

In the most extended description of my social-political ideas, the book *Die Sozialistische Entscheidung*, I have developed a many-sided image of a transformed society in which the economic element is definitively subordinated.[45]

His ideas about economics can only be grasped in his broadened humanistic perspective. In his view of a transformed order, which is basically socialist, some feudal and bourgeois elements remain.

Certain ideas about the economic order which were Marxist in inspiration disappeared from his writing and speaking after World War II. These ideas are present in the original edition of *The Protestant Era*, but absent or muted in the abridged edition and lacking from later speeches and writing on society. The social context in which he worked was different, and the "controlled capitalism" of the United States, with its powerful trade unionist movement, was not the Berlin of the interwar period. The concept of the

---

[44]Ibid., 240.

[45]Paul Tillich, "Rejoinder," *The Journal of Religion* 46/1/2 (January 1966): 190.

proletariat was obsolete in the United States. The problems of social injustice in the United States, primarily those of poverty and race, were problems of dehumanization which were not best addressed by the categories of early twentieth-century German religious socialism.

It was irrelevant to contend in the United States that (1) the masses were becoming more impoverished, or (2) that the increase of "unproductive capital in the banks"[46] drove the country into imperialism and war, or (3) that the rapidity of technological advance demanded by capitalism would necessarily mean increasing structural unemployment, or (4) that the proletariat was a revolutionary vanguard. However, the weakening of the persuasiveness of some of Marx's economic ideas did not allow his thought to be confined to the past. It had influenced modern thinking to the extent that an analysis of capitalist society, without reference to his thought, was unlikely to be productive. Tillich did not want to return to the illusions of harmony in the marketplace, or justify contemporary democracies on the basis of an idealism of progress.[47]

Tillich knew the extent to which the workers of the Berlin suburbs were reduced in many aspects of their being to a mass level. The system of production, which included a standardization of work, a standardization of a low wage, a uniformity of housing opportunities, and a sameness of education to prepare them for industry determined their lives. He thought Marx was right in emphasizing that the system of material production was fundamental. However, he criticized Marxists who would simply deduce all aspects of culture from the system of production. To the extent that Marx rigidly deduced the superstructure from the substructure of production, Tillich was critical of his theory, also. For Tillich:

> The economic sphere is itself a complex sphere, to which all other spheres essentially contribute, so that they cannot be derived from it, although they can never be separated from it.[48]

In economics, as elsewhere, his direct dependence on members of his discussion circle was acknowledged. Edward Heimann and Adolf Löwe, who had been members of his Kairos Circle in Berlin, for example, were the

---

[46]*Protestant Era*, 224.
[47]Ibid., 260.
[48]Ibid., 258.

mentors of the economic theory in *The Socialist Decision*. The setting of economic reflections in the broad social context was a characteristic of the Frankfurt School.

C. The Fellowship of Social Christians

The Reinhold Niebuhr family had assisted in Tillich's transition from Frankfurt to New York. So his transition into the Niebuhr-influenced Fellowship of Social Christians was one inevitable consequence of his move to New York City. When Tillich considered moving to Manchester, England, to join his colleague Adolf Löwe, Reinhold Niebuhr prevailed upon him to remain at Union so that they could found a school of theology there. They shared more in common in their social ethics than they did in their theology. They both were Christian realists and until the end of World War II both were socialists.

Tillich joined the group which had functioned earlier under different names. The fellowship became better known when it began publishing *Radical Religion* in 1935.[49] The fellowship evolved, with Niebuhr's leadership remaining a constant, as it changed its name to the Frontier Fellowship and then to Christian Action in September 1951. In 1954, the Christian Action form of the society had "850 members in 42 states and 9 countries."[50] Its projects included support for the Southern Tenant Farmers Union and the founding, funding, and support of the interracial Delta Cooperative Farm in Mississippi before the civil rights movement of the 1950s.

The central supports of the Fellowship of Social Christians and *Radical Religion* in its earliest days were Reinhold Niebuhr, Winnifred Wygal, Eduard Heimann, Joseph F. Fletcher, Sherwood Eddy, Paul Tillich, John C. Bennett, Harry Bone, and Rose Terlin. The work of the fellowship was that of social theology, and its political and economic commitments were in terms of socialism. The group was noncommunist but understood itself to be in debt to Karl Marx in terms of social philosophy, if not in metaphysics. The editor's philosophy included, in 1943, a program of socialization of major centers of property.

---

[49]John C. Bennett, "Tillich and the Fellowship of Socialist Christians," *North American Paul Tillich Society Newsletter* 16 (October 1980): 3.

[50]Reinhold Niebuhr, "The Significance of the Growth of Christian Action," *Christianity and Crisis* 14/4 (22 March 1954): 30.

It is quite obvious that these forms of "private" property which represent primarily social power, and the most potent social power of our day at that, cannot remain in private hands. The socialization of such property is a *sine qua non* of social justice.[51]

The earliest form of the society regarded Christian ethics as being in direct conflict with the ethos of capitalist individualism and its structures. The groups recognized the class struggle and called for "the aggressive assertion of the rights of the exploited and the disinherited." They hoped that class warfare could be avoided by all classes coming to recognize the need for radical social change. This position recognized the "covert and overt violence inherent in the present order."[52]

The declaration of objectives called for the application of Christian ethics to individual lives, to unite radical groups within the churches to strengthen their socialist influence, to encourage revolutionary social change, and to help the radical social movement to be more infused with "the religious spirit."

Members were obligated to take on Christian socialist discipline for social action and witness, including joining labor unions, organizing within their churches, joining in public social conflicts nonviolently, supporting socialist political parties, and paying on a "graded tax schedule" for causes that supported the aims of the "cooperative commonwealth" and the society itself. The "graded tax schedule" was highly progressive and required as contribution all the net taxable income of a family beyond $8,000. These taxes were eventually dropped as being overly legalistic.

Much of the work of the society retreats and publications was theological. Both Tillich and Niebuhr were writing their major theological works during the time of the society's life.[53] John Bennett listed five areas that he remembered as the major emphases of political-economic discussion in the society: (1) the continued evaluation of Soviet communism through the late 1930s; (2) response to the rise of fascism (both Tillich and Heimann were

---

[51]Note on A. T. Mollegen, "The Common Convictions of the Fellowship of Socialist Christians," *Christianity and Society* (Spring 1943): 28.

[52]"The Fellowship of Socialist Christians," reprinted in *Radical Religion* (Winter 1973): 7.

[53]Bennett, "Tillich and the Fellowship," 3.

refugees from Nazism); (3) response to World War II; (4) the movement away from the Socialist Party to the New Deal with Niebuhr himself campaigning for Franklin D. Roosevelt in the closing days of the 1936 campaign;[54] and (5) evolution in the thought about socialism. A. T. Mollegen's summary of 1943 had described the society as supporting autonomous public agencies like TVA, cooperatives, socialization of centers of economic power, and organized labor.[55]

In the closing years of the fellowship, as it merged into Christian Action, the membership grew to 1,200 and there were about a dozen local chapters. Much of the new organization's energy was put into combating the McCarthy movement and spirit in the early 1950s. Effort was also made to distinguish Christian social action from Marxism. Other foes that received critiques were the various movements trying to synthesize capitalist individualism and Christianity. The group also encouraged a positive relationship between Christian faith and democratic political participation, and they seemed to prevail in clarifying that issue.[56]

Though Tillich was closer personally to Wilhelm Pauck, in matters political he allied with his colleagues John Bennett and Reinhold Niebuhr. On one occasion he dropped a note to John Bennett requesting his political advice, writing: "What shall I do? You are my father confessor in politics and religion!"[57] Tillich did not shift as far away from religious socialism as Niebuhr. In 1955 he left the group as he moved to Harvard. He summarized the group's evolution noting that Niebuhr had changed the most with Eduard Heimann, his old friend from Berlin, close behind. Tillich thought he had changed less and John Bennett even less so. He indicated the need to join psychological insights to sociological ones to understand and resist the pressures of mass society. He noted that the group as a whole no longer trusted the socialist analysis while it still struggled politically for fragmentary

---

[54]Conversation with Charles Brown (2 June 1991), who presented evidence from Richard Fox, *Reinhold Niebuhr*, and independent confirmations of those who heard him speak.

[55]The five points are summarized in Bennett, "Tillich and the Fellowship," 3-5.

[56]Robert T. Handy, "Christian Action in Perspective," *Christianity and Society* 21 (Summer 1956): 10-14.

[57]Letter from Tillich to Bennett, 18 August 1959; copy in author's collection.

realizations of the Kingdom. He celebrated the fellowship and closed by exhorting the group to continue the prophetic spirit, but to "Do it better!"[58]

The leaders of Christian Action were involved in many other similar causes, in their denominations and in the ecumenical movement. Niebuhr was unable to give it as much energy after his 1952 stroke. The burden of financing a national office detracted from the work. Denominations were evolving their own social action programs, and the National Council of Churches was promising a vital program in social analysis and action. All these factors combined with a conviction that fresh analysis of the political economy was needed rather than the continued application of a fading Christian socialist consensus. *Christianity and Society* was discontinued in the summer of 1956, after the national office of Christian Action was closed in February. For about twenty years these ventures of publication, fellowship, study, and support of social action had received Niebuhr's support. They also had drawn the Union Theological students into expressions of social thought and action and become part of their education. During Niebuhr's lifetime, the intellectual legacy was continued by *Christianity and Crisis* while the political work was directed into Americans for Democratic Action and the Liberal Party. The mainline church expanding social action and education programs and staffs also continued much of the work of the fellowship. As for Tillich, his organizational work faded as he left Union and pushed to complete his *Systematic Theology*.

---

[58]Paul Tillich, "Past and Present Reflections on Christianity and Society" (May 1955) 4, Tillich Papers.

Chapter 10

Religious Socialism and Liberation Theology

The religious socialism of Paul Tillich preceded liberation theology and consequently never entered into dialogue with it. Liberation theologians of Latin America do not know much about Tillich's religious socialism and have not engaged it in dialogue. This chapter is an attempt to bring into dialogue two traditions which themselves have not engaged in conversation.

The North American Paul Tillich Society has maintained some conversation with both parties to the dialogue. Even in its prefounding days, when the Society existed as a consultation in the American Academy of Religion, attention was given to Tillich's social thought and its parallels to liberation theology. Several papers and published essays of the Society have either discussed parallels or suggested that the discussion between the two movements would be fruitful.[1] Similarly, the Society of Christian Ethics had religious-socialist members who were interested in both Tillich's social thought and in liberation theology. Enthusiasts for Tillich are in many cases, but not all, interested in keeping the memory of his religious socialism alive. There are individuals scattered throughout the continents who understand their analysis of social reality in a mixture of liberation and religious-socialist themes. In my mind's eye, I visualize a thin red line of Tillich scholars around the world who still work out of Tillich's socialist convictions. In the

---

[1]John B. Lounibos, "Paul Tillich's Structures of Liberation," in *Tilllich Studies, 1975,* ed. John J. Carey (Tallahassee: Florida State University, 1975). H. Frederick Reisz, Jr., "Liberation Theology of Culture: A Tillichian Perspective," in *Kairos and Logos,* ed. John J. Carey (Cambridge: North American Paul Tillich Society, 1978). Theodore Runyon, "Tillich's Understanding of Revolution," in *Theonomy and Autonomy,* ed. John J. Carey (Macon GA: Mercer University Press, 1984). James W. Champion, "Tillich and the Frankfurt School," in *Soundings* 169/4 (Winter 1986). Dennis P. McCann, "Tillich's Religious Socialism: 'Creative Synthesis' or Personal Statement?" in *The Thought of Paul Tillich,* ed. James Luther Adams, Wilhelm Pauck, Roger Lincoln Shinn (San Francisco: Harper & Row, 1985).

United States, as distinct from much of the rest of the world, religious socialism is not very alive. My friend, Dorothee Sölle, in a meeting of the late religious-socialist working group of the American Academy of Religion, referred to religious socialism in the United States as a discussion group "with neither a church nor a party."

The student of liberation theology will find only occasional references to Tillich in the literature. Rubem Alves's book *Protestantism and Repression*[2] utilizes Tillich extensively in delineating his ideal type of Right-Doctrine-Protestantism to show the repressive tendencies of modern Protestantism. But he makes no use of the liberating possibilities of Tillich's religious socialism. Gustavo Gutiérrez has not referred to Tillich's religious socialism in his writings. In liberation theology, references to the German situation of the Nazi period are largely in terms of Bonhoeffer or the Confessing Church.

The comparison between Gustavo Gutiérrez's and Paul Tillich's religious socialism seemed appropriate. They share many common emphases. They both emphasize personal dimensions of religious life as expressed in mysticism and in human psychology. Marxism, class struggle, social revolution, and socialism are significant in their thought. They are concerned to maintain their respective traditions while participating in reforming those traditions. They both express the characteristics Erik Erikson assigned to the term *homo religiosii*. They agonized personally over the inadequacies of their received traditions and in articulating new visions of religion transformed the human consciousness of many people with a worldwide impact.

The two belong to a type of religious social thought. Comparison between the two is within a type, it cannot express the degree of dissonance that Tillich's work between Buddhism and Christianity exhibited.[3] This examination of their social thought focuses on *justice* and *revolution* while touching on related concerns.

Justice

Ismael Garcia's dissertation directed by James Gustafson was published as *Justice in Latin American Theology of Liberation*.[4] The focus of the

---

[2]Rubem A. Alves, *Protestantism and Repression: A Brazillian Case Study* (Maryknoll NY: Orbis Books, 1985).

[3]Paul Tillich, *Christianity and the Encounter of the World Religions* (New York: Columbia University Press, 1963).

[4]Ismael Garcia, *Justice in Latin American Theology of Liberation* (Atlanta:

work is on Hugo Assmann, José Míguez Bonino, Gustavo Gutiérrez, and José Porfirio Miranda. Gutiérrez is regarded as the classical figure of the movement and his work is consulted most regularly in the book. The first major chapter entitled "The Centrality of Justice in Latin American Theology of Liberation" argues that justice is the central concern of liberation theology. However, Garcia is forced to argue that though "social justice is central to the reflection and practice of liberation theologians, they never present a clear statement of what they mean by this frequently used term."[5]

The argument develops that any formal definition of justice would come from the needs of the poor. Warnings are given against the dangers of an ahistorical understanding of justice. Justice may not be defined abstractly. The author admits even in the conclusion that the authors of liberation theology remain unclear about the meaning of justice, but that the elements necessary for a clear definition are available in their work. The elements may be there but the process of clarifying the relationship of those elements would still be a pretty abstract piece of work. Or maybe they cannot be clarified without more analysis.

Throughout Garcia's book the term *liberation*, which is defined abstractly, dominates the term *justice*. The work of liberation theology is focused mostly on conceptual work for overthrowing injustice rather than the building work of justice. Justice certainly presupposes order and liberation theology could not advocate order in any Latin American country at the present. Hannah Arendt's distinction between the working of fighting for freedom and structuring freedom is relevant here. Garcia may have been led to focus on justice because of the necessary fight against injustice.

Garcia's conclusion discusses aspects of justice from a liberation perspective. These aspects are as follows.

1. Justice is based on each person's equality of worth.
2. Justice reflects humanity's social nature.
3. Justice is based on a criterion of need.
4. Justice means "the eradication of all those forms of inequality that enable some to exploit and dominate others."
5. All are entitled to economic well-being and political freedom.

John Knox Press, 1987).
    [5]Ibid., 11.

6. Institutions which care for the poor deserve support in a just society.
7. Justice implies the rich nations helping the poor nations.
8. Well-being has a priority over freedom given the historical struggles.
9. In the Latin American context, only some form of socialism will lead to justice.[6]

The perspective of Garcia is that "justice can only be properly defined in the activity of bringing it about in light of the concrete situations that limit its realization."[7] This passion for the liberation process motivates this study and allows Jacques Maritain and other theorists who used natural law theory to define justice to be set aside. The natural law theory produced understandings of justice which informed Christian Democratic parties' reform efforts. But when reform has been overcome, Garcia argues, the process called for is liberation. If socialist liberation is not on the foreseeable horizon for most of Latin America, we are called back to look at alternative definitions of justice. For many countries striving to creep out from under military government or aspiring to moderate one party government some of the more traditional definitions of justice may still be helpful.

Karen Lebacqz[8] finds the contributions of Miranda and Gutiérrez to a theory of justice to be in their staying close to a biblical meaning of righteousness. She explains that for Miranda and Gutiérrez justice is real, right relationships. This requires special attention to the poor, for their situation must be altered. Justice is seen by their denunciations of injustice, particularly the injustices done to the poor of Latin America. The world is characterized by injustice and God's work is particularly the righting of the wrongs that oppress the poor.

The important contribution of Gutiérrez requires an understanding of the Peruvian context which his translated works do not provide. The social research of his institute is published in Peru in *Paginas*. The Las Casas Center is located in Rimac, a barriada of Lima. Tillich suggested that the writings of socialism are unintelligible without a commitment to the social struggle

---

[6]Ibid., 190-93.

[7]Ibid., 120.

[8]Karen Lebacqz, *Six Theories of Justice* (Minneapolis: Augsburg Publishing House, 1986).

reflected in socialism. Moreover, the writings of Gutiérrez are not intelligible without a commitment to solidarity with the poor to change their social situation. The poverty of Peru which leads to starvation and exploitation is the necessary context for understanding Gutiérrez's work. A remarkable book by Curt Cadorette[9] is a necessary introduction to the Peruvian poverty of which Gutiérrez writes. Cadorette makes clear to North American readers the context of the sharp contrast between the poverty of the poor Indians of Lima and the benefits of capitalism to the wealthy of Lima. Moreover, he puts meaning into the footnotes of Gutiérrez to Peruvian thinkers upon whom Gutiérrez draws. For years Gutiérrez taught a course based on the ideas of Mariátegui of adapting Marxist analysis to a critical dialectical understanding of Peruvian society and religion.[10] Similarly, Gutiérrez's friendship with and utilization of the Peruvian social-novelist José Maria Arguldas reveals the depth of the truth captured in the title of Gutiérrez's book *We Drink from Our Own Wells*. His work draws upon these Peruvian thinkers and current sociological-anthropological research, including the work of his own institute. His utilization of Marxist critiques of society was indigenous, drawing upon a long history of its critical application to the society of Peru. In the immediate context it had to take account of the new reality of Christian base communities in which he invested his life, the shifts in ecclesiastical politics, the realities of the threat from *Sendero Luminoso*, or Shining Path guerilla movement, the possibilities of the Alan Garcia regime, the ever-present threat of military coup, the major players of international business, and the intervention by outside governmental pressures. Given the fluidity of all of these realities, Gutiérrez's realism led to shifts in his emphasis while continuing to look for openings in the situation which could give his people, the poor, a chance to improve their situation. His writings on justice and revolution are within the perceptions of a radically unjust, repressive social situation.

Gutiérrez writes of "institutionalized injustice" following the frequent use of it at the Pueblo conference. One finds more references to institutionalized injustice in his writing than institutionalized justice. One of his clearest paragraphs on justice is that the proclamation of Jesus of the Kingdom of God

---

[9]Curt Cadorette, *From the Heart of the People: The Theology of Gustavo Gutiérrez* (Oak Park IL: Meyer-Stone Books, 1988).
[10]Ibid., 76.

is the proclaiming of a Kingdom of justice and liberation. Justice for him is absolute:

> The only justice is the one that assaults all the consequences and expressions of this cleavage in friendship. The only justice is the definitive justice that builds, starting right now, in our conflict-filled history, a kingdom in which God's love will be present and exploitation abolished.[11]

Justice is used to denounce the present, and as a perspective from which all oppressors will be overthrown. Liberation or the overthrow of the structures dominates the writing, rather than justice as something that the rulers could now deliver.

In his meditations on *Job*, Gutiérrez makes it clear that though justice is essential to the meaning of God, the meaning of God is not circumscribed by any theories of justice. Job has been freed in the end from "the temptation of imprisoning God in a narrow conception of justice."[12] The theology of retribution is abandoned but the obligation of doing justice with God is affirmed. We seem to lack in Gutiérrez that which Karen Lebacqz and Ismael Garcia were looking for—"a theory of justice."

Justice was not the central term of Paul Tillich's religious-socialist polemic against capitalism. He did not often judge capitalism by the criteria of justice; rather, he assumed the contradictions within capitalism were going to destroy it. He regarded the spirit of capitalism as the proclamation of a self-sufficient finitude, and his basic argument with it was that it was not open to the experience of the unconditioned. Capitalism encouraged alienation, competition, and meaninglessness, and it was self-destructive. Justice became a central concept for Tillich in his American experience when the socialist cause or at least the expression of it in the categories of the young Marx seemed irrelevant to the American social scene.

Exceptions to the above generalization are three of Tillich's writings: "Grundlinen des Religiosen Sozialismus" (1923);[13] "Man and Society in Reli-

---

[11]Gustavo Gutiérrez, *The Power of the Poor in History: Selected Writings*, trans. Robert R. Barr (Maryknoll NY: Orbis Books, 1983) 14.

[12]Gustavo Gutiérrez, *On Job* (Maryknoll NY, Orbis Books, 1987) 91.

[13]*Blatter für Religiosen Sozialismus* IV, Heft 8/10 (1923); also GW 2 (1962); translated by James Luther Adams and Victor Nuovo as "Basic Principles of

gious Socialism (1943);[14] and "Die Sozialistische Entscheidung" (1932).[15] These writings do not push the discussion of justice to the ontological depths of his later work. None of the works use the criteria of justice as a weapon by which to criticize society the way Reinhold Niebuhr did during the same period. It further could be said that the Hegelian background is just below the surface in the 1923 work and the 1943 essay is more reminiscent of the political-philosophical discussion in England and America.

According to the 1943 essay, human nature bears the claim that every human being be recognized as a person.[16] There is a natural equality that is the equality of claim to express one's creativity—later he would say "power of being." "This is the ultimate criterion of justice."[17] Justice concedes to finitude that the contingent characteristics of human *existence* prevent absolute equality. But justice requires that all accidental differences— by which Tillich meant sex, race, intelligence, strength, birth—ought not infringe upon *essential* equality. Therefore, all the structures that reinforce *essential* inequality were to be opposed. Fascism, monopolistic capitalism, and class-determined education all result in dehumanization, or the violation of the opportunity to express one's power of being, and therefore they were opposed to justice.

Justice plays an important role in Tillich's most profound socialist writing. *Die sozialistische Entscheidung (The Socialist Decision)* was written in 1932 under the pressures of the reactionary seizure of power in Berlin by Chancellor Franz Von Papen and the romantic-revolutionary gains by the Nazis. In Tillich's analysis, neither party represented the claims of justice. They both appealed to myths of the origins of life and not to a future shaped by the critique of justice. Tillich argued for an understanding of socialism that would be religious in its respect for the origins of being and prophetic in its insistence on justice. The symbol of the future is "expecta-

---

Religious Socialism," in *Political Expectation*, ed. James Luther Adams, 58-88 (New York: Harper & Row, 1971; repr.: ROSE 1, Macon GA: Mercer University Press, September 1981).

[14]*Christianity and Society* 8/4 (1943): 10-20.

[15]GW 2 (1962): 219-363; later translated as *The Socialist Decision*, trans. Franklin Sherman (New York: Harper & Row, 1977; repr.: Washington DC: University Press of America, 1982).

[16]*Christianity and Society* 8/4 (1943): 17.

[17]Ibid.

tion." Expectation expresses the direction of humanity; it is the power of human transformation. He finds the power of expectation in the longings of the proletariat to overcome the demonic condition under which they survive. In the book, the discussion of expectation is elaborately developed. It is a powerful precursor to the later theologies of hope. This development of expectation, which is a presentation of eschatology in secular-autonomous terms, obscures the importance of justice in the argument. Still, justice, though not elaborated, is central. The call of the future is that of justice. Justice is the demand arising in human consciousness that calls for the future to be different. Justice requires expectation. As Tillich puts it, "The ought is the fulfillment of the is. Justice is the true power of being."[18]

Justice means "the dignity of being free, of being the bearer of the fulfillment implied in the origin. This recognition of the equal dignity of the 'Thou' and the 'I' is justice."[19] Here, though not stated, is the definition of justice as the second commandment of Jesus: "Love your neighbor as yourself." Similarly, to the religious reader the trusting in expectation for the proletariat is similar to really living as if one expected an answer in history to the daily prayer "Thy Kingdom come." Tillich's argument in the book depends upon the proletariat and the proletariat's ability to understand its possibilities of transforming its historical situation. The book is committed to the possibilities of the proletariat. Of course very few of the proletariat could have understood the book if they had read it. Nazi suppression of the book in 1933 made even an attempted reading of it a near impossibility.

Beyond the justice rooted in the I-Thou encounter, Tillich speaks of justice as the consent to the social contract. Justice is therefore necessary to power as distinct from force. Consent to power, in the long run, depends upon the recognition of justice.

> Consent is given because those who assent to the exercise of power consider the way in which the unified will is executed to be just. The exercise of power appears to be just when all members of a society can acknowledge that their own will is contained in the will of the whole.[20]

---

[18]*The Socialist Decision*, 6.
[19]Ibid.
[20]Ibid., 139.

Tillich perhaps overestimated the need for assent to a successful party's version of justice by other groups. The Nazis demonstrated the power of terror and force in dissuading groups with alternative visions of justice from competing for power. Tillich's hope in linking justice to power was to dissuade socialists from utopian politics of justice that neglected power. For him, "the problem of power proves to be the problem of a concrete justice."[21] In his perspective, the Social Democrats had failed to "exercise and consolidate" power when it had come to them. Socialism in his view had been stronger in working on elaborating justice than it had been in exercising power. The state depends upon both justice and power, and effective politics required an understanding of their mutual dependence. Justice for Tillich in this 1932 writing was the movement toward the classless society and the planned economy. It was antithetical both to the revolutionary Nazis and the reactionary Junkers. It depended upon the emergence of both a tougher and a more religious socialism. The failure of such a movement to emerge permitted the Nazis to win and consolidate power without justice and for barbarism to reign in a formerly Christian Europe.

Tillich's 1954 work *Love, Power, and Justice* is his most systematic discussion of justice. Here he unites reflection on justice to two concepts on which he had worked for years, love and power. He attempted to find a way between cynics who would reduce justice to the meaning of power and idealists who would assert the demands of justice without reference to power. He sought to overcome dichotomies in Protestant ethics between justice and love without collapsing them into each other.

The method of the volume may be confusing.[22] I would regard the method as that of conceptual analysis of basic categories of ethics and politics. Tillich asserts that such elaboration is the work of ontology. Consequently he calls what I would regard as conceptual analysis of terms that have ontological implications as well as other meanings, ontological analysis. Also much of the method is etymology, but Tillich in his search for "root" meanings of terms also regards this as ontology. This difference in naming the method Tillich uses does not vitiate the results for me. It does mean, however, that the following of Tillich's argument leaves the conclusions as

---

[21]Ibid., 141.

[22]See Alistair M. Macleod, *Paul Tillich: An Essay on the Role of Ontology in His Philosophical Theology* (London: George Allen & Unwin, 1973).

to the relationship of love, power, and justice as one model reflecting several human, even political, decisions rather than seeing it as a conclusion necessarily rooted in the way things ultimately are. Tillich's Protestant principle forces him to agree with the above conclusion.

"Justice is the form in which the power of being actualizes itself."[23] In Tillich's ontology, all beings drive towards transcending themselves. This drive toward transcendence produces competition, and justice is the form that allows creativity to be expressed without destroying the whole.

The principle of justice is love that contains (a) adequacy, (b) equality, (c) personality, and (d) liberty. Community or fraternity was rejected as part of the formal definition of justice by Tillich, yet his rejection of it seemed to slight the importance of the issue. Community is certainly more than "an emotional principle adding nothing essential to the rational concept of justice."[24] All through the discussion of the principles of justice, Tillich can be seen analyzing the concepts as they appeared historically, but also stipulating his preferred meanings. The stipulations reflect his existentialist background and his protest against dehumanization.

The principles of justice are applied at various levels of justice. He lists (a) the intrinsic; (b) the tributive, including (i) distributive, (ii) attributive, and (iii) retributive; and (c) the transforming. The transforming level of justice is where the biblical roots of Tillich's discussion of justice are most clear. Creative or transforming justice is the form of reuniting love that does what is necessary for the reunion of beings.

> Love does not do more than justice demands, but love is the ultimate principle of justice. Love reunites; justice preserves what is to be united. It is the form in which and through which love performs its work. Justice in its ultimate meaning is creative justice, and creative justice is the form of reuniting love.[25]

The background of Tillich's discussion of justice reaches through his entire thought, but perhaps enough has been said to provide a context for understanding his aim. The influence of Hegel is particularly strong in *Love,*

---

[23]Paul Tillich, *Love, Power, and Justice*, (New York: Oxford University Press, 1954) 56.

[24]Ibid., 62.

[25]Ibid., 71.

Power, and Justice, and the fragment on love is particularly in the background. Tillich's oft-repeated statement that the relationship between theology and politics was the driving force of Hegel's system applies only a little less accurately to Tillich.

Tillich recognized the need for a socialist ethic while promoting socialism, but he did not write it. Consequently his term *justice* was underdeveloped in his most socialist period. Despite Garcia's claim for its centrality in liberation theology, it appears there to be subsumed under the categories of liberation. Only in the older Tillich does it become a central term and here it is expressed as the form that allows life to flourish and not as a denunciation of the present. Tillich's discussion of justice can be read from his earlier commitments of passionate, religious socialism, but the book itself is not written that way. The formal presentation of justice, which the liberation theologians avoided, seems to lose its force of moral indignation against the present in Tillich. In this book, particularly, the absence of the proletariat is felt. Tillich did not find a proletariat in America and the force of his socialism was lost. He did not have the liberation special class of the poor. His groups are national groups, not classes, in this writing. Tillich does not expect fulfillment in history; Gutiérrez demands social fulfillment and righteousness. It may be just this passionate zeal for overthrowing structures of injustice that prevented Gutiérrez from presenting an adequate formal definition.

Revolution

As a religious socialist Paul Tillich supported the revolution that ended the German Empire. He hoped the revolution would both push the social changes in a socialist direction, and become more consciously a religious movement. He tried in the pre-Nazi period to defend the humanistic gains of the revolution, and in 1932 he urged it to deepen its socialist commitments. If one regards the Nazi coup of 1933 as a revolution, Tillich participated in losing a revolution. His urging the defeat of National Socialism from 1933 to 1945 could be seen as a counterrevolutionary struggle by a political exile, though I would rather regard his efforts as a continuation of the religious-socialist revolution that was never achieved.

In his *Systematic Theology*, Tillich discussed revolution as part of historical ambiguity in relationship to the Kingdom of God. Sentences recall his fight with Emmanuel Hirsch, for example, "Demonic consequences result from absolutizing the fragmentary fulfillment of the aim of history within history."[26] Also, the discussions of personal bitterness and the disruption of human ties must refer to the conflicts with his friend turned enemy.[27] Other sentences are reminiscent of his own socialist revolutionary essay: "In such movements of expectation, however unrealistic they may be, the fighting Kingdom of God scores a victory against the power of complacency in its different sociological and psychological forms."[28] By the time of publication of this volume, Tillich had lived a long time with revolution (1918–1963), and he can neither deny the hopes of revolutionaries nor expect the fulfillment of those hopes. He remembers his own excesses and also the power of hope. There is no general solution: the status quo movements and churches need the spirit of transformation, the prophetic movements and churches need the reminder of the ambiguity of history and of individual fulfillment in the Kingdom of God.

Revolutions are sometimes the only way to release new creativity. They may be crushed in counterrevolution, and suppression may mean less creativity than before the struggle. Tillich rejected the antirevolutionary bias of much of the tradition of the church while cautioning of the dangers of revolution.[29]

Gutiérrez regards theology of liberation as a style of reflection in solidarity with the poor who are struggling to abolish injustice. It is in alliance often with Marxists. Its goal is to assist in building a new society. In the new society, the ownership of the means of production will not be in private nor foreign hands. Obviously in *A Theology of Liberation* a revolution overthrowing the present rulers was a goal. The theology itself will be verified "by active, effective participation in the struggle which the exploited social classes have undertaken against their oppressors."[30] Gutiérrez's early writing is clear enough to be understood as advocating the church changing sides, raising consciousness, forming a critical-supportive theology of revolution by the poor. Often his own perspective is hidden in his exegesis of the

---

[26]Paul Tillich, *Systematic Theology*, 3 vols. (Chicago: University of Chicago Press, 1951–1963) 3:390. (Hereafter cited as ST with volume and page numbers.)

[27]ST 3:343-44.

[28]ST 3:391.

[29]ST 3:388-89.

[30]Gustavo Gutiérrez, *A Theology of Liberation*, 15th anniversary ed. (Maryknoll NY: Orbis Press, 1988) 174.

revolutionary potential of the documents of Medellion and Pueblo which he had a hand in writing. His advocacy of social revolution is clearest in the section "Towards a Transformation of the Latin American Reality."[31]

By the time *A Theology of Liberation* was published in English, his writing in Spanish eliminated any doubt as to his meaning.[32] The poor were being heard but only by those engaged in the revolutionary struggle against the Latin American order. The poor were to end the class society, appropriate the means of production, undertake their own political order, and engage in the creation of a new consciousness.[33] The coming into the revolutionary practice he described as "the *most important fact* in the life of the Latin American Christian community."[34] Admitting some dependence on the theologies of revolution, Gutiérrez distinguishes the popular movements from such theologies. For here in the popular movements the thinking is by the people within the struggle rather than it being thought outside and applied to the struggle. This distinction is not easily grasped, but it does, I believe, point to a distinction between Gutiérrez's theology of transformation and Tillich's philosophy of transformation.

Gutiérrez really is more of the people than Tillich ever was of the proletariat. Tillich's early ministry was with the proletariat, but his life was with the intellectuals after World War I. Gutiérrez's research and much of his teaching is with the poor. Of course the programs of both were dependent on the potency of the class for which they articulated socialism. Tillich's proletariat seemed to disappear in postwar America. Gutiérrez's poor seem unlikely to disappear in Latin America. Given the immediacy of the suffering, and the program of revolution, we need only to see if Gutiérrez maintains any of Tillich's sense of ambiguity about revolution. The ambiguity is not present in his early writing. The task of liberation theology was to assist Christians into the Latin American revolutionary process.[35]

In Gutiérrez's later writing, however, the theme of joining the revolutionary process is muted. Obviously he could not urge Christians to join the

---

[31]Ibid., 63-68.

[32]See *Power of the Poor in History: Selected Writings*, 37; from an essay first published in Spanish in 1973.

[33]Ibid., 37-38. It is probable that this description of the goals of the revolutionary society is Gutiérrez's meaning of justice.

[34]Ibid.

[35]*A Theology of Liberation*, 173.

Shining Path which led a revolutionary struggle in his own country. The national security states have destroyed revolutionary movements throughout Latin America. A sadder, more contemplative Gutiérrez is read in his lectures in Peru in 1982, *We Drink from Our Own Wells*.[36] The mystic, nonactivist writer Henri Nouwen wrote the introduction and seemed to value the spiritual crisis of Central America as "something more than political conflict."

The turn toward spirituality was a possible development from *A Theology of Liberation*. It was only one possible development; Gutiérrez could have developed his theology in terms of social ethics or deeper social analysis. But many have been killed and his writing reflects their martyrdoms, though he does not reflect on Che Gueverra and Camilio Torres as he did in his earlier work. My colleague Gonzalo Castillo speaks of a Gutiérrez evolving out of his emphasis on social revolution. Perhaps such an evolution is necessary as revolution in a socialist direction is not imminent and the persecution is terrible. In his most recent book of meditations, *On Job*, Gutiérrez has also dropped the theme of social revolution. There are cold winds of repression blowing from the Vatican. Finally, if the theology of liberation is to truly be the second act, it must wait upon social revolution in South America to mature before it can reflect upon it. Gutiérrez wrestles with *Job*, finding there an innocent suffering, but he still is calling one to join God in struggling for justice. The choice of *Job* rather than *Exodus* for commentary is significant, however. When Gutiérrez writes here of his Peruvian context, he writes of the incredible suffering, deprivation, terrorism, and oppression. Then he writes: "What we must deal with is not the past, but, unfortunately, a cruel present and a dark tunnel with no apparent end."[37]

Themes of kairos and utopia are still present in Gutiérrez's writing, but they are muted. Kairos refers to a favorable time,[38] but the moment is of the Lord's knocking on the doors of the Latin American church community calling to solidarity, prayer, and deeper spirituality with the poor. The theme of utopia is still of a people building a new world, but the denunciation is

---

[36]Gustavo Gutiérrez, *We Drink from Our Own Wells: The Spiritual Journey of a People* (Maryknoll NY: Orbis Press, 1984).

[37]*On Job*, 102.

[38]*We Drink from Our Own Wells*, 136.

more sorrowful than it was a decade earlier. The annunciation is not so clear. "The process is only beginning."[39]

The muted nature of these once powerful themes is familiar to students of Tillich. Kairos and utopia in Gutiérrez both required the transformation of the condition of the poor. Likewise in Tillich the connection between the proletariat and socialism saved socialism from utopianism. Only through the transformation of the proletariat could socialism arise. In his later years, the waiting expectantly in the sacred void while fighting evil replaced the expectation of the transformation of the proletariat. *The Socialist Decision* and *A Theology of Liberation* are both affirmative of utopian politics even though Tillich avoids the term. Tillich's later affirming of the "spirit of utopia" while avoiding utopianism is more cautious. The religious socialism of the two remains much less demanding in their later years. In both cases it has been brutalized and defeated, in Tillich's case by National Socialism, and for the present, in Gutiérrez's case by the national security state in Chile, by terrorism and murder in other states, and by the dynamics of Peru.

The complexity and the richness of the minds of the two thinkers also contributed to their changing emphases. The frustration of religious socialism in Tillich's case freed him to evolve with more emphasis on psychology and religion and to write his *Systematic Theology*. In the case of Gutiérrez, his more recent writings and speeches are emphasizing spirituality and ecclesiology. The Marxist analysis has faded and his solidarity between the poor and a renewed church is within the bounds of approved Vatican social teaching.

Still, Gustavo's journey goes on.[40] God willing, new insights from the poor of Lima will continue to fertilize his mind. The fading of Marxist categories may lead to a more thoroughly indigenous, more thoroughly Christian, social philosophy.

The accounts of both Gustavo and Paulus reveal dynamic thinkers taking account of their times. Both agreed that discussion of religious socialism required sensitivity to the struggle of the underclasses though they focus on

---

[39]Ibid., 27.

[40]Robert McAffee Brown concludes his short biography of Gutiérrez with a chapter entitled "There Is No Conclusion: The Curtain Stays Up, the Play Goes On, and We Are on Stage," in *Gustavo Gutiérrez* (Atlanta: John Knox Press, 1980). (My use of Gutiérrez's first name in this paragraph is deliberate; it expresses our friendship and sense of comradeship in hope and faith.)

different classes as the bearers of their hopes. Both revealed possibilities in a humane Marxism far removed from a dogmatic reading of Karl Marx on the cruelties of pre-Gorbachev Russian socialism. Both of them require socialism to be open to full religious expression of the people. Both of them are indigenous, we may say, existentialist thinkers. Together they reveal different forms of Christian-oriented reforms of society which the world needs for its health. Christian social philosophy has possibilities for assisting the poor in their struggles and also for the promotion of peace among the more affluent.

The Christian social philosophies of both thinkers were overcome by revolutionary developments. Tillich was driven into exile by the revolutionary Nazis. The World War II victories of the market-oriented democracies of the West and the Communism of the Soviet Union crushed hopes for religious socialism. The counterrevolutionary forces of the Vatican and the United States thwarted liberation theology's political aspirations and sometimes killed its practitioners. But it was the nonviolent revolutions of Eastern Europe and Russia in the late 1980s and early 1990s that really ended socialism and left market-oriented economies as the victors. Latin America rushed to market-oriented reforms, abandoning state-planned or run economic corporations.

So, given the dominance of mixed-economy, market-driven systems, where is Christian social philosophy to turn? It seems that the reform-oriented action philosophies of a Tillich or a Gutiérrez have their heirs still in the parties of the left in Latin America, the socialists in France, Social Democrats in Germany, the Labor party in Great Britain, and liberals in the Democratic party in the U.S. Their commitments will be to emphasize the religious dimensions of depth and justice against the faces of secularism and capitalist greed. The struggle will continue to be to humanize the social organization of the world in the name of God. For the present, reform, not revolution, is the Christian social goal.

Chapter 11

Fundamentalism, Feminism, and Pluralism

Fundamentalism is not simply a religious stance or a theological approach but also a strong political influence in society. Both locally and globally, fundamentalist groups work to silence and resist feminist actions and interreligious endeavors. In the immediate area of my hometown, Louisville, Kentucky, three women have been forced to resign from positions of leadership in various Christian institutions—one from Southern Baptist Seminary, one from St. Meinrad's Roman Catholic Seminary, and one from the Presbyterian Church (U.S.A.), all under pressure from conservative groups inside those denominations. At the United Nations Fourth World Conference on Women and the corresponding NGO Forum on Women in China in 1995, conservative voices called for and in some cases achieved a pulling back from rights that had been championed for women at the United Nations Conference on Population in Egypt in 1994. Interreligious dialogue is attacked through calls for conversion of non-Christians and books that attack academic analyses of pluralism on nonacademic grounds.[1]

Clearly, these conservative and fundamentalist voices cannot be dismissed as insignificant or powerless. Understanding and responding to these conservative and fundamentalist movements is important to political efforts for justice and to theological explorations of truth in a multireligious world.

The relationship of event and symbol in Christology provides a good focus for comparing conservative and liberal approaches. Understanding the

---

[1]Examples include statements by conservative Christians about evangelizing Jews and efforts to convert Mormons in relation to the Southern Baptist Convention in Salt Lake City, Utah, in June 1998. Daniel B. Clendenin's *Many Gods, Many Lords* (Grand Rapids MI: Baker Books, 1995) offers a fundamentalist attack on religious pluralism.

fundamentalists' approach to Jesus as the Christ brings us into the center of their theology and can evoke meaningful comparisons with more liberal theologies. Given the biblicist tendencies of fundamentalist approaches, Tillich's Christology provides a helpful counterpoint. With feminist and pluralist Christologies on the other pole, Tillich's Christology offers a middle position. Finally, all of these approaches are evaluated in terms of the relationship between religious truth and justice.

Setting the Context:
Fundamentalist versus Feminist and Pluralist

Fundamentalist Approach to Christology. In their introduction to *Fundamentalism and Gender*, John S. Hawley and Wayne Proudfoot argue that fundamentalists are not simply literalist interpreters of the Bible but rather are inerrantists who move between literal and nonliteral interpretations.[2] Kathleen C. Boone describes inerrancy as meaning that "the Bible is wholly without error, whether doctrinal, historical, scientific, grammatical, or clerical."[3] Thus, the Bible must be read as the absolute authority, and any apparent contradictions must be resolvable.[4] For many fundamentalists, to suggest that the Bible has error or that portions should be read as not absolute or as symbolic is to undermine its objective certainty and authority.[5] As Proudfoot and Hawley point out, whether fundamentalists read literally or not has to do with preserving this inerrancy.[6]

For fundamentalists, one cannot separate the authority of Christ from the authority of the scriptures. Christ fully supports the authority of scriptures;[7] and the authority of scriptures confirms the authority of Christ. Within this scriptural approach, Boone shows that it is Christ's death that

---

[2] John S. Hawley and Wayne Proudfoot, "Introduction," *Fundamentalism and Gender*, ed. John S. Hawley (Oxford, New York: Oxford University Press, 1994) 13.

[3] Kathleen C. Boone, *The Bible Tells Them So: The Discourse of Protestant Fundamentalism* (Albany NY: State University of New York Press, 1989) 13.

[4] Ibid.

[5] Ibid., 23.

[6] Hawley and Proudfoot, *Fundamentalism and Gender*, 14.

[7] Ibid., 33.

has primary significance, more than his words or deeds, and that more emphasis is put on the Epistles than on the Gospels.[8]

Four of the five fundamentals usually associated with fundamentalism affirm this emphasis on the event of Christ, more than on Jesus' teachings or deeds: the virgin birth, Christ as atonement for sins, physical resurrection, and the second coming of Christ. While some liberal theologians might take all of these terms as symbolic, fundamentalists emphasize their literal and physical meaning. As one conservative writer states, "For Paul and the early Christian community the gospel was not myth, metaphor, or poetry; it was literal, historical narrative."[9] That statement hits at the heart of our issue—event and symbol, portraying them as alternative rather than integrated interpretations.

Feminist and Pluralist Approaches to Christology. While the fundamentalist emphasizes the historical reading of the New Testament as part of the Bible's inerrancy, several feminist and pluralist thinkers focus on the symbolic and metaphorical meanings that can be pulled from the Gospel narratives. For example, Sallie McFague reflects on the metaphor of God as Lover to reflect the passionate love of the world shown in Christ.[10] "God as lover values the world and all its creatures so passionately and totally that God enters into the beloved, becoming one with them."[11] She argues that salvation involves becoming disciples of Jesus, participating in the love and healing of the world, rather than being something that is received.[12] Jesus, then, is not the only figure who reveals passionate, inclusive love; Christians and non-Christians can reveal it in their lives and deaths.[13]

In *Journeys by Heart*, feminist theologian Rita Brock rejects interpretations that focus on the Christ as the individual Jesus.[14] She argues: "I

---

[8]Boone, *The Bible Tells Them So,* 51.

[9]Daniel B. Clendenin, *Many Gods, Many Lords; Christianity Encounters World Religions* (Grand Rapids MI: Baker Books, 1995) 144.

[10]Sallie McFague, *Models of God; Theology for an Ecological, Nuclear Age* (Philadelphia: Fortress Press, 1987) 129. In developing and supporting this metaphor, McFague analyzes biblical stories of Jesus as well as other biblical texts and later theological tradition.

[11]Ibid., 144.

[12]Ibid., 145.

[13]Ibid., 150.

[14]Rita Brock, *Journeys By Heart: A Christology of Erotic Power* (New York: Crossroad, 1991) 52.

believe the individualizing of Christ misplaces the locus of incarnation and redemption. We must find the revelatory and saving events of Christianity in a larger reality than Jesus and his relationship to God/dess or any subsequent individual Christ."[15] Jesus participates in Christ/Community, but he did not start it and does not control it.[16] Central to Brock's Christology, though, are the crucifixion and the resurrection—not as historical events but as images of pain and broken hearts (crucifixion) and the need for community and solidarity, people living with and for each other (resurrection).[17]

Another strongly metaphorical reading of Christ can be found in John Hick's pluralist theology. He argues that one must give up a historical and an ontological understanding of Christ in order to hold a fully pluralist theology.[18] He sees both the historical and ontological approaches as entailing an absolutist claim about Jesus as the Christ that leads to rejection of non-Christian religions. Although the focus in his pluralist works is on the noumenal "Real," a metaphorical or mythical understanding of religious claims is central to his theory as well. In *An Interpretation of Religion*, he argues that "we speak mythologically about the noumenal Real by speaking literally or analogically about its phenomenal manifestations."[19]

These feminist and pluralist theologies challenge the fundamentalist approach to the Bible by emphasizing the metaphorical or symbolic meanings in the biblical narratives rather than reading them as historical descriptions. The stories of the events of Jesus' birth or incarnation, the crucifixion, and the resurrection provide the symbolic context within which the feminist and pluralist theologies are developed. But for Brock and Hick, a literalist reading *prevents* the liberating, transforming message of the gospels. To a fundamentalist, such liberal readings threaten to undermine the absolute authority of the inerrant Bible. Although conservative efforts against women and renewed Christian exclusivism stem from political and social agendas as much as from religious issues, these feminist and pluralist

---

[15]Ibid., 68.

[16]Ibid., 52.

[17]Ibid., 100.

[18]John Hick, *A Christian Theology of Religions: The Rainbow of Faiths* (Louisville KY: Westminster/John Knox Press, 1995) 87-95.

[19]John Hick, *An Interpretation of Religion* (New Haven CT and London: Yale University Press, 1989) 351.

theologies add fuel to the fundamentalist fires of rhetoric against feminism and pluralism.

Comparison. The differences here are rooted in the interrelationship of event and symbol. Even when fundamentalists feel a need to offer a nonliteralist reading of a biblical text, in order to maintain their doctrine of biblical inerrancy, they still do not move to a fully symbolic or metaphorical reading. To extend the length of a day in the creation story in Genesis 1 is not to see a day as a metaphor but rather to extend the meaning in God's time rather than human time. The biblical stories still are read as setting forth events, as presenting scientific, historical truth.

However, the Bible itself contains symbolic and allegorical interpretations of other biblical texts. Paul's interpretation of Christ's death and resurrection in relationship to baptism and the Lord's Supper is a primary example of symbolic interpretation. Thus, the reliance of fundamentalist interpretations on the Epistles privileges Paul's symbolic interpretation above the more direct narrative of the gospel writers. The events of Christ's death and resurrection are central to fundamentalist theology, but the understanding of those already assumes Paul's symbolic interpretations. Since Paul himself had no direct experience of Jesus' death and resurrection as historical events, one might ask how closely tied to the events is his Christology? In contrast to Brock's or Hick's approach, Paul's Christology affirms the death and resurrection both as historical events and as ontological events in which Christians can participate. Brock and Hick, on the other hand see salvation and religious transformation as ontological and historical *in the people* who experience them, but they do not root those events in an ontology that privileges Christ above all others or in a claim of historical truth for the events.

Between these two positions, Tillich's approach is closer to the symbolic interpretations. It is well known that Tillich was deeply critical of fundamentalist and biblicist approaches to theology. Fundamentalists have had no time for Tillich's theology either.[20] Tillich's Christology does have some affinity with the feminist and pluralist thinkers cited here, but there also are important differences that place Tillich in a middle position on the issue of event and symbol in Christology.

---

[20]Boone, *The Bible Tells Them So*, 84.

Event and Symbol in Tillich's Christology

Objective Side. Tillich argues that the event of "Jesus as the Christ" has two sides to it: (1) the fact, Jesus of Nazareth, and (2) people's acceptance of Jesus as the Christ.[21] Although not easily separated in a Christological discussion, the objective, factual side relates to historical and ontological issues while the subjective, receiving side relates to symbolic meanings. Underlying both sides is the relationship of Tillich's Christology to the biblical texts. Rather than the Bible itself being the theological norm, as it is for fundamentalists, Tillich argues that the theological norm is "derived from the Bible in an encounter between Bible and church."[22] Such encounters cannot and should not escape the religious and cultural situation of the church and its theologians.[23] Tillich's theory for developing theological norms includes a central role for the theologian's response, not only to the Bible and the broader Christian tradition but also to his or her particular historical, cultural situation. The Bible, then, is not absolute in itself, but directs the reader toward ultimacy.

Tillich incorporates both the objective and subjective sides of the event in his theological norm of the New Being in Jesus as the Christ. In contrast to fundamentalists but parallel to Brock's and Hick's approaches, Tillich's emphasis is on the subjective response of people rather than on the objectivity and historical accuracy of the biblical texts.

Tillich does address briefly the historical issues relating to Jesus of Nazareth. He argues that the historical fact of the New Being present in a particular human life is central to Christian faith (or else the quest for healing power would have continued).[24] He argues that the actual occurrence of the event of Jesus as the Christ in time and in history provides an "unshakable objective foundation" for revelation and salvation.[25] Yet Tillich also notes that efforts to find the historical Jesus have not provided strong grounding for Christian faith. Historians of early Christianity do assert some "facts"

---

[21]Paul Tillich, *Systematic Theology*, 3 vols. (Chicago: University of Chicago Press, 1951–1963) 2:97. (Hereafter cited as ST, with volume and page numbers.)

[22]ST 1:50-51.

[23]ST 1:52.

[24]ST 2:98.

[25]ST 1:146.

about Jesus with high degrees of probability, but those facts do not provide the basis for Christian faith that Jesus is the Christ.[26] The failure to produce a scientific, mutually accepted scholarly picture of Jesus of Nazareth stems from the nature of the biblical texts as texts of the believing community.

The biblical texts present the early Christian versions of Jesus' words and deeds. For Tillich, the significance of Jesus' words, deeds, and sufferings is not in their content or specific details but rather in their ontological meanings, showing his unity with God and his sacrifice of self.[27] Jesus' teachings and actions are "expressions of the New Being," not qualities that make him the New Being.[28] Given the weak conclusions of scholarly efforts to discover the historical Jesus, Tillich argues that we cannot absolutize the deeds and words of the historical Jesus. Jesus' ethics, doctrines, and ideals for personal and communal life provide examples that point toward absolute ideals but they should not be taken as absolute in themselves.[29] Jesus' words and deeds point to the New Being, but they remain expressions of it rather than absolute forms.

Tillich argues further that Jesus' self-sacrifice "means that in following him we are liberated from the authority of everything finite in him, from his special traditions, from his individual piety, from his rather conditioned worldview, from any legalistic understanding of his ethics. Only as the crucified is he 'grace and truth' and not law."[30] He sees this approach as condemning a Jesus-centered religion or theology. What Tillich focusses on in the biblical picture of the Christ is the "continuous self-surrender of Jesus who is Jesus to Jesus who is the Christ."[31] The event of Jesus as the Christ, then, is not the events of Jesus' life but rather the ontologically significant reality of the New Being manifest in Jesus' negation of himself, symbolized in the Cross.

Thus, when Tillich talks about the *event* of "Jesus as the Christ," he assumes that it has a historical root, but his focus is on the ontological event, the event of the Logos becoming flesh.[32] That event is concrete,

---

[26]ST 2:104.
[27]ST 1:135, 137.
[28]ST 1:135-36.
[29]ST 1:151.
[30]ST 1:134.
[31]ST 1:134.
[32]ST 1:16.

rather than merely mythical or mystical, because the event is a particular, personal life.[33] The distinctive quality of the event of Jesus as the Christ, for Tillich, is the simultaneity of absolute concreteness with absolute universality. The Logos brings the universal dimension while its manifestation in the flesh, in a personal life, brings the concreteness. But the details of that personal life are not central to the theological claim of Jesus as the Christ. The particularity of the event of Jesus as the Christ is ontologically significant because it "has the power of representing everything particular."[34] That Paul can claim to be *in Christ* shows the possibility of participating in the particular event of Jesus as the Christ. Tillich, then, is drawing universal meaning from the concreteness even as he emphasizes the importance of revelation in a particular person.

The facts of Jesus' life cannot be proved absolutely. One cannot even be sure that the name of the New Being was Jesus of Nazareth.[35] Certainty does not stem from the objective, historical side of the event of Jesus as the Christ. Tillich sees all humans and all events as historically conditioned and subject to the limits of finitude. By contrast, fundamentalist approaches exempt both the Bible and their interpretations from historical conditioning and finite limits. Certainty is given through the absoluteness and inerrancy of the biblical texts; by association, their theologies are affirmed as certain and absolute as well.

It is interesting to note that both Tillich and the fundamentalists follow Paul in giving more significance to the death and resurrection of Jesus than to Jesus' words and deeds. Certainly, Tillich goes further in this regard than the fundamentalists because of his emphasis on Jesus' self-sacrifice. Fundamentalists may ignore Jesus' extraordinary treatment of women and the poor and even deny his call to give up family values by leaving one's family. But they are willing to emphasize Jesus' words when they support their own social and religious values, such as Jesus' words about no one coming to the Father except through him. Both conservative and liberal Christians pore over the text of the New Testament to find passages to prooftext their political ideologies and actions.

Tillich avoids such an approach because he emphasizes Jesus' sacrifice of himself to himself as the Christ. Jesus' words and deeds are accepted as

---

[33]ST 1:16, 150.
[34]ST 1:16.
[35]ST 2:114.

finite even though they also are seen as expressions of the New Being and as transparent to divine mystery. Does Jesus' sacrifice of his finite self on the Cross also include his words and deeds? Yes. Tillich sees all aspects of the finite Jesus sacrificed because no finite aspect can be absolutized. It is the sacrifice of absoluteness on the cross that enables the words and deeds to be transparent to the divine. Thus, for Tillich, Jesus' words and deeds are useful to the extent that they point beyond themselves, but potentially dangerous to the extent that they are absolutized.[36] As we shall see in his discussion of the receptive side of the event of Jesus as the Christ, Tillich's fear of idolatry penetrates his whole Christology.

Subjective Side. Tillich argues that the receiving side of the event of Jesus as the Christ needs equal emphasis with the factual, historical Jesus.[37] In fact, Tillich places more emphasis on the subjective, receiving side than the objective side. Or more accurately, the receiving side confirms the objectivity of the event. Tillich argues that Christianity is based on the witness of early Christians to Jesus' messianic character, not on a "historical novel."[38] The early Christians were not writing a history but sharing their experiences of faith. But their subjective experience of faith becomes a ground of certainty for the reality of the New Being. Faith cannot guarantee the historical aspects of that reality, such as the name of Jesus, but it does guarantee, for Tillich, the transformed reality in a personal life that is expressed in the biblical picture of Jesus as the Christ.[39] In volume 3 of his *Systematic Theology*, Tillich argues that the particular concreteness of Jesus as the Christ is the event that affirms fully and universally the historical dimension.[40]

Thus, the encounter of faith is central to Jesus being the Christ. Tillich emphasizes this subjective side of the event as necessary. Without acceptance as the Christ by people, both at the time of Jesus, through the

---

[36]This point can be important to feminist and pluralist hermeneutics because it suggests an element of freedom in interpreting the biblical texts. Efforts to read "behind" the text or to give voice to the previously voiceless Christians would be given some legitimacy as long as they relativized their interpretations and used them to point to ultimate meaning beyond the finite narratives.

[37]ST 2:99.

[38]ST 2:105.

[39]ST 2:107, 114.

[40]ST 3:368.

centuries, and now, Jesus is not the Christ. In other words, there is an ongoing "revelatory correlation" of people's acceptance with the event of Jesus as the Christ.[41] Granting that this ongoing revelation is a dependent revelation, in contrast to an original revelation (Peter's or Martha's encounters), Tillich emphasizes the importance of ongoing encounters to the claim of Jesus as the Christ.

Because all encounters with Jesus as the Christ occur in a historical and cultural context, Tillich's approach rejects the absolutist approaches of biblicism or orthodoxy that see theology as capable of escaping our historical conditioning or our human finitude. It is Tillich's emphasis on experience that sets him apart from fundamentalist or biblicist understandings of the Christ. That the norm of theology should be the event of Jesus as the Christ would get little debate from fundamentalist Christians. But fundamentalist epistemologies do not allow a normative role for historical and cultural experiences but rather derive their certainty from the absolute authority of the biblical text.

Fundamentalists do emphasize the receptive side of the event of Jesus as the Christ. Religious experience is important to Christian faith—but only as long as that experience is expressed in traditional, personalist terms that abstract from the concrete situation of the person. The "born-again" person is one more person who has participated in the universal experience of the saving grace of Christ. The concreteness and particularity of the person is finally irrelevant and should not become part of the interpretation of the norm to others. Yes, people are encouraged to share their stories of conversion, but the transformation focused on is abstracted from their personal situations, and that transformation is seen as absolute.

In contrast, Tillich notes that the reception of revelation and salvation is always fragmentary under the conditions of finite existence. "Revelation and salvation are final, complete, and unchangeable with respect to the revealing and saving event; they are preliminary, fragmentary, and changeable with respect to the persons who receive revelatory truth and saving power."[42] Experience is the medium for receiving revelation, and as such, the reception is always limited. The receiving side of the event of Christ is the root of the symbols associated with the event, both in the New Testament and in the theological tradition.

---

[41]ST 1:126.
[42]ST 1:146.

Symbol. For the most part, Tillich does not emphasize Christ or the New Being as symbols. He does speak of the "symbol of the Christ" in a few places in the second volume of his *Systematic Theology,* but for most of the volume, Tillich uses the term symbol to refer to specific terms in the New Testament, such as Son of God, Son of Man, Cross, or Resurrection.[43] Donald Dreisbach suggests that Tillich wants to say that the Christ or the New Being is more than a symbol.[44] Richard Grigg argues that the New Testament picture of Jesus as the Christ, including various stories and symbols, is "a unified whole and is to be understood as itself a symbol, a symbol that empowers what Tillich terms "New Being."[45] Tillich is unclear on this point, although his theory of symbols would seem to require him to understand the Christ, the New Being, as symbolic, as both Dreisbach and Grigg argue.

Tillich sees "tremendous symbolic power" in the simultaneity of the disciples' acceptance of Jesus as the Christ and Jesus' rejection by the powers of history.[46] That symbolic power is rooted in the basic Christological paradox of unity with divine power and sacrifice of himself, in the human Jesus being called "the Christ."[47] Thus the *symbol* of Jesus as the Christ is rooted in the factual Jesus (or some such factual person) but given its power and meaning through people's acceptance of Jesus as the Christ. The event includes the symbol, and the symbol includes the event. Both rest on a paradox, uniting divine and human, universal and concrete, unity with divine power and self-sacrifice, particular finite person and acceptance of him as the Christ.

Jesus' followers respond to him as the Christ, but Tillich argues that the cross negates the focus on the person as the medium of revelation. "In his cross Jesus sacrificed that medium of revelation which impressed itself on his followers as messianic in power and significance."[48] Tillich argues that

---

[43]ST 2:109, 158, 159.

[44]Donald F. Dreisbach, *Symbols and Salvation; Paul Tillich's Doctrine of Religious Symbols and His Interpretation of the Symbols of the Christian Tradition* (Lanham MD: University Press of America, 1993) 142-45, 157-66.

[45]Richard Grigg, *Symbol and Empowerment: Paul Tillich's Post-Theistic System* (Macon GA: Mercer University Press, 1985) 74.

[46]ST 2:97.

[47]ST 2:98.

[48]ST 1:134.

Jesus is the Christ only because he is crucified. "Any acceptance of Jesus as the Christ which is not the acceptance of Jesus the crucified is a form of idolatry."[49] Clearly, Tillich wants to avoid a Christology that undermines the centrality of the Cross.

The Cross then becomes a criterion of all symbols and of the truth of faith. In *Dynamics of Faith*, Tillich states that "the criterion of the truth of faith, therefore, is that it implies an element of self-negation. That symbol is most adequate which expresses not only the ultimate but also its own lack of ultimacy."[50] And that criterion, rooted in the Cross, in turn becomes his basis for claiming the superiority of the Christian symbol of the Cross in contrast to all other religions.[51]

Symbols associated with Jesus as the Christ must meet this criterion of self-negation or transparency in Tillich's view. This approach does not cut off new expressions of the event of Christ or new symbols; rather it encourages new theological expressions. That all symbols and expressions should be tested against the criterion is Tillich's effort to avoid idolatry. But because he emphasizes the importance of the subjective, receptive side of faith and the importance of ongoing response to the event of Christ, he speaks of the importance of new theological expressions.[52] Yet all such expressions will stand under the criterion of the self-negation of the Cross.

Because fundamentalists affirm an objective, historical understanding of the Christ, rooted in their assumption of the inerrancy of the Bible, they reject theologies based on the subjective, receptive side of the event of Christ. Like Tillich, they see the relativity and finite limits of human experience. For them, efforts to form a theology from human experiences, even religious experiences of the Christ, would be idolatrous of those human experiences. One could note that Paul does precisely that in his letters, but the assumption of biblical inerrancy removes the finite limits from Paul's experiences and theology. In the fundamentalist view, the biblical texts cannot be read as human expressions of faith, subject to the limits of culture, history, and finitude. Such a historical-critical perspective rejects the absoluteness of the biblical text and removes all certainty from theology, the fundamentalists argue.

---

[49]Paul Tillich, *Dynamics of Faith* (New York: Harper & Row, 1957) 98.
[50]Ibid., 97.
[51]Ibid., 97-98.
[52]Ibid., 71.

Similarly, for fundamentalists, to emphasize the symbolic character of Christological events is to undermine the absoluteness of the event of Christ as well as the historical and scientific inerrancy of the Bible. The event of Christ, particularly the incarnation, Jesus' atonement through the cross, and his physical resurrection, must be stressed as real, historical events or else faith has no absolute grounding. The event of Jesus as the Christ is historical, but the biblical reports of it are treated as nonhistorical, as not subject to historical and cultural limits. But those historical and cultural limits do apply to all religious thinkers who do not agree with fundamentalist theology or biblical inerrancy. Fundamentalists and biblical inerrantists, however, are exempt from their historical, cultural conditions because they see themselves as merely repeating the inerrant, biblical truths.

There is little basis for dialogue between thinkers positing symbolic theologies and fundamentalists who insist on the absoluteness of their theologies. Correlations in meaning between the symbols and fundamentalist interpretations are irrelevant because the focus on symbols already undermines the fundamentalist assumptions. So even though both Tillich and fundamentalists might agree on the centrality of the Cross, for example, that would not be a basis for dialogue because Tillich emphasizes the *symbolic* meaning of the Cross. Both share in the modern emphasis on historical and cultural conditioning and reject idolatry, but they differ on what can be called idolatry because they differ on the locus of absoluteness. Where Tillich would see idolatry in fundamentalist biblicism, fundamentalists would see idolatry in the authority Tillich gives to human experience. Tillich's response would be that the authority of human experience must always stand under the criterion of the self-negation of the Cross, that human experience never has absolute authority.

Critical Evaluations and Conclusions

Event. For some feminist approaches to the biblical material, Tillich's lack of interest in the words and deeds of Jesus is problematic. His fear of idolatry seems to relegate Jesus' words and deeds to mere expressions of the New Being—expressions that Tillich wants to make sure do not get turned into absolute ethics, doctrines, or ideals. But to the extent that Jesus' words and deeds are liberating, not just from individual estrangement, but for whole groups of people (women and the poor), many feminists want those teachings and actions brought into more prominence. To set forth the liberating implications of Jesus' words and deeds for our own time is to challenge the tendencies toward absolutization that exist in our religious and social institutions as well as in our cultural attitudes. That Jesus was a feminist, as Leonard Swidler argues, or that Jesus sided with the poor, as Latin American liberation theologies emphasize, is not just an expression of the New Being in Jesus as the Christ but sets forth religious and ethical ideals for people today. Jesus' actions and teachings, then, can be given normative power for Christians today, without absolutizing them. Their meaning is not just existential but has become social and political today; like all meanings and actions, they stand under the critique of idolatry and the ambiguity of life.

Other feminists would see liberating dimensions in Tillich's de-emphasis on the finite characteristics, words, and deeds of Jesus. Having been victim to theologies and church structures that absolutize Jesus' maleness or the maleness of his "official" disciples, they recognize the negative results of absolutizing the human Jesus. They would share in Tillich's rejection of biblicism because such an inerrantist approach also absolutizes the hierarchical, social teachings in the Epistles and denies leadership to women.

John Hick clearly finds the traditional interpretation of Jesus as the unique Son of God very limiting and arrogant. Such an absolute view of Jesus limits the approach to the Real and cuts off all other approaches as invalid or at least inadequate. Hick prefers instead to see Jesus as "a man who was open to God's presence to a truly awesome extent and was sustained by an extraordinarily intense God-consciousness."[53] References to God as incarnate should be understood as metaphorical or mythological, not literal. The event, then, for Hick, is the historical person Jesus who had a very strong consciousness of God. But the event itself is not absolute or unique in relation to events in other religious traditions. Like Tillich, Hick gives a strong role to Christ as symbol or metaphor, but Hick rejects the claims of final revelation in Christ that Tillich still holds.

Symbol of Self-sacrifice. The emphasis Tillich places on Jesus' self-sacrifice can have both negative and positive meanings for feminist work. Some feminists, like Mary Daly in *Beyond God the Father*, have pointed to the destructive consequences of women internalizing self-sacrificial behavior.[54] And while it is also true that some oppressed people have found

---

[53]Hick, *A Christian Theology of Religions*, 92.
[54]Mary Daly, *Beyond God the Father* (Boston: Beacon Press, 1973) 45-49.

comfort and hope in Jesus' suffering and self-sacrifice, we have to be careful not to use self-sacrifice in a way that prevents fulfillment of self. Self-sacrifice and emptiness of self can allow fullness, but they can also be misused to control and subdue others.

But there is another sense of self-negation that brings empowerment to others rather than just giving in to the domination of others. When Jesus sacrifices himself on the Cross, it not only allows his fulfillment as the Christ, but it also empowers others, allowing them also to be fulfilled. It is precisely in that self-negation of the finite characteristics of Jesus that the Cross opens up the possibility of other bearers of the New Being, of anyone participating in the transformation of the New Being. For when the event is no longer tied just to the human Jesus, the possibility is created for the event to occur for anyone. And when it does occur for others, they can become bearers of the New Being as well. Paul's theology recognized this in his theory of participation, but the implications of that are often lost in the focus on the event of the individual Jesus Christ. When the event of Christ is tied to the self-negation on the Cross, then the particularity of Jesus is extended to other particular beings. Cannot the poor or women, then, become bearers of the New Being as is suggested in some liberation theologies? Just as Buddhist or Taoist emptiness is what makes fullness possible, so Jesus' self-negation makes fullness available for others. If the individual Jesus is glorified and absolutized, then there is no room for others to be empowered and to be bearers of the New Being.

This issue is precisely what underlies the Christologies of Brock, McFague, and Hick. Brock's emphasis on incarnation and redemption, as located more broadly than in the individual Jesus, opens up spiritual transformation for many and allows them to be the bearers of hope and transformation for others. McFague's Christology extends the love of God to the whole universe, not just as objects of God's love but as bearers of that love to others. McFague argues that one can see the depths of divine love and love's "inclusive, healing work, in the destabilizing inclusive, non-hierarchical life and death of Jesus of Nazareth," but she also adds that "one sees it as well in the lives and the deaths of others."[55]

If one extends this same idea to pluralist theologies, one can argue that the self-negation of Jesus opens up the possibility of non-Christian bearers of the New Being. To the extent that Jesus is not absolutized, revelation and

---

[55]McFague, *Models of God*, 144.

salvation need not be tied to Jesus. John Hick uses the idea of metaphor to explain the Incarnation in a way that frees it from absolutization in Jesus only. The idea of metaphor already contains the element of self-negation in it; a metaphor both is and is not. Hick's relativizing of Jesus by placing him on the phenomenal level in contrast to the noumenal Real is extended to other religious forms of revelation. Hick is then able to emphasize the transformative power of salvation or liberation through a variety of religious traditions rather than any one religious form.

Criteria of Symbols. It might seem that this application of Jesus' self-negation on the Cross would open up any reality or symbol as bearer of revelation and salvation. To the extent that the emphasis is on the symbolic meaning rather than on a particular event it might seem to make all theological proposals and religious meanings valid. But if one continues Tillich's use of self-negation to also include the critique of idolatry, one has other criteria for judging truth.

The structure of symbols, as finite and yet directed toward and participating in ultimate meaning, shows that they have the potential to be distorted into idols. But that same structure also sets a criterion of maintaining the paradox of the symbol, the finite and ultimate at the same time. To the extent that the paradox is broken and idolatry occurs, to that extent religious and theological truth is distorted. Or put differently, to the extent that the metaphorical or symbolic dimension is forgotten, to that extent the idea or image becomes an idol.

But there is another dimension here, brought out in the examples from McFague, Brock, and Hick—the effect of symbols on whole communities or even the world. Each thinker calls for an extension of the traditional view of salvation and redemption to groups or realities that have been treated as "other" and as outside the salvific effects of Jesus as the Christ. For all three, Jesus is radically relativized to being *one* bearer of the healing, reconciling reality in order to recognize other bearers of empowerment and salvation.

For Tillich, when one shifts from the individual context to the historical and cultural contexts, one also shifts from focus on the New Being to focus on the Spiritual Presence. The community of the New Being, the Spiritual Community, "is created by the divine Spirit as manifest in the New Being in Jesus as the Christ.[56] As such, the Spiritual Community is a community

---

[56]ST 3:155.

of faith, love, and unity among all members, irrespective of their "sex, age, race, nation, tradition, and character."[57] It is in the communal realm, under the impact of the Spiritual Presence, that judgment of inequality and the aim for justice are experienced. Under the Spiritual Presence, all are equal, but that ultimate equality is often "invisible and ineffective" in actual social situations.[58] The Spiritual Presence, then, can empower people to work for equality and justice. Tillich's extension of the healing power of the New Being in Jesus as the Christ occurs through the Spiritual Presence.

If we combine Tillich's Christology and pneumatology, in order to include the social as well as individual realms, we can suggest another critique to complement the critique of idolatry, namely, a critique of injustice. As Tillich suggests and we have elaborated in chapter 6, section B, idolatry is connected with injustice. This combination of critiques is directed not only toward ideas and symbols but also toward individual and social actions. This approach allows the teachings and actions of Jesus (or other bearers of New Being) that call people to social justice and social transformation to be normative for followers, but it also holds their application under a criterion of self-negation and a criterion of justice. The particulars of the event as well as the symbolic meanings can be taken seriously but not absolutely. Jesus' words and deeds can both model and call people to internal and external transformations, even though all efforts will have ambiguous results.

When applied to fundamentalism, the critiques point up several problems. Fundamentalists claim to absolutize the Bible but in fact absolutize those parts that fit with their fundamental beliefs and conservative, hierarchical, and patriarchal social agendas. In analyzing the way that authority actually works for fundamentalists, Boone shows that "biblical inerrancy becomes in actual practice a political tool whereby one's questions or objections can be deferred to the text."[59] Their fear of absolutizing feminist or pluralist or any individual experiences fits with the critique of idolatry. But their inability to turn that critique of idolatry toward their own absolutes leaves them subject to idolatry and contributing to injustice. They need both to take more seriously the New Being expressed in Jesus' words and deeds, including those parts where Jesus challenges existing social and religious structures, and to put their own words and deeds under the self-negating

---

[57]ST 3:157.
[58]ST 3:262-63.
[59]Boone, The Bible Tells Them So, 111.

meaning of the Cross in order to see their own idolatry. They are right that feminists and pluralists need to be subject to this critique as well. And fundamentalists as well as feminists and pluralists need to subject their words and deeds to the critique of injustice that stems from the critique of idolatry and the symbols of Christ and the Cross. For the event of Christ to be an ongoing event, negation of absoluteness must continue not only in the symbols we accept but in the actions and structures of our communities.

Chapter 12

The Aims of World War II

The author of Ecclesiastes provides three texts on war:

For everything its season, and for every activity under heaven its time: . . . a time for war and a time for peace (3:1, 8)

It is not in man's power to restrain the wind and no one has power over the day of death. In war no one can lay aside his arms, no wealth will save its possessor. (8:8)

Wisdom is better than weapons of war, and one mistake can undo many things done well. (9:18 NEB)

Though Tillich is more hopeful than the world-weary preacher of Ecclesiastes there were for him seasons of war. Both World War I and II called him to participate, and while I interpret him as a theologian of peace, he was also a theologian of war. War came upon him with irresistible force and though he would act as a philosopher of war, he knew also of the weapons of war, particularly the ideological weapons.

A major motif of Tillich's thought about war is found in his various writings on war aims. War aims correspond closely to one of the points of just-war theory: the goal of a war must be just. Tillich chose to organize much of his thought about war around this teleological point. What are the appropriate aims of the war? The aims of the war would then assist in organizing the way the war should be fought and strategies chosen.

There are five major locations for his discussion of war aims. His articles on war aims in *The Protestant Digest*, his papers for the Federal Council of Churches Commission on a Just and Durable Peace, his statement of purpose for the Council for a Democratic Germany, his speeches to German listeners in Europe from March 1942 to May 1944, and his essay on "The World Situation" are the major sources for these discussions of aims. The five contexts affect Tillich's presentations of the goals of the war, but all five portray a consistency. All five contexts reflect his urging warfare upon armies in which relatives served, his own beloved homeland, his universities, and the culture for which he had fought thirty years earlier.

The Coming of War

The closing months of 1938 and the spring and summer of 1939 were busy months of international diplomacy. The democracies of France and England vacillated before the determined, aggressive diplomacy of Italy, Japan, and Germany. The United States remained ineffective, and the Soviet Union contemplated various security arrangements that would further its interests. In retrospect, it was a time of deciding when the war would come and who would be allies.

Located between the major powers, the weaker countries, including Finland, Estonia, Latvia, Lithuania, Poland, and Czechoslovakia, were the bargaining chips of the deadly game being played. Earlier appeasement in the Far East, Africa, and Spain had encouraged the fascists to risk belligerency.

The Munich pact of September 1938 sacrificed Czechoslovakia to Hitler and encouraged Stalin to divide Poland with Hitler the following summer. The French and English bought peace in Munich, and Russia bought peace from Ribbentrop in Moscow in August 1939. The two pacts for peace insured that war would come.

Tillich knew that no compromise was possible with Nazism. In 1938, aware of the relativities of judgment and ambiguity of political action, he had called for a life-and-death struggle against Nazism.[1]

Commenting on the Munich agreement before the outbreak of war, Tillich isolated five factors as presuppositions of the situation. Those people operating in nineteenth-century categories of continual progress were unprepared to understand events of the twentieth century. The foreign policies of the various countries depended upon the interests of the ruling classes. The politics of leftist forces in the democracies were inept. Fascism promised an answer to the insecurities of the present. Collective security had not worked, and the Munich settlement recognizing a German protectorate over central Europe was unstable.[2]

---

[1]Paul Tillich, "The Gospel and the State," *Crozer Quarterly* 15/4 (1938): 241-61.

[2]Paul Tillich, "The Political Situation in Europe since the Munich Conference," Tillich Papers.

War seemed inevitable. The encirclement policy that followed Munich was a reaction of the old empires to the new German empire. The policy depended upon Russia, and Tillich feared that dependence on Russia was foolhardy.

Several contradictory conditions in Germany were obvious to Tillich. There was a contradiction between the mass movement of Nazism and its foundation of terror. Capitalism was being both preserved and transformed. Economic problems were being resolved by a war economy, but the economy was threatened by a war conducted by a mass society. The rhetoric was of both nationalism and supranational imperialism. All these instabilities in Germany were overcome by repression.

Tillich thought in 1939 that there was still a chance that the emergence of a German empire in central Europe would be tolerated by the democracies. However, if Germany reached agreement with Russia, war would follow. He recognized that the Russian-German alliance must be prevented, but that it was probably too late to stop it, and he supported the growing toughness of Roosevelt's foreign policy.

Religious leadership, he felt, had been largely irresponsible in the face of the developing situation. In a short discussion of power and justice, he refuted religious pacifism as a possible response. Democracy to survive would have to realize internal justice and not just observe the forms of legal justice. In the twentieth century, the emptiness of meaning and the lack of justice allowed demonic totalitarianism to rush into the vacuum. The German invasion of Poland on 1 September 1939, with the assistance of Russia, drove Tillich into a period of discouragement and despair. He had anticipated war and urged preparation for it, but the actuality of it brought back too many painful dreams and memories of his own time in the trenches of World War I. During this second world conflagration his actions were first to become an American citizen and then to join in the public debate over the aims and policies of the war, to continue to assist refugees, to write on the war, and to join the American propaganda war after the United States was brought into the conflict.

Tillich's work among refugees had emphasized the need for a real migration. He urged Germans to identify with their new country and to free themselves from illusory hopes for a return. On 4 March 1940, he became a U.S. citizen, and in an essay celebrating his new status, he affirmed his ability as a citizen to participate in building the future.[3] Europe, for him, became identified more and more with the past.

The Protestant

In 1941, Kenneth Leslie attracted Tillich to his journal *The Protestant Digest* (soon changed to *The Protestant*), and Tillich wrote several essays for it in 1941–1943. Leslie was a rather independent editor, and he was constantly in tension with his editorial board of which Paul Tillich became chairman. One of the disputes led Tillich to write a policy statement for the journal in 1942. It is one of Tillich's most succinct statements of the relationship of Christian faith to political action; it appeared under the title "Protestant Principles."[4]

1. Protestantism affirms the absolute majesty of God alone and raises prophetic protest against every human claim, ecclesiastical or secular, to absolute truth and authority.
2. Protestantism affirms the Christian message as the ultimate expression of the nature of the Divine and protests against all attempts to dissolve this message into a complex of religious experiences, moral demands and philosophical doctrines.
3. Protestantism affirms Divine sovereignty over the institutions and doctrines of the Christian churches and protests against attempts to bind the Christian message to the life and law of any historical Church.
4. Protestantism affirms the direct reference of the Divine to every element of reality and protests against hierarchical meditations as well as against the separation of a sacred from a secular realm.
5. Protestantism affirms the independent structure of the different spheres of the cultural life and protests against encroachments upon their autonomy by churches and states.

---

[3]Paul Tillich, "I Am an American," *Protestant Digest* 2/4 (June-July 1941): 24-26. See also his "The Conquest of Theological Provincialism," in *The Cultural Migration: The European Scholar in America*, ed. Franz L. Neumann et al. (Philadelphia: University of Pennsylvania Press, 1953) 138-56.

[4]Paul Tillich, "Protestant Principles," *The Protestant* 4/5 (April-May 1942): 17.

6. Protestantism affirms the dependence of the spiritual meaning of all cultural activities on their religious foundation and protests against the separation of religious transcendence from cultural immanence.

7. Protestantism, while rejecting any definitive or final system of Christian ethics and politics, applies the Christian message to every historical situation as the principle of criticism and demand.

In a following issue of the journals Tillich commented on the principles in response to readers reactions.[5] He set out his belief that the essence of Protestantism, or prophetic religion, is the dual recognition of the transcendence and immanence of God. All of life has a religious base, but life itself is not divine. Religion has two senses: its special proclamation of its vision of God and the denial that its special proclamation is absolute. All of life points toward its source, but the source is not captured by any expression of life. Vital religion announces the "end of religion" in the sense of criticizing the absolute pretensions of religious communities, but vital religion continues to affirm the human need for religious symbols to express the ultimate.

This dialectical approach conditions Protestantism's relationship to both the church and the world. Both are affirmed, both are criticized. Therefore, in politics there is no absolute Christian answer, but continual Christian engagement in the pursuit of answers. "Protestantism is not bound to its past; therefore it is free for its future, even if this future should deserve the name 'Post Protestant Era.' "[6]

Tillich's first statement regarding appropriate war aims had appeared in 1941 in The Protestant Digest. He blamed the democracies for creating communism by nurturing social injustice and of having used fascism to combat communism. The war was a struggle by fascism to destroy the humanism of the West, he argued, and the appropriate war aim should be the creation of a planned economy in a European federal union, which could be liberal enough to prevent tyranny while assuring economic security to the masses of Europe. Liberal arbitrariness could be overcome without sacrificing freedom, he thought, and nationalism reduced by an economic

---

[5]The Protestant 4/7 (August-September 1941): 8-14.
[6]Ibid., 14.

federation. The war aims that appeared in serial form in the journal were brought together as a pamphlet and sold for a nickel to contribute to the American discussion of goals of the war.[7]

Eventually the sponsors of the journal differed over the editorial position regarding communism. *The Protestant* folded as a result of the dispute, and Leslie, who was too close to communism for many on the board, returned to his native Canada. The split among the sponsors of the journal was symptomatic of what happened to many of Tillich's projects in the war period, and beyond that, foreshadowed the tensions that would divide the victors of World War II and result in the cold war.

Against the Third Reich[8]

Paul Tillich prepared 112 five-page addresses in German for broadcast into occupied Europe from March 1942 through May 1944. Even his closest friends in the U.S. did not know of his secret work for the Allied cause. These addresses have been largely unknown in the U.S. except for specialists in Tillich scholarship. The essays in *Against the Third Reich* are among the most concrete and passionate of his political writings. They also show that this Protestant theologian who could announce the end of the Protestant era and castigate Protestantism so thoroughly was also a German Protestant theologian who saw the demonic, named it, and did what he could as a theologian to denounce it. The reader of these essays will learn that Tillich's analysis was not only profound, powerful, and polemical, but that it was also true. These radio speeches are the raw data of a theologian at war from 1942 to 1944, following the daily events and analyzing them theologically. These are not works from hindsight, but engaged, political-theological risk taking.

Tillich's address writing began at an Allied low point in the war, moved through the Axis defeats of 1942, and concluded before D-Day in mid-1944. Throughout this period, Tillich optimistically trusted in the ultimate Allied victory. The United States and the Soviet Union were both stronger than Germany. With the empire to draw upon, Britain's strength was

---

[7]Paul Tillich, *War Aims* (New York: Protestant Digest, 1941).

[8]*Against the Third Reich: Paul Tillich's Wartime Radio Broadcasts into Nazi Germany*, ed. Ronald H. Stone and Matthew Lon Weaver (Louisville: Westminster/John Knox Press, 1998).

certainly as great as Japan's, and the lesser nations of the world were drawn into functional alliances with the Allies. Tillich regarded the outcome as certain, but one to be achieved through much suffering and hard fighting. In terms of population and industrial production the Allies were too strong for the Axis powers. The military skills of the democrats and the communists were to be proven as in no way inferior to those of the Nazis, Fascists, and Japanese militarists. Tillich portrayed Hitler as a gambler who had taken a contest at bad odds. Having lost his gamble, Hitler compulsively tried to repair his losses, but when defeated his actions turned into an orgy of German self-destruction.

Should we regard Tillich as too optimistic? Probably not. Most Americans of Tillich's generation with whom we've spoken also regarded the outcome of the war as a foregone conclusion. After all, Pittsburgh itself would outproduce the Ruhr Valley. Once U.S. production was geared up, more aircraft and ships would flow from North American mills on the invulnerable continent than the Japanese could destroy. Tillich's judgments were shrewd, formulated from experience in the trenches of World War I. It is worth remembering that his rank in World War I was higher than either Hitler's or Eisenhower's. By the time of his writing, Hitler and Japan's mistakes had doomed their regimes. Hitler's "Barbarosa" invasion of the Soviet Union perhaps had a chance in 1941, if Japan had struck the U.S.S.R. in the East. But Japan's foolish attack on the U.S.A. and Hitler's declaration of war on the world's strongest industrial power sealed their fate. If Stalin, in the sure knowledge that Japan was committed elsewhere, had not been able to shift thirty-two divisions from the East to thwart the Nazis at the gates of Moscow in the first winter, things might have been different. But by March 1942, Tillich could see the Nazi defeat. The turning points for Germany came in North Africa in 1942 and at Stalingrad in early 1943. In addition to population, material, and military intelligence, will was needed to defeat the Axis. Both Japan and Germany in their terrible barbaric excesses aroused the will to fight in both communists and democrats.

Tillich for his part was trying to divide the will of his German listeners from the mania of their Nazi rulers. Again and again he hit on the theme Nazism is doomed; abandon it. He tried to persuade Germans to stop cooperating with their rulers. This attempt, of course, confronted the obedient character of the good German. Just by listening to his broadcasts a German or other European was engaging in resistance. A Czech theologian put it to me: "The broadcasts of the Voice of America were very important to us, but we could be executed for listening."

Tillich did not last long under Hitler. He was among the first professors dismissed by the Nazi regime from the University of Frankfurt in 1932. All the others of that first group of dismissed professors were Jews. His publication of "Ten Theses: The Church and the Third Reich" in 1932, combined with his support for Jews, his religious socialism, and his actions as dean at Frankfurt to expel rowdy Nazi students, earned him his quick dismissal. He urged in thesis 7 that Protestantism set "the cross against the paganism of the swastika" and testified that the cross was against the " 'holiness' of nation, race, blood, and power." Narrowly missing arrest, he was allowed to emigrate in response to the invitation from Union Theological Seminary and Columbia University. From his safe haven in New York he would direct his programs of Self-Help for Emigrés from Central Europe and the Council for a Democratic Germany and write the addresses collected in *Against the Third Reich.*

Tillich's great distance from the Confessing Church in rejection of Nazism consisted in two tendencies. He was closely associated with Jewish friends, intellectuals, and causes. His theology was political. The Confessing Church at Barmen and later was relatively apolitical and concerned primarily about the freedom of the church. For Tillich, Nazism was not to be submitted to, even in matters of the state; it was to be defeated. Christianity was grounded in and depended upon its Jewish roots, and to be anti-Jewish was to be anti-Christian. The Nazi fight with Judaism was of its essence and necessary to the space and blood-bound folk paganism of Nazism.

Tillich's resistance to Nazism also had its personal loyalties in his friendships with Jews from Berlin, Frankfurt and New York. Adolf Löwe and Eduard Heimann, members of his circle at both Berlin and Frankfurt, would join him in New York as would the Frankfurt philosophers Max Horkheimer, Herbert Marcuse, and Erich Fromm. His first political speech in English was to attack Hitler's anti-Semitism in a rally at Madison Square Garden in 1938. He appealed for unity between Jews and Christians on the foundation of prophetic religion. He opposed Nazi ideology with references to the universalism of German classicism and argued how dependent German thought was upon Jewish contributions. He urged solidarity with Jews and opposition to Nazism. Many of the themes of 1938 would reappear in the addresses of 1942-44.By mid-1942, Tillich joined with Reinhold Niebuhr in supporting a national homeland for Jews. They and three others composed the executive committee of the Christian Council on Palestine which promoted Zionist understanding and encouraged American clergy to support a homeland for Judaism.

His first speech to "My German Friends"—as Tillich began each of the "Voice of America" talks—was against anti-Semitism. It was logical for Tillich to begin his speeches with "the Jewish question," both existentially and intellectually. Nazi atrocities against Jews had begun prior to his exit from Germany in the early 1930s.[9] They were a fact of life that had to be confronted. Further, the historic identity of the Jewish people had a significant place in his theology as well as his philosophy of history. Theologically, they are the inspiration for his notion of the Protestant principle, that element of perpetual critique that stands against the ever-present threats of idolatry and utopianism.[10] Historically, Jewish prophetism is the vehicle for his argument of the dominance of time over space as the necessary prerequisite for the existence of justice.[11] Tillich began his speeches at this point because "the Jewish question" was central to his thought. Before 1942 was over, Tillich was writing of the Nazi actions of extermination of the Jews (12 September 1942 and 12 November 1942). In December of that year he was telling Germans of the trains of death, of the machine-gun executions of Jewish children and women, and of German physicians who joined in the slaughter in the camps. The Nazi guilt was a burden to the country that had become the tool for Nazism. So these essays march on from March 1942 to May 1944, detailing the guilt of all responsible Germans. Degrees of guilt are different and types of guilt can be distinguished, but Germany's guilt is detailed address by address and Tillich's own guilt fuels the passion of his writing.

Tillich does not ignore guilt for the breakdown of German democracy attributable to the other nations. But his focus on the guilt for the horror of the war, the extermination campaigns, the assault against humanity is on Germans. The faults in Germany are deep and he expounds on German character, myth, and history, but responsibility rests upon those who allowed Hitler to enslave them. The majority of the addresses urge Germans to act to liberate themselves from the Nazis. But historically the Germans could not

---

[9] Wilhelm Pauck and Marion Pauck, *Paul Tillich: His Life and Thought* (San Francisco: Harper & Row, 1976) 127-30.

[10] Paul Tillich, "The Protestant Principle and the Proletarian Situation," in *The Protestant Era* (Chicago: University of Chicago Press, 1948) 161-81.

[11] Paul Tillich, "The Struggle between Space and Time," in *Theology and Culture* (London: Oxford University Press, 1959) 31, 32; and idem, *The Socialist Decision* (Washington DC: University Press of America, 1977) 6, 20, 22.

liberate themselves, and the Russians had to bear the brunt of that liberation struggle. But though Russian Communism brought liberation from Nazism, it also brought a new tyranny to millions of Germans. The united, cooperative Germany that Tillich hoped for after the liberation had to wait until the 1990s.

The addresses are theology of culture. The culture is terribly evil, and though many are guilty, the Nazis utilizing the Germans are particularly guilty. Redemption could come if the Germans could liberate themselves, but it becomes apparent that they cannot. In fact, as the war closes in on its climax the conquest of Germany by the Allies promises only a partial liberation. Tillich's own political leadership in the German emigré organization, the Council for a Democratic Germany, falters on the clash between democrats and communists who will divide and oppress much of Germany. World War II was for a Tillich a war to liberate Europe and Germany from the Nazis. One could say it was a war to save Germany and Europe from the Nazis. But the results of the war of liberation turn out, as they almost always do, very ambiguously. It is a theology for very troubled nations upon whom judgment has come or is coming in its historically ambiguous character. The hope for self-liberation is recognized by the author but not historically realized. Judgment and retribution against evil is more sure in this theology than liberation. Also, the question of Israel's salvation is close to the center of the story. Can poor Israel, crushed beneath the superpower, be liberated? For Tillich, by 1942, not much of European Israel would be saved, but a remnant for a restored home in Palestine was a hope. Even so, the plagues of Egypt forcing the freedom of Israel are compared to the scourges to come upon Germany in its oppression of Israel.

In one of his last addresses chosen for this volume, "One Hundred Speeches on Liberation from Nazism" (7 March 1944), Tillich tells his listeners he has tried to encourage them to separate from Nazism. He affirms he speaks for Germany to find liberation from Nazism or, in a cautionary note, at least from the spirit of Nazism. Expression of support for Germany while opposing Nazism would not be easily understood by American bureaucrats. Before the war ended Tillich would be blacklisted by the U.S. Army as pro-German. He was deeply pro-German and very deeply pro-Jewish and totally anti-Nazi.

War Aims in the Speeches

In the speeches more than in his other writings, the war becomes a struggle to destroy Nazism. It is seen as a war of Christian culture against evil. It is to be conducted with a holy passion against the evil of Nazism without hatred for the Nazis as persons (Sept. 12, 1942). The war was waged he assured his German listeners to liberate Germany from the Nazis. (Oct. 6, 1942) In addition to the breaking of the death machine of Nazism, the war criminals must be punished. For him this is the doing of justice. It is to punish crimes against humanity. It will be a worldwide judgment against their crimes, and he argued there would be no refuge in the whole world for their crimes against humanity. He returns to the need to punish the Nazis so often that it must be recognized as a war aim for him. "It is the response of that which is divine in the world to the attempt to distort it into that which is diabolical." (Oct. 20, 1942)

Repeatedly he describes the Germans as enslaved, and he calls for them to act against their enslavers. Victory in the war can mean freedom for Germans as well as their victims. Freedom for the allies was also a war aim and for Tillich it meant not only constitutional rights but the fulfillment of personal security in a fairer society represented by Roosevelt's domestic policies.

Another war aim articulated in the speeches is for the restoration of community among European nations and in the world. Technology and war have revealed the world to be one. Nazism violated the developing world community and the goal of the war is to restore that community with a de-Nazified Germany having a place in the unity of nations. In the speech of 17 July 1942, Tillich identified himself with the progressives, speaking of regional and world federations which would deny to the nations the rights or capacities to make war. He affirmed the developing plans for a stronger world organization than the previous League of Nations.

In summary, the speeches are less specific considering their length than the other sources on war aims. The first theme of the speeches is, "Germans, liberate yourselves from the Nazis." This is the first aim of the war to destroy Nazism; in the fervor of this goal Tillich declares a war that is of the crusade form, but he does not use the term. Other goals are the freedom of the nations of the world, European internal security, and social-economic security.

A Just and Durable Peace

One of the most creative responses of organized American Protestantism to the war was the work of the Federal Council of Churches' Commission on a Just and Durable Peace. Under the chairmanship of John Foster Dulles, the commission developed a philosophy of international relations and sponsored educational work in the churches on this complex subject. Dulles's moralism and his natural tendency as a lawyer toward legalism pervaded the commission's philosophy. The program of the commission was a program of those who expected to be victors in the war and who wanted to assume the responsibilities of power in creating a new order. It was very effective in lobbying for the replacement of the League of Nations with a stronger organization—what would become the United Nations.

The commission knew when it invited Tillich to deliver a series of lectures that his perspective of German religious socialism would be different. However, the gap between the commission's inclination toward a Calvinist legalism and the Lutheran theologian's dynamism was greater than Dulles anticipated.

Under the theme of the "Christian Basis of a Just and Durable Peace," Tillich delivered three addresses.[12] The first lecture interpreted the war as a world revolution and developed Tillich's theological perspective on international politics. He avoided both crusade and pacifist interpretations of Christianity, but he criticized the concepts central to the commission's ideas of "just" and "durable." Tillich's dynamism—inherited from Jacob Böhme, Luther, and Schelling—made it impossible for him to regard any imposed peace as either just or durable. In fact in his interpretation of the world revolution, he felt the grounds for World War III were already being laid.

In the second lecture, Tillich revealed his fears that after the war, the Leviathan of an uncaring, monopolistic capitalism would be enforced on Europe. Capitalism in control of technology would foster the very dehumanization process that nurtured Nazism. He saw a minor hope in the possibility of progressive elements (meaning the British Labour Party, the central

---

[12]Paul Tillich, "Christian Principles and Political Reality," "The Social Problem of a Just and Durable Peace," and "The International Problem of a Just and Durable Peace," Tillich Papers; published in *Theology of Peace*, ed. Ronald Stone (Louisville: Westminster/John Knox Press, 1990).

European underground forces, American New Deal proponents, and strong sections of the churches) cooperating with Russia for an alternative order; but his fears of Russia negated that hope. His greatest hope was that nations would achieve liberated state capitalism in which the "chaotic insecurity of monopolism is excluded" and in which individuals could participate creatively in production.

His final lecture dealt with the idea of a world order and the reality of competing nation-states. He certainly reflected no trust in balance-of-power politics, but the overcoming of nineteenth-century diplomacy by transformation to a new order was in the future. He could not visualize a center for an emerging world federation. A new order would require transforming the present technical-rationalistic manipulations of the human world into a new political-spiritual reality. In a very direct sense, Tillich called the work of the Dulles commission superficial. He expressed his fears that Europe would be reduced to a colonial hinterland of the emerging superpowers. Never spoken, but underlying his words, was his concern about the fate of the villages in which he had grown to maturity. It was in the spirit of prophetic religion, he claimed in his conclusion, that he destroyed the moralism of the Commission on a Just and Durable Peace. The theological terms of grace and tragedy, he said, were more adequate categories than the moralistic principles of the Commission to describe the present broken order.

Council for a Democratic Germany

Paul Tillich served as chairman of the Council for a Democratic Germany, a group of anti-Nazi German refugees. The council published its founding philosophy, "A Program for a Democratic Germany," in *Christianity and Crisis* in May 1944, just before the D-Day invasion of June 6.[13] Though no author's name appears, the document was written by Tillich and represents political thought identical to that expressed elsewhere under his own name. Signers of the declaration included professors, ministers, business people, politicians, actors, and writers, many of whose names are well known today. Also among the signers were those who had contact with the German underground resistance. American supporters of the statement included John C. Bennett, Norman Cousins, John Dewey, Harry Emerson

---

[13]"A Program for a Democratic Germany," *Christianity and Crisis* (15 May 1944): 3-5.

Fosdick, Rufus M. Jones, Reinhold Niebuhr, William Scarlett, Dorothy Thompson, and Jonah B. Wise.

The statement presupposed that cooperation between the West and Russia was a necessary precondition for the reconstruction of Europe. Many of the signers, including the author, however, knew that such cooperation was only a precarious possibility. There were four major emphases.

Germany was part of the European problem. The defeat of Nazism and the liquidation of the Nazis were prerequisites to any solution of the problem. Also, those who supported the Nazis had to be deprived of political power. Though it assumed a disarmed Germany, the statement warned against a dismembered Germany, fearing irredentism.

The economic power of Germany should be conserved to avoid widespread poverty and future unrest. The German economic system had to be integrated with the rest of Europe to reduce the danger of German economic hegemony and rearmament.

The democratic forces in Germany must be allowed to assert themselves and encouraged to carry out the program of denazification. The vestiges of Nazism had to be expurgated from all aspects of life by the Germans themselves.

The education of the German people had to be carried out by Germans in a context that provided security and democracy. Nazism and its spurious idea of Germany must be removed from schools, universities, books, libraries, and other cultural media. Historical experience was the primary teacher, and the imposition of American education on Germans, particularly in the absence of social justice, would be folly.

The document pleaded, as Tillich emphasized everywhere, for Americans to recognize and nurture healthy elements in German society so that the evil elements could be removed without creating a vacuum into which new evil forces would move.

The brief life of the council, 1944–1945, was characterized by internal divisions, and the refugees were unable to agree upon policy for postwar Germany. The council's basic opposition to extreme measures of punishment for Germany was criticized, and for a short time Tillich was blacklisted by the U.S. Army. Eventually, the tensions represented in the developing cold war drained the council of its life, and it expired. What policy it had depended on a united Germany and some cooperation between the U.S. and the U.S.S.R. With division and antagonism, it had no program. In later years when Tillich would refuse to participate in some political activities, he would point to his chairmanship of the council and attribute his withdrawal from active politics to its failure.

He had actually argued for a theology of liberation: the liberation of Europe by the Allied armies and the equipping of Germans for self-liberation in a Nazi-free Germany. With the imposition of military rule and the return of monopoly capitalism after the war, Tillich's dream of a liberating religious socialism had almost no chance for realization.

The World Situation

Since 1934 Tillich had met semiannually with a body that called itself the Theological Discussion Group. The gathering included the Niebuhr brothers, Roland Bainton, Robert Calhoun, John Bennett, Henry P. Van Dusen, Douglas Steere, George F. Thomas, John Mackay, Georgia Harkness, Benjamin Mays, John Knox, Theodore M. Greene, Samuel McCrea Cavert, Edwin E. Aubrey, Wilhelm Pauck, and others. Originally a young gathering, the group gradually came to represent something of an establishment in American theology. Its members considered the group an important channel of cross-fertilization of ideas. The meetings were generally informal and consisted of discussions of scholarly papers.

Henry Van Dusen sensed an emerging consensus among the group, and in 1945 he edited a collection of essays by its members entitled *The Christian Answer*.[14] Tillich contributed the lead piece, "The World Situation." This essay represents Tillich's most complete social analysis of the late war years. The outcome of the war was clear by the time he wrote in 1944, but the atomic bomb and the overt split between Russia and the U.S. were not yet in evidence.

Though Van Dusen's introduction to the volume emphasizes the original process by which the essays were written, criticized, and rewritten, the content of Tillich's essay is not really new. Much of the argument is from *Die religiöse Lage der Gegenwart*, which had been published in Germany in 1926 (ET: *The Religious Situation*, 1932), and other material is from a manuscript that remained in fragment form. Tillich had begun work on a volume on "Religion and World Politics," which was to be published in German by a Dutch publishing firm. The outbreak of the war ended that

---

[14]Paul Tillich et al., *The Christian Answer*, ed. Henry P. Van Dusen (New York: Charles Scribner's Sons, 1945).

project, but much of the conceptual argument appears in "The World Situation" and the original fragment is available in German.[15] Some of Tillich's characteristic dialectic disappeared under Van Dusen's editing, and the claims for the ecumenical church sometimes seem to owe more to Van Dusen than to Tillich.[16] However, the essay, which has been reprinted for popular distribution,[17] remains one of Tillich's most important statements on social philosophy from his American writings.

The work is an attempt by a Westerner to discover the meaning of a revolution that is absorbing the whole world. The determining fact of the emerging, interconnected world is seen as the bourgeois triumph over feudalism and subsequent control over the fate of the world and, most importantly, the ensuing revolt against bourgeois life. World War II is presented as the absorption of the world in the struggle of forces arising out of the failure of bourgeois society to provide security and meaning.

In monopoly capitalism armed with technology, humanity had created a Leviathan that was nearly irresistible. The chaos of bourgeois economic life and the wars of the twentieth century, says Tillich, refute the myth of laissez-faire harmony, and society is now in revolt against liberal capitalism. In Italy and Germany it is a fascist revolt; in the U.S. and England it takes the form of New Deal planning and mild socialist measures; and in Russia, communism expresses the revolt. Humanity could not return to the capitalism of recurrent depressions, Tillich argues, so planning is inevitable. Tillich, however, hopes for an order that will avoid "totalitarian absolutism" and "liberal individualism." The danger he sees ahead is the modern Leviathan, totalitarianism.

In "The World Situation," Tillich shows how personality and community evolve together. His analysis ranges over art, family structure, and education, revealing that the political-economic substance of a culture dominates these cultural expressions. Politics and economics are interdependent, he says, and cannot be separated. Much of postwar Christian social ethics would have had more depth if this interdependence of economics and politics had been kept in view.

---

[15]Tillich, *Gesammelte Werke* 9:139-92.

[16]Reprinted as *The World Situation*, Social Ethics Series 2 (Philadelphia: Fortress Press/Facet Books, 1965).

[17]Ibid., 24.

Throughout the essay, Tillich's concern for structures that would protect the masses from economic insecurity emerges. His own early experience among the workers in Berlin after the First World War inclines his writing in favor of security for the masses, and he calls for breaking the power of "large vested interests.[18] Christianity, he argues, must be committed in its struggle against dehumanization to an alliance with the masses for economic reorganization of the system.

Tillich was not an absolutist in defense of democracy as a constitutional form of government. He thought that liberal democracy demanded prerequisites that were not present in most of the world. The basic principle of his political ethics was the rendering of justice to the "dignity of every human being."[19] A distinction must be made, he argued, between the constitutional system of democracy and democracy as the protection of human dignity. Christianity was allied to the latter cause, but not necessarily to any political form. His colleague Reinhold Niebuhr wrote *The Children of Light and the Children of Darkness* at about this same time. As an American with a different experience of democracy, Niebuhr offered a more thoroughgoing defense of democracy. The two were very close in politics, but Niebuhr was more of a radical democrat than Tillich and, after the war, more prone than Tillich to a cold-war defense of democracy. Christianity for Tillich could not sanction forms of democracy that hid the "destruction of community and personality."

The old balance-of-power politics of nineteenth-century Europe was inadequate for the twentieth century. Tillich saw hope resting in a federation of nations not overly dominated by the victorious allies, but the world lacked the unifying spirit to make such a federation a reality. Christianity had to commit itself to the building of a common spirit within the world. Such a task required an inclusive, ecumenical Christianity. Existential and universal truth would need to be unified within an inclusive church if the church were to rise to the occasion demanded by the world situation.

He summarized the situation: a world revolution was under way against a decaying bourgeois order. Christianity had to protect the masses from meaninglessness and insecurity by promoting a new order. Such an agenda required an ecumenical, progressive Christianity, which remained realistic in the midst of tragedy and eschewed utopian solutions. Tillich's vision during

---

[18]Ibid., 26.
[19]Ibid., 27.

the closing years of the war was essentially the same as during the years of the Wiemar Republic. The victory of an autonomous humanity was affirmed in all its radicalness. Solutions of returning to totalitarian heteronomy were to be avoided even when autonomy was threatening, but humanity had to move on to a theonomous culture in which a modern solution for people in community could be found.

Across the street from the Union Seminary Tower in which Tillich wrote his philosophy, another group was working on the atomic bomb. The headquarters of the Manhattan Project, located on the campus of Columbia University, was visible from Union. The detonation of the world's first two atomic bombs on Japan would close the war, but plunge humanity into a new, revolutionary, world situation.

Conclusion

The most passionately expressed war aim of Paul Tillich is the destruction of Nazism. This is paralleled by the liberation of Europe which is to be also the liberation of Germany. As in classical just-war theory there was the just cause and also the punishment of evil. In the speeches of *Against the Third Reich* these goals are expressed with a fervor and connection with the ultimate reality giving them the character of crusade.

Aims which dominate other writings and also appear in *Against the Third Reich* are the establishment of a world federation, federation in Europe including Germany, social-economic security for the masses, and freedom in its human rights forms and also in its constitutional forms.

He saw the outcome of the war as a victory for Christianity over both Nazism and secularism and as a victory for Anglo-American democracy and Russian socialism. He dreaded the colonization of Germany by the victors, hoped for its avoidance and did not share these fears with his German listeners who already feared the consequences of losing the war.

Elsewhere I have written on Tillich as a theologian of peace. In this war he was a participant against the evil dominating his homeland. He was not a fully developed just-war theorist, though he believed World War II to be both necessary and justifiable on the part of the allies. His attempts to persuade Franklin D. Roosevelt not to pursue unconditional surrender and to listen to the needs of the German resistance for less demanding terms were rebuffed. His protests against the attacks on civilians were not considered. In the end he acquiesced and interpreted the destruction of their cities as punishment for Nazi evil and told his listeners that they could not expect to negotiate with the democracies before surrendering their arms.

Tillich's is the Christian realism that seeks peace as far as it is possible, and then participates in war with few illusions about limiting the violence. Yet he seeks to limit it. In trying to define the war aims he hopes to help shape the war settlements toward longer periods of no war.[20]

Tillich's articulation of war aims for World War II in various contexts still provides an agenda for the coming century. The world still seeks ways to provide human security for the masses. Increasing numbers of people suffering from malnutrition and the denial of resources to become human thwarts claims for justice or peace. Still we seek to mold a Europe that will contain a pacified Germany. Can we contain Germany in a larger NATO and a European Union? The goal of a world organization that can restrain nations from war still eludes us. The fate of the Jewish people still hangs in the balance though now it is dangers in the Middle East rather than in Europe that threaten them. Our ecumenical religious unity that could undergird world ethics for peace and promote human solidarity remains a dream threatened by ethnic murderous idolatries. So many of Tillich's ideals couched in realism remain utopian. But the very process of articulating and defining war aims remains a needed exercise. Failure to be clear about war aims leads to disaster in Vietnam, Somalia, Central America, unclarity and vagueness in Iraq, and uncertainty in the former Yugoslavia.

Peacemakers too, whether at the United Nations or in the United States, need reinforcement in the pursuit of rigor in defining how and when they will defend peace or fight for peacemaking and justice.

---

[20]The chapter utilizes edited pages from Ronald H. Stone, *Paul Tillich's Radical Social Thought* (Atlanta: John Knox Press, 1980); Ronald H. Stone, ed., *Theology of Peace* (Louisville: Westminster/John Knox Press, 1990); and Ronald H. Stone, Matthew Lon Weaver, eds., *Against the Third Reich* (Louisville: Westminster/John Knox Press, 1998); and with pages original to this essay.

Chapter 13

Niebuhr, Tillich, Bennett, and the Bomb

Church leaders and the public knew nothing about the development of the atomic bomb as decisions were made by scientists, military people, and a few civilian officials, particularly Presidents Roosevelt and Truman.

On some other war-related issues, church leaders were ahead of the political leadership. Reinhold Niebuhr, for example, had told of the murder of Jews in camps as early as 1933. Paul Tillich had denounced the anti-Semitism of Nazism before it was understood in the United States. John Foster Dulles, as chairman of the Federal Council of Churches Commission, had met with President Roosevelt advocating an international organization. In 1944–1945 the church was developing American opinion to reverse its shortsighted rejection of the League of Nations, and to support a new and strengthened United Nations. Church leaders had denounced obliteration bombing of cities and questioned demands for unconditional surrender. But on the development of nuclear weapons they were silent in their innocence. On the coming of the new nuclear age they did not see the signs of the times. Paul Tillich's brilliant *The World Situation*, published in 1945, for example, has no mention of the new warfare soon to be revealed. Meanwhile the Manhattan project was going ahead across the street from Union Theological Seminary.

The president of Union Seminary and the editorial board of *Christianity and Crisis* had, in June 1945, spoken out against the single-minded slogan of unconditional surrender and against obliteration bombing. Henry Pitney van Dusen directed these two criticisms of the administration in the issue of *Christianity and Crisis* dated 6 August 1945.

George Kennedy Bell, Anglican bishop of Chichester, wrote:

There are certain deeds which science should not do. There are certain actions for which scientists should not be made conscripts by any nation. And surely the extermination of any civilian population by any nation is one of these.[1]

By October 1945, Reinhold Niebuhr saw that neither world control of atomic energy nor the outlawing of the bomb was going to be realized. He had some hope for sharing atomic knowledge in a thoroughgoing settlement of issues with the Soviet Union, but he knew that too was beyond immediate political realization.[2]

The earliest semiofficial church statement on atomic warfare was the release in the spring of 1946 of the report of the Federal Council of Churches Commission on the "Relation of the Church to the War in the Light of the Christian Faith." The report is widely referred to by the name of its chairman, Robert L. Calhoun, professor of Historical Theology, Yale University, as the "Calhoun Report." The Commission's membership included nearly two dozen leading professors of theology and Christian ethics, mostly from the eastern corridor of schools, including one woman and one African-American. John C. Bennett served as secretary and drafted most of the report. (Throughout Bennett's long career he would continue to write, teach, and debate on these subjects.) Also, both of the Niebuhr brothers were present.

The theology of the report is theocentric with God understood as creator, redeemer, and judge. The report, after a theological analytic preface, begins with repentance.

We would begin with an act of contrition. As American Christians we are deeply penitent for the irresponsible use already made of the atomic war.[3]

The "surprise bombings" without warning were specifically regarded as "morally indefensible." Further argument referred to the discussion among scientists of an alternative demonstrative use. Japan's position in 1945 had been hopeless, but the report conceded the bombing may have shortened the war.

---

[1]*Christianity and Crisis* 5/15 (17 September 1945): 7.

[2]*Christianity and Crisis* 5/17 (15 October 1945): 7.

[3]"Atomic Warfare and the Christian Faith" (New York: Federal Council of Churches, 1946) 11.

The report put the atomic bomb in the context of the pre-atomic obliteration bombing and rejected the arguments of military necessity alone deciding the issues. They pointed to U.S. Air Force studies which were showing that obliteration bombing had not been, on the whole, a military success.

Four theses were put forward: (1) these new methods are intolerable to Christian conscience and Christians need to resist their use; (2) war itself is the problem; (3) the U.S. was urged to stop production of atomic bombs and to promise no first use; and (4) U.N. control of atomic weapons was needed.

The church's role was in helping the spirit of worldwide community to grow. Penitence for wartime crimes was called for. Temptations to overpunish the vanquished enemies needed to be overcome. Hiroshima and Nagasaki should be rebuilt and the churches could lead the financial drive. The report concluded with the final third of the report being theological analysis of ultimate issues of faith.

Robert C. Batchelder has called attention to the conditioning of the report by World War II with the expectation that war would be total war. Therefore, the war problem itself was attacked. The report focused on the tilting of the advantage to aggressive rather than defensive war and the advantage to the attacker of surprise attack or treachery.

Conant-Niebuhr Exchange

The theologians denouncing the nuclear attacks on Hiroshima and Nagasaki led James Conant, the president of Harvard University, to respond sharply to Reinhold Niebuhr. If Niebuhr had been innocent of knowledge of uranium's potential before the atomic bomb, Conant had led in the development of the bomb from the beginning. Serving as scientific advisor to President Roosevelt and as a member of the "top policy group" on atomic weapons, he at several points had played a central role in advancing the weapons. As an early scientific negotiator with the British Conant had advised Churchill, as well as Roosevelt, and after the war he would discuss scientific cooperation with Stalin and the use of nuclear energy for peace. Conant was an active interventionist against Nazism before Pearl Harbor and a militant articulator of the policies of unconditional surrender. He approved of the use of the bomb on Hiroshima, as well as the firebombing of Tokyo. His relationship with Niebuhr was one of friendship and admiration. He had courted Niebuhr to come to Harvard as a university professor. Niebuhr's pragmatism and realism were both sympathetic to the president of Harvard's own intellectual commitment. Conant's son, Theodore, described Niebuhr's wartime book, *The Children of Light and the Children of Darkness*, as his father's guiding philosophy. "If he had an equivalent of the Old Testament for an orthodox Jew it was *The Children of Light and the Children of Darkness*."[4]

Conant would write to Niebuhr three times in March 1946. Conant's letters were personal, but they were also symptomatic of his broader postwar campaigns to justify the bombings. He urged and corrected the McGeorge Bundy ghost-written essay for Stimson justifying the bombing. He tried to stop and participated in altering an MGM film about Hiroshima, and generally was very active in publicly arguing for the decision to drop the weapon which he had urged forward and helped to manage. The campaign he and others promoted to win acceptance of the bombing and consequently of the weapons was largely victorious. By 1950 most of the church leaders who had condemned the bombing were learning to accept the weapons themselves and deterrence.[5] It awaited further work by ethicists and historians to refute the arguments that the bomb itself stopped the war and led to Japan's surrender or that the bomb was necessary to prevent a costly United States' invasion of Japan.

Conant responded to the *New York Times* account of the Commission of the Federal Council of Churches' report and Niebuhr's participation. Some of Conant's concerns might have been alleviated if he had read the whole report. But, even so, after Niebuhr's responses he had to conclude that the two were still in disagreement.

Conant's first complaint was that the report did not adequately relate the atomic bomb to the accepted practices of strategic or area bombing. If we were to be penitent for the atomic bomb and the incendiary destruction of Tokyo then "the whole method of warfare used against the axis powers" was questioned.

---

[4]James G. Hershberg, *James B. Conant: Harvard to Hiroshima and the Making of a Nuclear Age* (New York: Alfred A. Knopf, 1993) 284.

[5]Robert C. Calhoun and Georgia Harkness of the original critics dissented from the Dunn Commission of 1950 which represented the theologians' acceptance of the weapons. See Robert C. Batchelder, *The Irreversible Decision 1939–1950* (Boston: Houghton Mifflin Co., 1961) 237-69.

Moreover, he feared that the Protestant leaders would cut themselves off from the majority of American opinion which supported the atomic bomb as "part and parcel of the total operation of that war." Then he asked where does the argument take us. Sarcastically he added: "Are we to scrap all our armament at once?"[6]

In the last paragraph of his letter to Niebuhr, Conant states that he is "a great believer in eliminating the atomic bomb as a potential weapon for a surprise through international control."[7] But, of course, that would be very difficult to achieve. A postscript is even more barbed. He mentions recommending Niebuhr's book, *Children of Light and Children of Darkness*, to a clergyman who denounced him for his role in the atomic bomb. But then he adds: "I can't reconcile this book with your signature on the document in question."[8]

Niebuhr's response was irenic. He pointed out that the report made "no absolute distinction" between the levels of destructiveness achieved by different weapons. He referred to the reports mentioning that Air Force studies showed that obliteration bombing was not very effective.

Then he pointed out that the majority of the committee objected to the use of the bomb without warning. They had believed the bomb should have been demonstrated and Japan warned. He then went on to say that the conviction of most of the committee was that the bomb could have eventually been used and justifiably so for the "shortening of the war." The ordinary argument about saving the lives of thousand of American soldiers who would die on the beaches in an invasion was also affirmed.

Then he wrote a long paragraph about the guilt that good people incur in defeating tyranny. He signed the report he wrote "to admit the moral ambiguity of all righteous people in history, who are, despite the good they do, involved in antecedent and in marginal guilt."

The tone of Niebuhr's letter is pacifying, the tone of the report had been alarming and condemnatory. Sentences of the report were as threatening as Carl Sagan's *The Nuclear Winter*. If Conant had seen the whole church report and not just the newspaper accounts he would have understood that the practice of obliteration bombing was judged immoral

---

[6]Quotes from letter of James B. Conant to Reinhold Niebuhr, 6 March 1946, Library of Congress.

[7]Ibid.

[8]Ibid.

and against the laws of God. The line the church leaders wanted to hold after the war between obliteration bombing of cities and attacks on military targets was one that the president of Harvard did not discern or, at least, acknowledge. Neither did President Truman in his writing and speeches on the bomb make that distinction.

Paul Tillich shared the dilemma of the church statements following the bomb that rejected total war, but did not completely renounce the bomb. The Federal Council report of the Dunn Commission of 1950 saw the need for deterrence and they would not give up even the first possible use of the bomb. Batchelder reports that the Catholic moralists who wrote *The Ethics of Atomic War* in 1947 saw the dilemma and affirmed both the immorality of bombing a city and the possible necessity for so doing. Similarly the British Council of Churches' *The Era of Atomic Power* could neither sanction the use of atomic weapons or demand their abandonment in the present situation. Batchelder believes the Federal Council of Churches' Commission of 1950 of which Bennett, Niebuhr, and Tillich were members escaped the dilemma by drawing the line between bombing of cities and other uses of nuclear weapons. The moral distinctions are not between instruments in warfare. Atomic bombs may, under some circumstances, be used, but their indiscriminate use had to be avoided. Niebuhr's introduction to the statement in *Christianity and Crisis* calls attention to four aspects of the report.[9]

(1) The report is set in context of historical responsibilities to defend Western civilization.
(2) No absolute distinction among kinds of weapons is made morally. So the report refuses to denounce specifically all possible first uses of atomic weapons.
(3) The primary task is to avoid war through development of non-Communist worlds, unity of allied nations, and international courage. Preventive war and/or inevitable war understandings are rejected.
(4) The difference between destruction of military targets and mass destruction of civilian population was central to the report.

---

[9]*Christianity and Crisis* 10/21 (11 December 1950): p. 161.

Two pacifists on the Dunn Commission who refused to sign the final report published their dissent. The context of the Dunn report was the beginning of the Korean War and though this expressed itself in the sentences affirming the struggle with Communism it failed to note that the present wars were limited and the nuclear weapons, while relevant, were unlikely to be used. Batchelder is very critical of these church studies in their failure to focus on limited wars. The pacifists felt that not enough distinctive Christian guidance was given and that a more thorough theological document was needed. The 1950 document was more aware of the Cold War and the Korean War and less critical of atomic weapons in themselves than the 1946 piece. The church was learning to live with the weapons.

Paul Tillich joined his Union colleagues Reinhold Niebuhr and John Bennett in signing the report. Niebuhr had endorsed the "no first use of hydrogen weapons" in 1950 while conceding that in the Cold War context the United States could not refrain from developing them after the Soviet Union had detonated an atomic bomb. Seeing the Baruch plan defeated and finding little hope in nuclear disarmament negotiations with the U.S.S.R., he pleaded for restraint in U.S. planning to rely on the bomb.[10] The arguments of no first use were the strongest recommendations of the Dunn Commission.

In Tillich's own writing he argued that a war fought with nuclear weapons could not be justified. It was not permissible to enter a war that included the intention to use nuclear weapons. Such a war would only bring mutual destruction and no intended goal of the war could be fulfilled. He noted that Western allies could, if they had the will, develop conventional armaments adequate to deter any Communist invasion in Europe. He leaned toward a position of no first use of nuclear weapons as the Commission had declared, but he also allowed the West some ambiguity in announcing such a policy. Until adequate conventional forces were created, "maybe it was safer to keep the Communists uncertain about first use."[11] However, the logic of deterrence meant that

---

[10]Reinhold Niebuhr, "The Hydrogen Bomb," *Christianity and Society* (Spring 1950): 5-7.

[11]Paul Tillich, "Correspondence," *Partisan Review* 39/2 (1962): 311-12.

Our intention to answer any nuclear attack with nuclear weapons must be absolutely clear, and it must also be clear that we have the power to do so.[12]

A remarkable short statement on the hydrogen bomb by Tillich was published in 1954 in *Pulpit Digest*. It consisted of only five points.

(1) Humanity may destroy itself by the tensions in itself.
(2) The meaning of history is not dependent on how humanity is annihilated.
(3) Resistance to self-destruction is called forth by all persons who are aware of humanity's suicidal instincts.
(4) The resistance must be carried out in all levels of politics, morals, and religions including "a new expression of the ultimate concern which transcends as well as determines historical existence."[13]
(5) Finally, the acts of resistance must unite all these different levels of concern and be done with wisdom and courage.

The emphasis on resistance to human self destruction was new and it did not simply follow Niebuhr and Bennett.

Correspondence in the Harvard Tillich Archive indicates that Tillich was repeatedly requested by the American Friends Service Commission, the National Committee for a Sane Nuclear Policy, and other organizations to endorse their positions against weapons testing and for nuclear disarmament. He refused to give any of the organizations wholehearted support, and he especially resisted their pacifist leanings. In 1957 he did sign a statement of the Committee for a Sane Nuclear Policy calling for arms control and the abolition of nuclear testing. The statement was published in *The New York Times* on 15 November 1957. Other signatures included long-standing pacifists, anti-war activists, religious leaders, Eleanor Roosevelt, and John Bennett whose guidance Tillich often sought on these questions. Reinhold Niebuhr, who was a little more of a cold warrior than John

---

[12]Ibid., 312.
[13]Reprinted in Paul Tillich, "The Hydrogen Bomb," *Theology of Peace* (Louisville: Westminster/John Knox Press, 1990) 158-59.

Bennett, refrained from signing, though on most issues Bennett, Niebuhr, and Tillich were agreed.

Tillich's Harvard secretary, Grace Leonard, was a member of SANE, and through her influence Tillich agreed to SANE's 1961 use of his statement in the *Pulpit Digest* on resistance to the hydrogen bomb.

After Reinhold Niebuhr's stroke in 1952, John Bennett, the younger colleague of both Niebuhr and Tillich, took the lead in writing the frequent articles and essays in *Christianity and Crisis*. Though mindful of the full context of the Cold War, Bennett would focus his direct attention on the problems of the weapons themselves. Niebuhr always accentuated not the weapons but the conflict that gave rise to the weapons. Tillich made shorter contributions to the discussion which revealed great passion and deep concern about the problem, but he was not the leader. Bennett's recollection, shortly before his death in 1995, was that Niebuhr's thought provided the leadership on this issue. But it was Bennett who edited the book *Nuclear Weapons and the Conflict of Conscience*;[14] Niebuhr wrote a very laudatory review of it.

Niebuhr's major contribution to the discussion was the chapter "The Cold War and the Nuclear Dilemma" in his 1959 volume, *The Structure of Nations and Empires*.[15] He could find no way out of the dilemma, which was the necessity of possessing the weapons and the moral impossibility of using them. All three of the Christian realists recognized the need in a nuclear age for deterrence, but all of them were horrified at thoughts of first use, preventive war, or preventive strike use of the weapons. Accepting that neither side intended to initiate a major conflict, it could still come upon them. Even so the prospects for either disarmament or arms control seemed minor until the hostilities of the Cold War faded. Capitulation of the allied side seemed unrealistic to Niebuhr, though some in the West advocated it. He did not expect capitulation from the Communist side except in the long range of hundreds of years. Attempts to limit the conflict to tactical weapons in Europe as Henry Kissinger had proposed did not seem realistic to Niebuhr in 1959, though he had hailed Kissinger's book when it first came

---

[14]*Nuclear Weapons and the Conflict of Conscience*, ed. John Coleman Bennett (New York: Scribner's, 1962).

[15]Reinhold Niebuhr, *The Structure of Nations and Empires: A Study of the Recurring Patterns and Problems of the Political Order in Relation to the Unique Problems of the Nuclear Age* (New York: Scribner's, 1959).

out. His one hope was in the waning of the communist fervor as the original generations of revolutionary idealists faded from the scene. We were not fated to confront fanatical communism forever, but communism was perceived to have advantages in the Third World, and he did not see its demise in the foreseeable future. Occasionally reports of scientific dialogue between scientists from the USA and the USSR, the ABM treaty, or the partial test-ban treaty would raise his hopes that incremental steps might add up to significant progress in relationships with the USSR, but his overall perspective was pessimistic and he expected ongoing conflict mediated by fears of mutual annihilation and processes of wise diplomacy.

The dangers of the 1961 Berlin crisis led to Paul Tillich's participation in the debates again. It is hard for us to remember the sense of danger that accompanied the years of the Kennedy presidency. I was in Europe during the summer of 1961, and I particularly remember the sense of crisis and the foreboding dark fears of pessimism of Norman Vincent Peale with whom I was visiting in Interlaken. Informed people knew that Berlin was near the crux of the Cold War and that the young president was being tested very threateningly by Khrushchev. Tillich with the realism of his own theology and his central European experience could not regard shifts in the borders of Berlin or its politics as the ultimate issue. His appearance on a panel discussion program of Eleanor Roosevelt's with Henry Kissinger, James Reston, and Max Freedman revealed the deep caution with which Niebuhr, Bennett, and Tillich all regarded the use of nuclear weapons. The panel was dominated by the hard-line cold warriors. A few days later James Reston attacked Tillich for Tillich's refusal to support defending Berlin with nuclear weapons.[16]

For Tillich, defense was a moral necessity, but to defend something in actions which meant its destruction violated the reason for defense. Particularly noteworthy in Tillich's analysis—a theme that appeared elsewhere in his writing during this period—is the insight that even retreat is not the end. Retreat is a normal strategic move. Tillich knew and wrote in *Partisan Review* in 1962 that in the long run the West was militarily superior to the Warsaw Pact nations. The avoidance of retreat was no excuse for relying on nuclear weapons in a suicidal manner.

---

[16]*The New York Times* (25 October 1961).

Writing in *Christianity and Crisis*, the Christian realists quickly picked up the debate in November 1961.[17] Bennett led by calling for more significant participation in these nuclear moral issues and cautioning about any violation of the firebreak between conventional and nuclear weapons use. Niebuhr added a short response agreeing that the only use of the weapons for the West was in deterrence or in a second strike to prevent any further attacks by an enemy who had already unleashed nuclear weapons. Kenneth Thompson, in the same issue of *Christianity and Crisis*, refused to go to the no-first-use position and cautioned Bennett against strident moral protest. Tillich published the statement that had led to the attacks on his recommendation of no defense of his home city of Berlin with nuclear weapons. Tillich's statement was a shortened form of his own formulation of the justified war. Proportionality was built into the requirement that any recourse to war must serve creative justice. Atomic war, Tillich concluded, cannot be justified ethically. Therefore, while defense was required, temporary retreat until the allies could redress the conventional forces was an ordinary tactic and was preferred to any initiation of a nuclear exchange. The criticism directed against this no-first-use policy of these Christian realists was that it invited attack to telegraph beforehand that you would not defend a vulnerable position with nuclear weapons. For their part the Christian realists regarded the first use of atomic weapons as wrong and they did not want to be the first to use them ever again.

Summary

Christian realism, as I understand it from my reading of Tillich and Niebuhr and the additional contributions of Bennett, had several distinctive emphases. The atomic bombing of Hiroshima and Nagasaki was morally wrong. Cities should never be the object of nuclear-weapon attack or obliteration bombing in warfare. It was necessary to retain nuclear weapons as long as one's enemy possessed them. It was morally wrong to use nuclear weapons first. The danger of war remained even though neither superpower intended to begin a nuclear exchange. Incremental reduction of the danger of war and the decrease of nuclear terror were possible through creative diplomacy and the probing of the other's position to find out where agreement was possible. They did not foresee any near end to the Cold

---

[17]*Christianity and Crisis* 21/19 (13 November 1961): 200-204.

War, and they did not trust much in disarmament negotiations while the political issues were divisive.

After the assassination of President Kennedy, Tillich's public political role decreased, though he did, as a systematic theologian, issue a denunciation of Goldwater partially because of Goldwater's saber-rattling stances. Niebuhr followed the debates until his death in 1971, growing increasingly concerned about the dominance of the military under Presidents Johnson and Nixon in the context of the Vietnam war. Bennett's debates with Paul Ramsey continued the in-house Christian-realist debates. Bennett exalted over the collapse of the USSR and the decrease in the nuclear dangers. In his last Christmas letter he quoted Simeon, "Now let thy servant depart in peace."

In conclusion, I find a lot of wisdom in this review of Christian realism. During his lifetime I disagreed with Reinie on the evil of communism, now I think he was more correct than I was. Bennett was not in agreement with my criticism of deterrence as immoral. Its intention to be used under certain circumstances against enemy civilians rendered it morally indefensible as I argued in The Peacemaking Struggle (1985), Presbyterians and Peacemaking: Are We Now Called to Resistance (1985—both with Dana Wilbanks), and Christian Realism and Peace Making (1988).

I do not think Reinhold Niebuhr or Paul Tillich would have put it the way I did either. Niebuhr left it at the dilemma level with the only possible use in defensive strike; Tillich stayed with the use of war only as an act of creative justice and did not reject deterrence. I thought and still think that the Christian moralist must reject nuclear deterrence morally and then urge creative solutions moving us away from reliance on nuclear weapons. I do not think the moral rejection of deterrence means policies of surrender or immediate unilateral disarmament. That is not how policy works. The Christian moralist fulfills the vocation as clearly as possible saying what is intolerable and working with others to find ways to move out of morally impossible structures.

Niebuhr warned us as well as anyone about the imponderables, surprises, and ironies of history. I will not criticize him now for not foreseeing the early end of the Soviet empire. My own reading is that the collapse was mostly due to the failure of the ideas of communism and this is quite ironic for a historical-materialist system. Maybe he was a little too pessimistic about arms control agreements, but not very much. His optimism was probably more misplaced in his hopes for UNESCO and the Alliance for Progress.

At this point it seems useful to me to note that this Christian Realism was quite different from government policy, though William McNamara's strategies brought the government closer to the realist sense of morality. Though it often found wisdom in Kissinger, Herman Kahn, and other mainstream nuclear theorists, the moral reservations and critique were present. Notes of unilateral initiatives recommended by Bennett and Tillich's resistance to nuclear weapons and the necessity of relying on conventional defense took these Christian realists a long way from harder realism or realpolitik, and U.S. government policy.

Finally, Tillich's refusal to regard even atomic warfare as ultimate kept it in perspective. Ultimately, there was God, not decisions by politicians or generals.

Bibliography

Primary Bibliography[1]

Tillich, Paul. *Das System der Wissenschaften nach Gegenständen und Methoden: Ein Entwurf*. Göttingen: Vandenhoeck & Ruprecht, 1923. In *Gesammelte Werke*, volume 1. Stuttgart: Evangelisches Verlagswerk (1959) 109-293. ET: *The System of the Sciences according to Objects and Methods*. Translated by Paul Wiebe. Lewisburg PA: Bucknell University Press, 1981. Also translated earlier by Emile Grünberg and partly revised by James Luther Adams as "The System of the Sciences." Undated typescript in Harvard Tillich Archives.

_____. "Religionsphilosophie." In *Lehrbuch der Philosophie*, two volumes, edited by Max Dessoir, 2:765-835. Berlin: Ullstein, 1925.

_____. *Die religiöse Lage der Gegenwart*. Berlin: Ullstein, 1926. ET: *The Religious Situation*. Translated by H. Richard Niebuhr. New York: Henry Holt and Co., 1932. Various reprints.

_____. *The Interpretation of History*. Translated by N. A. Rasetzki and Elsa L. Talmey. New York/London: Charles Scribner's Sons, 1936.

_____. "The Gospel and the State." *Crozer Quarterly* 15/4 (1938): 241-61.

_____. "The Religious Symbol." Translated by James Luther Adams. *Journal of Liberal Religion* 2 (Summer 1940): 13-33.

_____. *War Aims*. New York: Protestant Digest, 1941.

_____. "I Am an American." *Protestant Digest* 2/4 (June–July 1941): 24-26.

_____. "Symbol and Knowledge." *Journal of Liberal Religion* 2/4 (1941): 202-206.

_____. "Protestant Principles." *The Protestant* 4/5 (April–May 1942): 17.

_____. "Man and Society in Religious Socialism." *Christianity and Society* 8/4 (1943): 10-20.

_____. "Nietzsche and the Bourgeois Spirit." *Journal of the History of Ideas* 6 (June 1945): 309.

---

[1]Works by Tillich are organized (generally) by date of publication, but note that a number of his earlier works were not published until after his death.

_____ et al. *The Christian Answer*. Edited by Henry P. Van Dusen. New York: Charles Scribner's Sons, 1945.

_____. "The Two Types of Philosophy of Religion." *Union Seminary Quarterly Review* 1 (May 1946): 3-13.

_____. "The Problem of Theological Method." *The Journal of Religion* 27 (January 1947): 16-26.

_____. *The Protestant Era*. Translated by James Luther Adams. Chicago: University of Chicago Press, 1948.

_____. *The Shaking of the Foundations*. New York: Charles Scribner's Sons, 1948.

_____. "Beyond Religious Socialism." *Christian Century* 66 (15 June 1949): 732-33.

_____. *Systematic Theology*. Three volumes. Chicago: University of Chicago Press, 1951–1963.

_____. *The Courage to Be*. New Haven: Yale University Press, 1952.

_____. "The Conquest of Theological Provincialism." In *The Cultural Migration: The European Scholar in America*, edited by Franz L. Neumann, 138-56. Philadelphia: University of Pennsylvania Press, 1953.

_____. *Love, Power, and Justice*. New York/London: Oxford University Press, 1954.

_____. "Past and Present Reflections on Christianity and Society." May 1955. Tillich Papers.

_____. *Biblical Religion and the Search for Ultimate Reality*. Chicago: University of Chicago Press, 1955.

_____. "To the Editor." *Christianity and Crisis* 16/3 (5 March 1956): 24.

_____. *Dynamics of Faith*. New York: Harper & Row, 1957.

_____. *Theology of Culture*. London: Oxford University Press, 1959.

_____. "The Christian and Marxist View of Man." Second edition. Harvard Archive: Universal Christian Council for Life and Work, 1959.

_____. "How My Mind Has Changed." *The Christian Century* 77 (7 December 1960): 1435-37.

_____. *Love, Power, and Justice*. New York: Oxford University Press, 1960.

_____. "Kairos und Logos." In volume 4 of *Gesammelte Werke*, 43-76. Stuttgart: Evangelisches Verlagswerk, 1961.

_____. "Sin and Grace in the Theology of Reinhold Niebuhr." In *Reinhold Niebuhr: A Prophetic Voice in Our Time*, edited by Harold Landon, 27-41. Greenwich: Seabury Press, 1962.

_____. "Correspondence." *Partisan Review* 39/2 (1962): 311-12.

_____. *Christianity and the Encounter of the World Religions*. New York: Columbia University Press, 1963. Repr.: Minneapolis: Fortress Press, 1974.

_____. *Theology of Culture*. New York: Oxford University Press, 1964.

_____. *Ultimate Concern: Tillich in Dialogue.* Edited by D. Mackenzie Brown. New York: Harper & Row, 1965.

_____. *The World Situation.* Social Ethics series 2. Philadelphia: Fortress Press/Facet Books, 1965.

_____. "Rejoinder." *The Journal of Religion* 46 (January 1966): 190.

_____. "The Significance of the History of Religions for the Systematic Theologian" (12 October 1965 lecture). In *The Future of Religions*, edited by Jerald C. Brauer, 80-94. New York: Harper & Row, 1966. Repr.: In *Theological Writings*, 431-46. Main Works volume 6 / Hauptwerke band 6. Berlin/New York: de Gruyter; Berlin: Evangelisches Verlagswerk, 1992.

_____. *A History of Christian Thought.* Edited by Carl E. Braaten. New York: Simon and Schuster, 1968.

_____. "The Conquest of the Concept of Religion in the Philosophy of Religion." In *What Is Religion?*, edited by James Luther Adams. New York: Harper & Row, 1969.

_____. "The Philosophy of Religion." In *What Is Religion?*, edited by James Luther Adams. New York: Harper & Row, 1969.

_____. "On the Idea of a Theology of Culture." In *What Is Religion?*, edited James Luther Adams and translated by William B. Green, 55-181. New York: Harper & Row, 1969.

_____. *My Travel Diary: 1936.* New York: Harper & Row, 1970.

_____. "Rechtfertigung und Zweifel." In volume 8 of *Gesammelte Werke.* Stuttgart: Evangelisches Verlagswerk, 1970.

_____. *Political Expectation.* Edited by James Luther Adams. New York: Harper & Row Publishers, 1971. Repr.: ROSE 1. Macon GA: Mercer University Press, 1981.

_____. *The Socialist Decision.* Translated by Franklin Sherman. New York: Harper & Row, 1977.

_____. *The Meaning of Health.* Edited by Perry LeFevre. Chicago: Exploration Press, 1984.

_____. *The Theology of Peace.* Edited by Ronald H. Stone. Louisville: Westminster/John Knox, 1990.

_____. "A Dialogue between Paul Tillich and Hisamatsu Shin'ichi." In *The Encounter of Religions and Quasi-Religions*, edited by Terence Thomas, 75-170. Lewiston NY: Edwin Mellen Press, 1990.

Secondary Bibliography[2]

Abe, Masao. *Zen and Western Thought*. Honolulu: University of Hawaii Press, 1985.

Adams, James Luther. *Paul Tillich's Philosophy of Culture, Science, and Religion*. New York: Schocken Books, 1965.

Adams, James Luther, Wilhelm Pauck, and Roger L. Shinn, eds. *The Thought of Paul Tillich*. San Francisco: Harper & Row, 1985.

Alves, Rubem A. *Protestantism and Repression: A Brazilian Case Study*. Maryknoll: Orbis Books, 1985.

Amelung, Eberhard. "Religious Socialism as an Ideology: A Study of the Kairos Circle in Germany between 1919 and 1933." Ph.D. dissertation, Harvard University, 1962.

Baird, Robert D. *Category Formation and the History of Religions*. The Hague: Mouton, 1971.

Barth, Karl. *The Word of God and the Word of Man*. New York: Harper & Row, 1956; orig. 1928.

_____. *The Epistle to the Romans*. Translated and edited by Edwyn C. Hoskyns. London: Oxford University Press, 1933.

_____. *Church Dogmatics*. Four volumes. Edited by G. W. Bromiley and T. F. Torrance. Edinburgh: T.&T. Clark, 1958.

Batchelder, Robert C. *The Irreversible Decision 1939–1950*. Boston: Houghton Mifflin Co., 1961.

Bell, George Kennedy. "Bishop Bell Condemns Use of Atomic Bomb." *Christianity and Crisis* 5/15 (17 September 1945): 7.

Bennett, John C., editor. *Nuclear Weapons and the Conflict of Conscience*. New York: Scribner, 1962.

_____. "Tillich and the 'Fellowship of Socialist Christians.' " *North American Paul Tillich Society Newsletter* (1 October 1990): 3.

Berger, Peter. *The Heretical Imperative*. London: Collins, 1980.

Boone, Kathleen C. *The Bible Tells Them So; The Discourse of Protestant Fundamentalism*. Albany NY: State University of New York Press, 1989.

Brock, Rita. *Journeys By Heart: A Christology of Erotic Power*. New York: Crossroad, 1991.

Brown, Robert McAffee. *Gustavo Gutiérrez*. Atlanta: John Knox Press, 1980.

Bullough, Vern. *The Subordinate Sex*. New York: Penguin, 1974.

---

[2]Multiple works by an author are organized by date of publication.

Burns, Rita. "Breaking the Grand Silence: A Diocesan Practice," volume 1 of *Women in the Church*. Edited by Madonna Kolbenschlag. Washington: Pastoral Press, 1987.

Cadorette, Curt. *From the Heart of the People: The Theology of Gustavo Gutiérrez*. Oak Park: Meyer-Stone Books, 1988.

Carr, Anne. *Transforming Grace*. San Francisco: Harper & Row, 1988.

Champion, James W. "Tillich and the Frankfurt School." *Soundings* 169/4 (Winter 1986): 512-30.

Clendenin, Daniel B. *Many Gods, Many Lords; Christianity Encounters World Religions*. Grand Rapids MI: Baker Books, 1995.

Commission on the "Relation of the Church to the War in the Light of the Christian Faith." "Atomic Warfare and the Christian Faith." New York: Federal Council of Churches, 1946.

Conant, James B. Letter to Reinhold Niebuhr. 6 March 1946. Library of Congress.

Council for a Democratic Germany. "A Program for a Democratic Germany." *Christianity and Crisis* (15 May 1944): 3-5.

Crossman, Richard C., editor. *Paul Tillich: A Comprehensive Bibliography and Keyword Index of Primary and Secondary Writings in English*. Metuchen NJ/London: American Theological Library Association and Scarecrow Press, 1983.

Daly, Mary. "Return of the Protestant Principle." *Commonweal* 90 (6 June 1969): 338-41.

_____. "If You Could Make One Change in the Church, What Would It Be?" *Commonweal* 92 (1 May 1970): 161.

_____. "After the Death of God the Father." *Commonweal* 94 (12 March 1971): 7-11.

_____. "The Church and Women: An Interview with Mary Daly." *Theology Today* 28/3. (October 1971): 349-54.

_____. "The Spiritual Revolution: Women's Liberation as Theological Reeducation." *Andover Newton Quarterly* 12 (March 1972): 163-76.

_____. *Beyond God the Father: Toward a Philosophy of Women's Liberation*. Boston: Beacon Press, 1973.

_____. "A Short Essay on Hearing and on the Qualitative Leap of Radical Feminism." *Horizons* 2 (Spring 1975): 120-24.

_____. *The Church and the Second Sex*. New York: Harper & Row, 1975.

_____. *Gyn/Ecology: The Metaethics of Radical Feminism*. Boston: Beacon Press, 1978.

_____. *Pure Lust: Elemental Feminist Philosophy*. Boston: Beacon Press, 1984.

Dion, Michel. *Liberation feministe et salut chretien: Mary Daly et Paul Tillich*. Quebec: Editions Bellarmin, 1995.

Dreisbach, Donald F. *Symbols and Salvation: Paul Tillich's Doctrine of Religious Symbols and His Interpretation of the Symbols of the Christian Tradition.* Lanham MD: University Press of America, 1993.

Driver, Tom. "The Case for Pluralism." In *The Myth of Christian Uniqueness,* edited by John Hick and Paul Knitter, 203-18. Maryknoll NY: Orbis Books, 1987.

Eliade, Mircea. *The Sacred and the Profane.* New York: Harcourt, Brace, and World, 1959.

Fishman, Hertzel. *American Protestantism and a Jewish State.* Detroit: Wayne State University Press, 1973.

Gadamer, Hans. *Truth and Method.* New York: Seabury Press, 1975.

Garcia, Ismael. *Justice in Latin American Theology of Liberation.* Atlanta: John Knox Press, 1987.

Gay, Peter. "Weimar Culture: The Outsider as Insider." In *Perspectives in American History* 2 (1968).

Gilkey, Langdon. "Plurality and Its Theological Implications." In *The Myth of Christian Uniqueness: Toward a Pluralistic Theology of Religions,* edited by John Hick and Paul F. Knitter, 37-52. Maryknoll NY: Orbis Books, 1987.

_____. *Gilkey on Tillich.* New York: Crossroad, 1990.

Grigg, Richard. *Symbol and Empowerment: Paul Tillich's Post-Theistic System.* Macon GA: Mercer University Press, 1985.

Gutierrez, Gustavo. *The Power of the Poor in History: Selected Writings.* Maryknoll: Orbis Books, 1983.

Gutiérrez, Gustavo. *We Drink from Our Own Wells: The Spiritual Journey of a People.* Maryknoll NY: Orbis Books, 1984.

_____. *On Job.* Maryknoll: Orbis Books, 1987.

_____. *A Theology of Liberation.* Maryknoll NY: Orbis Books, 1988.

Halpern, Ben. "Zionism,"In *International Encyclopedia of the Social Sciences.* New York: Macmillan, 1968.

Hammond, Guyton. *Man in Estrangement: A Comparison of the Thought of Paul Tillich and Erich Fromm.* Nashville: Vanderbilt University Press, 1965.

_____. "Tillich and the Frankfurt Debates about Patriarchy and the Family." In *Theonomy and Autonomy,* edited by John J. Carey, 89-110. Macon GA: Mercer University Press, 1984.

_____. "Tillich and the Frankfurt School on Protestantism and the Bourgeois Spirit." In *Religion et Culture,* edited by Jean Richard, 327-38. Quebec: Les Presses de L'universite Laval, 1987.

_____. "Why Did Westerners Become Fascists? Fromm, Tillich, and Horkheimer on Character Types." *Papers from the Annual Meeting of the North American Paul Tillich Society* (September 1990): 8-12.

_____. *Conscience and Its Recovery: From the Frankfurt School to Feminism.* Charlottesville VA: University Press of Virginia, 1993.

Handy, Robert T. "Christian Action in Perspective." *Christianity and Society* 21 (Summer 1956): 10-14.

Hawley, John S., and Wayne Proudfoot. "Introduction." In *Fundamentalism and Gender*, edited by John S. Hawley, 3-46. Oxford/New York: Oxford University Press, 1994.

Heimann, Eduard. *Kapitalismus and Sozializmus*. Potsdam: Alfred Protte, 1931.

Hershberg, James G. *James B. Conant: Harvard to Hiroshima and the Making of the Nuclear Age*. New York: Alfred A. Knopf, 1993.

Heyward, Carter. *The Redemption of God: A Theology of Mutual Relation*. Lanham MD: University Press of America, 1982.

Hick, John. *God Has Many Names*. Philadelphia: Westminster Press, 1980.

_____. "Whatever Path Men Choose Is Mine." In *Christianity and Other Religions*, edited by John Hick and Brian Hebblethwaite, 171-90. Philadelphia: Fortress Press, 1980.

_____. "On Grading Religions." *Religious Studies* 17 (1981): 451-67.

_____. "Christology in an Age of Religious Pluralism." *Journal of Theology for Southern Africa* 35 (June 1981): 4-9.

_____. "The Theology of Religious Pluralism." *Theology* 86 (September 1983): 335-40.

_____. "Religious Pluralism." In *The World's Religious Traditions*, edited by Frank Whaling, 147-64. Edinburgh: T.&T. Clark, 1984.

_____. "Religious Pluralism and Absolute Claims." In *Religious Pluralism*, edited by Leroy S. Rouner, 193-213. Notre Dame IN: University of Notre Dame Press, 1984.

_____. *An Interpretation of Religion*. New Haven CT: Yale University Press, 1989.

_____. *A Christian Theology of Religions: The Rainbow of Faiths*. Louisville KY: Westminster/John Knox Press, 1995.

Horkheimer, Max. *Werk und Wirken Paul Tillichs*. Stuttgart: Evangelisches Verlagswerk, 1967.

Hunt, Mary E. *Fierce Tenderness: A Feminist Theology of Friendship*. New York: Crossroad, 1992.

Jay, Martin. *The Dialectical Imagination: A History of the Frankfurt School and the Institute of Social Research, 1923–1950*. Boston: Little, Brown, and Company, 1973.

Jenson, Robert W. "Religious Pluralism, Christology, and Barth." *Dialog* (Winter 1981): 31-38.

Kaufman, Gordon. *The Theological Imagination*. Philadelphia: Westminster Press, 1981.

_____. "Religious Diversity, Historical Consciousness, and Christian Theology." In *The Myth of Christian Uniqueness*, edited by John Hick and Paul Knitter, 3-15. Maryknoll NY: Orbis Books, 1987.

Knitter, Paul. *No Other Name? A Critical Survey of Christian Attitudes toward the World Religions*. Maryknoll NY: Orbis Books, 1985.

Kolbenschlag, Madonna. "Spirituality: Finding Our True Home." In volume 1 of *Women in the Church*, edited by Madonna Kolbenschlag, 197-213. Washington: Pastoral Press, 1987.

Lebacqz, Karen. *Six Theories of Justice*. Minneapolis: Augsburg Publishing House, 1986.

Lounibos, John B. "Paul Tillich's Structures of Liberation." In *Tillich Studies 1975*, edited by John J. Carey, 63-74. Tallahassee: Florida State University, 1975.

Macleod, Alistair M. *Paul Tillich: An Essay on the Role of Ontology in His Philosophical Theology* London: George Allen & Unwin, 1973.

Marcuse, Herbert. *Eros and Civilization*. Boston: Beacon Press, 1955.

McCann, Dennis P. "Tillich's Religious Socialism: 'Creative Synthesis' or Personal Statement?" In *The Thought of Paul Tillich*, edited by James Luther Adams, Wilhelm Pauck, and Roger Lincoln Shinn, 81-101. San Francisco: Harper & Row, 1985.

McFague, Sallie. *Models of God: Theology for an Ecological, Nuclear Age*. Philadelphia: Fortress Press, 1987.

Mollegen, A. T. "The Common Convictions of the Fellowship of Socialist Christians." *Christianity and Society* (Spring 1943): 28.

Moltmann-Wendel, Elisabeth. *The Women around Jesus*. New York: Crossroad, 1982.

Niebuhr, Reinhold. Review of Tillich's *The Religious Situation*. *World Tomorrow* 15/23 (21 December 1932): 596.

_____. Review of Tillich's *Interpretation of History*. *Radical Religion* 2 (Winter 1936): 41-42.

_____. "The Contribution of Paul Tillich." *Religion in Life* 6/4 (Autumn 1937): 574-81.

_____. "Jews after the War." *The Nation* (21 February 1942): 214-16, 253-55.

_____. "The Atomic Issue." *Christianity and Crisis* 5/17 (15 October 1945): 7.

_____. "The Hydrogen Bomb." *Christianity and Society* (Spring 1950): 5-7.

_____. "Christian Conscience and Atomic War." *Christianity and Crisis* 10/21 (11 December 1950): 161.

_____. "The Significance of the Growth of Christian Action." *Christianity and Crisis* 14/4 (22 March 1954): 30-32.

_____. Review of *Biblical Religion and the Search for Ultimate Reality*. *Union Seminary Quarterly Review* 11/2 (January 1956): 59-60.

_____. "Editorial Notes." *Christianity and Crisis* 16/1 (6 February 1956): 2-3.

_____. "New Hopes for Peace in the Middle East." *Christianity and Crisis* 16/9 (28 May 1956): 65.

_____. *Pious and Secular America*. New York: Charles Scribner's Sons, 1958.

_____. *The Structure of Nations and Empires: A Study of the Recurring Patterns and Problems of the Political Order in Relation to the Unique Problems of the Nuclear Age*. New York: Scribner, 1959.

_____. "Nuclear Dilemma—A Discussion." *Christianity and Crisis* 21/19 (13 November 1961): 202.

_____. "Biblical Thought and Ontological Speculation in Tillich's Theology." In *The Theology of Paul Tillich*, edited by Charles W. Kegley and Robert W. Bretall, 216-27. New York: Macmillan, 1961.

_____. "Reply to Interpretation and Criticism, by Reinhold Niebuhr." In *Reinhold Niebuhr: His Religious, Social, and Political Thought*, edited by Charles W. Kegley and Robert W. Bretall, 429-51. New York: Macmillan, 1961.

_____. "The Response of Reinhold Niebuhr." In *Reinhold Niebuhr: A Prophetic Voice in Our Time*, edited by Harold Landon, 119-23. Greenwich: Seabury Press, 1962.

_____. *Man's Nature and His Communities*. New York: Charles Scribner's Sons, 1965.

_____. Letter to Will Scarlett. 5 November 1968. Washington Papers of Reinhold Niebuhr, Library of Congress.

_____. "Mission and Opportunity: Religion in 'Pluralistic Culture'." In *Social Responsibility in an Age of Revolution*, edited by Louis Finkelstein. New York: Jewish Theological Seminary of America, 1971.

Nishitani, Keiji. *Religious and Nothingness*. Berkeley: University of California Press, 1982.

O'Faolain, Julia, and Lauro Martines, eds. *Not in God's Image*. New York: Harper & Row, 1973.

O'Keeffe, Terence. "Tillich and the Frankfurt School." In *Theonomy and Autonomy*, edited by John J. Carey, 67-87. Macon GA: Mercer University Press, 1984.

Pauck, Wilhelm, and Marion Pauck. *Paul Tillich: His Life and Thought*. San Francisco: Harper & Row, 1976.

Plaskow, Judith. *Sex, Sin, and Grace: Women's Experience and the Theologies of Reinhold Niebuhr and Paul Tillich*. Lanham MD: University Press of America, 1980.

Rahner, Karl. "Christianity and the Non-Christian Religions." In volume 5 of *Theological Investigations*, 115-34. London: Darton, Longman & Todd, 1966.

_____. "Observations on the Problems of the 'Anonymous Christian." In volume 14 of *Theological Investigations*, 280-94. London: Darton, Longman & Todd, 1976.

_____. "The One Christ and the Universality of Salvation." In volume 16 of *Theological Investigations*, 199-224. London: Darton, Longman & Todd, 1979.

Riesz, H. Frederick, Jr. "Liberation Theology of Culture: A Tillichian Perspective." In *Kairos and Logos*, edited by John J. Carey, 300-13. Cambridge: The North American Paul Tillich Society, 1978.

Romero, Joan Arnold. "The Protestant Principle: A Woman's-Eye View of Barth and Tillich." In *Religion and Sexism: Images of Woman in the Jewish and Christian Traditions*, edited by Rosemary Radford Ruether, 319-40. New York: Simon and Schuster, 1974.

Ruether, Rosemary Radford. Review of *Beyond God the Father*. *Journal of Religious Thought* 30/2 (1973): 71-73.

_____. *New Woman New Earth: Sexist Ideologies and Human Liberation*. New York: Seabury, Crossroad, 1975.

_____. *To Change the World: Christology and Cultural Criticism*. London: SCM Press, 1981.

_____. *Sexism and God-Talk: Toward a Feminist Theology*. Boston: Beacon, 1983.

Runyon, Theodore. "Tillich's Understanding of Revolution." In *Theonomy and Autonomy*, edited by John J. Carey, 267-80. Macon GA: Mercer University Press, 1984.

Scharlemann, Robert. "The Scope of Systematic: An Analysis of Tillich's Two Systems." *The Journal of Religion* 48 (April 1968): 136-49.

_____. *Reflection and Doubt in the Thought of Paul Tillich*. New Haven CT: Yale University Press, 1969.

Schüssler Fiorenza, Elisabeth. "Symposium: Toward a Theology of Feminism." *Horizons* 2 (Spring 1975): 117-18.

_____. *In Memory of Her*. New York: Crossroad, 1983.

Second Vatican Council. "The Church Today." In (*Gaudium et Spes*) *The Documents of Vatican II*, 227-28. New York: America Press, 1966.

Slater, Peter. *The Dynamics of Religion*. New York: Harper & Row, 1978.

Smart, Ninian. *Worldviews*. New York: Charles Scribner's Sons, 1983.

Smith, Wilfred Cantwell. *Questions of Religious Truth*. London: Victor Gallancz, 1967.

_____. *Towards a World Theology*. Philadelphia: Westminster Press, 1981.

Soulen, R. Kendall. *The God of Israel and Christian Theology*. Minneapolis: Fortress Press, 1996.

Stenger, Mary Ann. "Paul Tillich's Theory of Theological Norms and the Problems of Relativism and Subjectivism." *The Journal of Religion* 62/4 (October 1982): 359-75.

_____. "The Significance of Paradox for Theological Verification: Difficulties and Possibilities." *International Journal for Philosophy of Religion* 14 (1983): 171-82.

_____. "Relative Absoluteness: An Approach to Religious Pluralism." In *The Theology of Langdon Gilkey: Systematic and Critical Studies*, edited by Kyle Pasewark and Jeff Poole, 239-58. Macon GA: Mercer University Press, 1999.

Stone, Ronald H. *Paul Tillich's Radical Social Thought*. Atlanta: John Knox Press, 1980.

_____. "The Zionism of Paul Tillich and Reinhold Niebuhr." In *Tantur Yearbook 1980–1981*, 219-33. Jerusalem: Tantur, 1981.

Stone, Ronald H., and Matthew Lon Weaver, eds. *Against the Third Reich: Paul Tillich's Wartime Radio Broadcasts into Nazi Germany*. Louisville: Westminster/John Knox Press, 1998.

Stumme, John R. *Socialism in Theological Perspective: A Study of Paul Tillich, 1918–1933*. Missoula MT: Scholars Press, 1978.

Stryk, Lucien, and Takashi Ikemoto, eds. *Zen Poems of China and Japan: The Crane's Bill*. Translated by Lucien Stryk and Takashi Ikemoto. New York: Grove Press, 1973.

Surin, Kenneth. "Revelation, Salvation, the Uniqueness of Christ, and Other Religions." *Religious Studies* 19 (Summer 1983): 323-43.

Tillich, Hannah. *From Time to Time*. New York: Stein and Day, 1973.

Vatican Declaration. "Women in the Ministerial Priesthood." *Origins* 6/33 (1977):523.

Von Oppen, Beate. *Religion and Resistance to Nazism*. Princeton NJ: Princeton University Center for International Studies, 1971.

Weaver, Mary Jo. *New Catholic Women*. San Francisco: Harper & Row, 1986.

Wilson-Kastner, Patricia. *Faith, Feminism, and The Christ*. Philadelphia: Fortress Press, 1983.

Indexes

Index of Names

Subject Index